INFORMAL JUSTICE IN ENGLAND AND WALES 1760–1914

INFORMAL JUSTICE IN ENGLAND AND WALES 1760–1914

The Courts of Popular Opinion

Stephen Banks

THE BOYDELL PRESS

© Stephen Banks 2014

All Rights Reserved. Except as permitted under current legislation
no part of this work may be photocopied, stored in a retrieval system,
published, performed in public, adapted, broadcast,
transmitted, recorded or reproduced in any form or by any means,
without the prior permission of the copyright owner

The right of Stephen Banks to be identified as
the author of this work has been asserted in accordance with
sections 77 and 78 of the Copyright, Designs and Patents Act 1988

First published 2014
The Boydell Press, Woodbridge

ISBN 978 1 84383 940 8

The Boydell Press is an imprint of Boydell & Brewer Ltd
PO Box 9, Woodbridge, Suffolk IP12 3DF, UK
and of Boydell & Brewer Inc.
668 Mount Hope Ave, Rochester, NY 14620-2731, USA
website: www.boydellandbrewer.com

A catalogue record for this book is available
from the British Library

The publisher has no responsibility for the continued existence or accuracy
of URLs for external or third-party internet websites referred to in this
book, and does not guarantee that any content on such websites is, or will
remain, accurate or appropriate.

This publication is printed on acid-free paper

Contents

Acknowledgements vi

Preface vii

    Introduction 1

1. Law, Symbolism and Punishment 20
2. Localism, Justice and the Right to Judge 33
3. The Forms of Rough Music 62
4. Sex, Gender and Moral Policing 83
5. Defending Economic Interests 107
6. Political Resistance 127
7. Resistive Communities 154
8. Performance and Proscription 175

    Aftermath 200

Select Bibliography 205

Index 218

Acknowledgements

In preparing this monograph I have received assistance from so many of the all-too-often unsung archivists and local historians who inhabit these isles that it would be invidious to single anyone out. Thanks to you all. Particular appreciation should be shown, however, to those in the Folklore Society who have done, and continue to do, so much to preserve the lives and learning of the ordinary people of our past – those who are too often swept aside in the grand histories of their times. I must express my gratitude to Kate McIntosh, without whose excellent suggestions and contributions this book would not have seen the light of day. Thanks also to Lawrence McNamara and Sam McIntosh for friendship, beer and a great deal of wise counsel. Finally, the biggest debts of all are owed to my parents, to my children, Oliver and Theo, and above all to my long-suffering wife Sanjeeda. I promise this thing is finally written and I will come out of the garage now.

Preface

This is a book about justice. It is not about justice as observed in the courtroom (unless it be a 'courtroom' of an unorthodox variety) but about unofficial justice as visited upon malefactors by the collective actions of private citizens. Justice is a difficult word, and I should say at the start that for my purposes the term 'unofficial justice' is taken to exclude deeds of furtive vengeance (however much deserved). I am not concerned here with those occasions upon which offenders were simply set upon in the dark and given a good beating – though it is likely that such instances occurred often enough. Rather my interest is in those occasions upon which groups acted openly, publicly and unapologetically against wrongdoers. Unapologetically because they claimed that they were doing so by right and in accordance with customary practices that supposedly legitimated group responses to moral defects. Reference will indeed be made to some actions that were both public and yet quite indiscriminate in respect of the violence visited upon the wrongdoer. However, it will soon become apparent that most public collective acts were intended primarily to shame their victims rather than to harm them, and that they were performed within an understood rubric of customary practice that served (in the main) to contain the violence inherent in group action. This study, then, is primarily focused on public shaming rituals – and these generally (though not invariably) involved a noisy perambulation through an offended community. During the course of these processions the participants tried to attract as much attention as possible by beating on pots, pans, kettles . . . anything suitable that came to hand. Hence these phenomena are broadly subsumed under the title 'rough music' – rituals that were widely distributed and known variously at the time as 'skimmingtons', 'stang ridings', 'ceffyl prens' and by many other terminologies besides.

'Rough music' has to date been much better studied in respect to its role in early modern England, in particular by those interested in gender and gender history. Since rough music was commonly employed against those exhibiting inappropriate gender behaviours, its history has often been connected with the use of the brank, the ducking stool and the like – as a tool to discipline women. Martin Ingram has observed that unofficial species of punitive procession in the early modern period were closely related to official punishments such as the judicial ridings, used (particularly in London) to punish prostitutes, scolds and other unfortunates. Such ridings were also used to punish those convicted of a wide range of economic offences.

Whilst some scholars have pursued the later history of rough music, few have gone right into the world of modernity itself. E. P. Thompson did pioneering work on the nineteenth century whilst examining the moral authority of the crowd. His work, though, was predominately political and historical rather than legal. In my introduction there is something of an appeal, suggested in part by the work of Thompson, for a new type of legal history: one that studies *beliefs* about the content of the law as much as the content of the law itself. Legal historians and lawyers have, in the main, focused on the doctrinal development of the law, the history of its institutions or the lives of its important personages, and have seen little reason to enquire into what ordinary people knew or believed about the law and how that influenced their personal behaviours. Lawyers are much more comfortable with official documents and prefer to leave things as insubstantial as beliefs to the domain of the folklorist, the sociologist or the anthropologist. Naturally, then, what was actually written in law seems to them of more consequence that what was *believed* to be the law. Furthermore, many lawyers seem to tacitly accept that 'The Law' did and does possess some special quality and authority, merely by virtue of being written down. My own view, however, is that the very deep rules of society are predicated upon world views that are rarely fully articulated in either the statutes or the cases. Not that I want for one moment to underestimate the importance of the study of written law, but rather wish to observe in addition that many acts in society are guided by legal thinking but not by legal knowledge. Such acts are often based upon suppositions as to what the law is, or should be. Such suppositions, advanced with enough conviction, can direct political discourse, influence economic activity, guide social behaviour and so on – in political debate, for example, what is thought to be in the law is often much more important than what is actually there. Throughout this book, evidence will be adduced that groups in penalising others operated with their own particular views of the legal environment and were not usually conscious of being part of an oppositional counterculture. They did not consider themselves as being outside the law trying to change it – but rather that they were inside the law and seeking to protect it. Legal belief can, in short, drive social action just as much as legal reality can – and therefore, in my view, it has just as much a place in the history of the law as the examination of the law's formal content or the operation of its often inaccessible institutions.

Generally speaking, the groups and communities surveyed here had a very developed sense of what was and was not permissible – although they often discovered after the fact that, from the point of view of authority, they were in error. The conflict of ideas that resulted interested Thompson as evidence of a clash between orders, one in which, from his point of view, real moral authority was invested in the crowd as opposed to vested interests.

For my part, this is not a political study – and in Chapter 1 I make the necessary but rather obvious point that, in the area of my research at least, the clash was as much between the new and the old as between the powerful and the powerless. The withdrawal of the state from the arena of shaming punishments during the course of the nineteenth century served to create the impression that the punitive practices of rural communities and labouring men and women were the product of their own unique culture, but in point of origin they in fact closely shadowed the officially licensed practices of years gone by.

Chapter 2 takes the enquiry into new territory. It argues that, with the benefit of hindsight, in the first half of the period under review the distinctions between formal and informal mechanisms of judgement and punishment can be overstated. As the operation of local and unofficial courts attest, the relationship between official and unofficial juridical systems remained – in rural communities in particular – complex, uncertain and contested. In the structure of the formal legal system, in its rhetoric and the manner of its dissemination, there was and continued to be much that gave succour to vibrant local justice traditions that blended elements of both the official and the unofficial. Communities contained within themselves their own juridical claims, which were often expressed during the conduct of festive life and the observance of calendrical customs. Communities coming together to celebrate and coming together to judge were closely connected. Rough music, then, was intimately associated with festivity both in terms of the conceptualisation of the activity and in terms of practical matters such as timing and location.

Chapter 3 considers the nuances of the rough music employed in communal punishments, the terminology associated with it and the three broad variant types augmented by certain specific regional practices. Whether the actual malefactor was dragged from his or her home and paraded, or a human substitute employed or an effigy displayed in their stead, what becomes apparent is that there were common views as to what was required to make these shaming rituals lawful. Thus, if it was performed in three parishes, or on three nights in succession, or first preceded by a march around the church – then the participants could be confident that they were acting within their 'rights'. Nonetheless, there were changes in rough music performance over time. Perhaps most importantly during the course of the nineteenth century, the beatings and duckings that characterised earlier practice became increasingly transposed into acts of purely symbolic violence.

Promiscuity, inappropriate gender behaviour or deviancy remained the avowed causes of rough music throughout the period under review. In Chapter 4, however, two caveats appear. First, in the field of marital relations punitive action against scolding wives seems to have been on the decline and, by the end of the nineteenth century, had clearly been overtaken in terms of frequency by actions taken against wife-beaters. I am sceptical, nonetheless, as to the claims of others that a consistent and coherent change in attitudes to gender relations can be discerned from this. Second, I urge some caution in respect of accepting at face value the reasons actually advanced for a performance of rough music. Whilst the avowed reason was almost certainly a contributing cause, evidence is advanced to suggest that the picture was often rather more complex. When confronted, for example, with an assertion that a skimmington had been staged because of a wife-beating, the intelligent question to ask is often why this particular wife-beater had been selected for chastisement as opposed to any other. Although, given the state of the sources, such questions are often difficult to answer there is enough evidence to suggest that, within communities, those seen as outsiders, non-conformists, teetotallers or otherwise suspect individuals were likely to be subjected to particular moral scrutiny.

Most works on rough music have, however, been content to characterise those participating in it as simply the representatives of homogenous communities, the members of which are assumed to share a common moral platform. This is challenged in Chapters 4 and 5, perhaps most particularly in the latter chapter where I show that shaming rituals had an important role to play in trials of representation staged between opposing interest groups. The community, in short, was a contested territory over which one might fight in order to establish one's own view of normative conduct. Coach drivers parodied their rivals, gentlemen staged mock executions to take their revenge upon revenue inspectors, and criminal gangs used humiliating parades to undermine the credibility of those who might testify against them. Even middling tradesmen sponsored street theatre in order to lambast larger operators, thereby attempting to defeat commercial ventures that were threatening to themselves, for instance by characterising a trader as involved in economic embezzlement. Rituals of popular justice then could readily be made to serve small vested interests and to express views not necessarily in harmony with those of the majority community.

Festive rituals and within them juridical and punitive practices had a strong affective power in an age not yet inculcated with ideologies and alternative group behaviours. In penalising individuals' abhorrent conduct they could be highly partisan but they could also serve as tools with which to unite communities in pursuit of general good. Rough music could both create and articulate the sorts of aspirations for change that were necessarily political. Chapter 6, then, explores the folkloric elements found in several kinds of resistance to established order: in food price protests, in the Swing disturbances and, most particularly, in Wales where the Rebecca Riots were most obviously an extension of the Welsh version of rough music – the 'ceffyl pren.' The chapter offers ample explanation as to why the authorities would wish to proscribe such practices.

The writ of the authorities did not, however, run with equal effect everywhere and the subsequent study of resistive communities in Chapter 7 suggests that there were particular places in which independent justice traditions were able to endure in the face of the increasing pressure created by, amongst other things, the spread of professional policing. In brief, it was in the industrial open villages that were distinguished by the presence of persons of some education – those that supported artisanal trades and where there was to be found a supply of labour that was skilled and granted a degree of autonomy – that ordinary men and women were best able to go about their business largely untouched by the hand of authority. A plurality of income streams accompanied by the exploitation of natural resources (often acquired by force majeure) allowed such communities considerable independence from landlords, whilst at the same time the somewhat precarious nature of their position encouraged a high degree of community cohesion and cooperation. Places such as Pockthorpe near Norwich managed themselves. The rural police were too thinly spread and their presence too transient to operate to any great effect and, as Laurie Lee memorably records in respect of a murder in his village of Slad, Gloucestershire, even in cases of the most egregious crimes it was difficult to break through the barriers erected against outsiders.

The subsistence of independent justice traditions in groups of skilled and semi-skilled labour is one justification for extending the study of rough music into the twentieth century. As this book will show, it was through the activities of quarrymen, colliers and the like that shaming rituals came to make an important contribution to nascent working-class culture and the emerging labour movement. The 'white-shirting' of blacklegs, for example, and the mockery and waving of women's apparel by women themselves, are both testimony to the continued importance of reputation in labouring communities. Even into the 1930s shaming practices that would not have been out of place in the eighteenth century can be seen to be informing school strikes and other working-class actions.

From here, Chapter 8 explores the campaigns against popular festivities, sports and shaming rituals that gathered pace in the second half of the nineteenth century. Of particular interest are the attempts to suppress the 'bonfire cultures', which with their immolation of effigies of contemporary hate figures mirrored the behaviours observed in rough music processions. I note that such practices were acceptable when subordinated to the purposes of national patriotic culture, and indeed perhaps as much effort was expended in taming and subverting anarchic popular celebrations to the cause of respectable patriotism as was expended in trying to completely suppress those that did not conform. Bonfire culture served as a catalyst for other types of collective action, as is observed through the operations of the 'Skeleton Army' at Worthing. Ultimately, though, as at Lewes, it could only endure by collaborating with the authorities. In doing so, its anti-authoritarian impulses were tamed and safely channelled into denunciations of national patriotic enemies such as the Pope, the Kaiser and so on.

Ultimately, I shall not agree with the assessment of others, however, that the authorities were just as active and successful in suppressing rough music proper in the rural environment. Examples illustrate that the intermittent and unpredictable nature of some of its forms meant that it was much harder to suppress than regular seasonal activities – however large they might be. Furthermore, there is much to suggest that the authorities felt themselves obliged to tolerate such activity as long as it was confined within certain bounds. The evidence will show that in a few locations rough music was still being performed and still having an operative effect upon its victims into the 1950s. Nonetheless, it was in terminal decline, the explanation for which lies not in the operations of the police or magistrates but rather in the dwindling rural consciousness. As Snell has shown, a world conceptualised through the medium of the parish began to pass away with the advent of the railway, the bicycle and the increased labour mobility that they brought. The parish as a juridical unit disappeared and with it rough music. Even in places where practices such as rough music endured, their affective force was undermined by the spread of education, increased autonomy, and social and geographical mobility.

In the closing pages I offer an instance where a rural community, still clinging to the assumptions of years gone by, attempted to shame an incumbent cleric and his wife but utterly misfired. The affair illustrates that in the absence of actual physical assault, rough music substantially depended on shared cultural understandings between the parties. It was the material, emotional, spiritual and psychological dependence of the victim on his or her community that gave any disapproval such potency. Where the victims were socially, educationally and culturally apart, as in the case of the clerical couple, the message of the music was indecipherable, inexplicable and even comic. However, for most of the period under review in this book, rough music and other justice rituals powerfully expressed collective disapprobation. The desire to preserve reputation, understood through traditional norms, was a significant determinant of conduct during the formation of working-class culture. Furthermore, when we consider how behaviour in rural environments and labouring neighbourhoods was managed into the twentieth century, too much can be credited to the thinly spread forces of authority. Much must be attributed to the power of shame, the virtues of self-governance and the operations of the courts of popular opinion.

Introduction: Inventing Law and Doing Justice

Many years ago, I found myself on a school trip to the now long-departed but not much lamented Soviet Union. Eager to further the cause of a history project I took advantage of some permitted shopping time in the state-owned GUM department store to purchase, for a remarkably small sum, an English translation of the 1936 Soviet constitution. For those unfamiliar with it, this was an astonishingly benevolent document guaranteeing universal suffrage, secret ballot and so forth. Even as a schoolboy, a moment's reflection that this was a constitution written by a committee headed by Joseph Stalin was enough to convince me that, sometimes, very little of the way that a society actually works can be captured by the study of its written laws or of the principles that purport to govern it. This was not a profound insight, but somehow in the world there still exists a very real belief in the innate power of words written down and, in particular, in the intangible power and authority expressed by written law. Perhaps this is an echo of our past.

The very first written laws were inscribed on stele, topped by the images of the gods. In truth we do not know if any of the early Sumerian and Akkadian law codes were ever actually enforced, but the message of the iconography was pretty clear – law had been given by the gods to the kings and was a sign of divine authority and therefore upheld by more than mere temporal sanction. Furthermore, to write something down was to bring it from one world into another. Whether it be the words inscribed upon stele, pierced into the clay of the omen texts, or much later scrawled upon the parchment of medieval prayers, curses and spells, for four millennia humanity has been seized by the sense that to write something down is in some measure to actualise it, to give it a potency both in this world and that of the gods.

To say that in the past the making of law was akin to a religious experience is not to deny ancient cultures their complexity. Cynicism about both the law and the gods is much documented, certainly within the classical tradition, where there was no shortage of spiritual and legal pragmatists. Even today though, in modern Western culture we still have not entirely shed a long-standing reverential mode of thinking about law. Law can still put on a show such that it can still inspire affective states akin to those aroused by religious devotion. Through its iconography, its architecture and its rhetoric, the law is still in the business of proclaiming that it is not merely about rules and about power but about something deeper and perhaps finer. Law maintains, at least in part, its power to inspire: it can still create and condition world views that, to cynics such as myself, can sometimes seem rather gauche.

I worked for a number of years in merchant shipping and became, so I thought, well acquainted with the many problems of this troubled and ineffectively regulated industry. I can still remember being portentously assured by a somewhat pompous trainee lawyer of my acquaintance that certain industry practices that were ubiquitous, and which I had myself often witnessed, could not possibly occur because they would be 'Against the Law!'. This statement was advanced with all the solemnity of a declaration of faith, as though it was invoking some mysterious potency, powerful in the realm of the real yet rooted in some authority much more intangible.

This book is a study concerned with law and justice viewed both pragmatically and reverentially. It is about what people in the eighteenth and nineteenth centuries believed and felt about law and justice, and about how they tried to go about actualising their beliefs outside the formal legal framework laid down by the superior courts. Although lawyers and courts will appear throughout this work, I predominantly consider the activities of people for whom the law formed part of their world view but was not consciously part of their daily business. I will be much more concerned with myths, fictions, understandings and misapprehensions, the power and perception of 'the law' in daily life rather than with law as a discrete doctrinal product. In particular, I look at transgressive behaviour and the ways in which groups visited their own forms of justice upon offenders. I will not be much concerned with justice as either an abstract philosophical concept or as an officially sanctioned outcome at the end of a judicial process. When I use the term 'justice' it will mainly be in order to capture the frame of mind of those delivering it rather than as a personal value judgement about their ethics in doing so. Along the way we will meet with community punishments, which may well arouse our approbation, such as the rough justice sometimes meted out to those who sought to profiteer by hoarding food in times of failed harvests. On the other hand, we will also encounter the collective bullying of eccentrics or unfortunates, which will likely seem utterly abhorrent.

What the variety of phenomena under consideration here will have in common is that their instigators appeal to claims of right or moral probity. Very often what will be observed is a struggle between contending views as to the content, spirit and disposition of the law as each party attempts to justify their actions by reference to an allegedly authentic tradition that contradicts the claims of their opponents.

Much of this book will be about those who, in a broad sense, 'lost': those who argued for local communal rights and powers, fixed prices, local tribunals and layered property rights in the context of an increasingly free market laissez-faire society. It is about the claims of those who were predominantly below the threshold at which erudite letters were created, memoirs composed and so on. It will consider the precarious relationship of communal legal visions as against the letters of the statutes and the operation of the courts. The relationships between law as expressed in ratio or written in statute, law as practised and law as an imagined social product will be shown to have been complex and interdependent.

This study is particularly concerned with excavating the world of legal fictions, of ideas about the content of the law. Before delving into my period proper, however, it might be appropriate to make some further general observations about the power of legal fictions to shape and constrain law and to make their own contributions to the broad species of legal knowledge.

Law's Fictive Body

In Britain the grand principles of the law are often invoked by means of aphorisms, observations that are really triggers used in order to ignite collective memories, aspirations or beliefs. My father, who comes from a very respectable working-class family in the Midlands, has often declared that 'An Englishman's home is his castle', although on what authority this is said he does not know. It is declared as a self-evident statement of what is, or, at the very least, ought to be. For men such as my father, individual laws may be subject to scorn and may be broken, yet the law as a whole remains a profound matter.

And this is not just true for an older generation. I have observed that my own young children and their friends use simple legal terminology and invoke the authority of the law in serious tones as a declaration of faith in a system of governance that cannot be disputed – an end point beyond which one cannot go. My eleven-year old, as solemnly as any judge, recently informed his eight-year-old brother that it was 'illegal' and indeed 'against the law' for someone still at primary school to have their own email account. Instrumentally, this in part accomplished his purpose of dissuading his sibling from seeking to share his iPad, but I am also fairly confident that he indeed believes this to be so, and that both children can envisage some unspecified dread and mysterious consequence that may well follow from ignoring such a prohibition.

Day-to-day, of course, our contact with the law is very likely to be rather more mundane and utilitarian: there is nothing very reverential about being on the end of a parking ticket! While lawyers spend their time dissecting and analysing legal rules, we all know and observe that there are flaws in the system: we know that there are partisan or avaricious judges, we regard with cynicism the passage of hurried and politically inspired statutes. Yet still the law can compel our allegiance. On this, as other things, the human mind is able to adhere to contradictory ideas or display seemingly contrasting affective moods according to time, place and circumstance.

It is possible to be an entirely hard-headed, realistic lawyer and yet in another mood feel a genuine emotional connection to the mythologised authority of the common law. There is always the danger of contradiction however. Reverence is generally inspired by mystery and nothing endangers mystery so much as knowledge.

As we shall see, there is nevertheless much value in propagating mystery, particularly when it serves to aggrandise the propagator. Fictitious views of the origin and authenticity of law are necessarily created by powerful interests as part of the project of legitimisation, but they also generate themselves – seemingly spontaneously – out of the soup of untested assertions, apocryphal stories, historical detritus, wishful thinking, misunderstood judgements, and sometimes genuine understanding that passes for social knowledge. Within the common law world, at least, one often observes attempts to substantiate broad views of the law by reference to particular points in real legal time. Unfortunately, such attempts are very often misplaced. It never ceases to surprise what some Americans suppose to be within their founding constitution or what conversely some British law students believe to be enshrined within Magna Carta!

Legal beliefs are not much studied; lawyers are not much interested in 'beliefs', they are much more comfortable with discussing the ratio of a case or the sections of an act or, more abstractly, the validity of Harteian rules of recognition. Legal anthropologists are a very rare breed indeed. Yet the fictitious statements commonly made about the law are far from unimportant. On the contrary, they are a key element in law's quasi-mythological construction as part of a collective habitus or world view. The statement 'An Englishman's home is his castle' comes suffused with a powerful attachment to notions of individual liberty. The least interesting thing to say about it is that, as a purported statement of some fundamental truth about the sanctity of one's home, the statement is so qualified in law as to have hardly any meaning at all. It nevertheless remains as a kind of rhetorical rallying point and an estimation of the general disposition of the law and its relationship to the individual. In the mind of the utterer, it stands as a foundational premise to which exceptions may be permitted but against which they must be judged.

Rational analysis of the actual content of the law makes little difference once an idea of the law – with all its affective power – informs core normative values. As an analogy, many things may in the future shake the British people's general adherence to the monarchy, but an intellectual exposition of the intrigues and accidents of the historical process is unlikely to prove itself one of them. Intellectually, I know that although I admire the Queen, she has no more 'right' to sit on the throne than my milkman, yet I sing 'God Save the Queen' as lustily as anyone and the 'Last Night of the Proms' stirs something very deep in me that I would not readily surrender.

It is sometimes necessary to remind ourselves that most people do in fact obey most of the laws most of the time – and this is not because of the content of the law books. Fear of being punished plays its part, and the rationality of a prohibition may make it more or less likely to be respected. For many people, however, it is still the case that the law represents a kind of *grundnorm*, it tells what 'ought' to be and invites an obedience that is primarily a habitual rather than an intellectual matter. The fact that we sometimes speed on the roads, or park in prohibited places, does not make this observation invalid. As a strategy for living it is necessary to have a world view, and there is in most (though clearly not all) of the population a sense of a kind of deep law that helps to tell us who we are and where we are placed in the scheme of things. Of course, not everyone will internalise the law in the same way; there may be general variations as between different persons, places and communities.

Consider for a moment the broad concept of Britishness. Although space prohibits the unpacking of all its baggage here, a vision of a particular kind of legal community is clearly an important item in the national kitbag. Yet that vision is not necessarily coterminous with the day-to-day operation of the legal system. This goes on its own way, for good or ill. Few follow its progress, unless they are very immediately involved, and interest groups frequently despair at their lack of success in interesting the public in legal issues. Civil liberties may be infringed, political arrangements changed, age-old institutions abolished or remodelled and still the public dog sleeps. Until that is, for no clear reason, it wakes. Exactly when it will do so is hard to predict, for it is not the most significant noises that make the dog stir. Very likely it will be a minor case, or a footnote in a government's legislative programme that is of no great social or economic import, that suddenly stirs the public mood. Core normative values are allegedly now under threat; letters are written to newspapers by people who do not normally write letters to newspapers, and the rhetoric of liberty or Britishness is brought down from the attic and dusted off. Law-abiding people with a thousand more pressing concerns of their own begin to demand the right to eat beef on the bone and wonder whether or not to start hunting foxes. In time the furore dies away but not before it has been made apparent that, in the minds of those who must be persuaded to obey it, the law is still an ideological construct, a statement of world belief as well as a pattern of rules. Simple power can sustain the law, but if the law wants or needs to rely on a degree of consent it has to create a world view or accommodate itself to one it finds already in existence.

I am concerned here with visions of the law as espoused by the people of the eighteenth and nineteenth centuries, visions that led on to consequent conduct. It is important from the first to give notice to the rather obvious point that alternate visions of the law were rather easier to sustain in a world where authority was less centralised and where local identity was much more important than today – although in the period under question this statement becomes progressively less true over time. The relationship between the central spine of law-making bodies and the regions of the kingdom was less direct, less certain in its transmission of legal information and more obviously obstructed by local jurisdictions, administrative problems and independent inclinations. Even more then than in the present day, there existed potential tensions between the legal expectations of communities and the law as practised amongst the common law judges. This tension between local interpretations of the law, and the law itself, will be very relevant to this study of the punishment of supposed wrongdoers by those whom, for the moment, I must beg to be allowed to call simply 'ordinary people'.

Communities had their own views of what constituted an offence and their own views of appropriate sanctions. Of course these were not always set in contradiction to a criminal justice system trying to lay down normative values. For the title of this book I chose the term 'informal justice' because my study will describe modes of doing justice that lay on both sides of the sometimes rather indeterminate legal divide. Sometimes communities responded to perceived offences in ways that were lawful and sometimes in ways that were unlawful (though this was not always apparent until decided by the courts after the fact). Both species of response, however, were often conceptually related and blended together into the local justice tradition.

At the start of the period in question there were many parts of the country where local tradition was still being upheld by formal institutions operating largely outside the ambit of the common law courts. Court-leets, swainmotes, verderers' courts, stannary courts and the like were staffed by those who were not legal professionals, and in them judgement was generally delivered upon the defendant by his or her peers. Local or occupational custom served as a powerful guiding principle and the proceedings were somewhat irregular by the standards of the common law lawyers. Still, the higher courts accepted the right of these courts to do justice within certain bounds.

In 1760 these courts were still penalising low-end misdemeanours, supervising weights and measures, upholding customary rights and work practices, arbitrating disputes, regulating markets and so on: matters not much accounted by history but undoubtedly important in the lives of the people who fell under their jurisdiction. However, most of these courts were already in decline, and by the end of the period those that remained were, by and large, shadows of their former selves, mere vestigial curiosities.

Existing alongside these courts, however, were traditions of juridical performance and systems of social sanction that were driven by common views of law, justice and right that were often founded upon legal fictions. Thus, one observes mock courts that had no legitimate authority yet acted as though they did; one sees shaming punishments, strict in their adherence to rules that allegedly made them lawful but that clearly ran contrary to established criminal case law; one observes labour agreements that were unenforceable yet imposed elaborate disciplinary frameworks upon collective labour; and also taxing customs (accompanied by penalties for avoidance) firmly anchored in specific time, place and tradition, that from the point of view of the common lawyer were little better than extortion.

There are many more examples that this book will explore, but it must be admitted that observing these informal social rules, fictions, self-constituted institutions, prohibitions and accompanying sanctions is much easier than assessing their true significance. It will be one of the contentions of this book that the extent to which the physical, juridical and psychological environments of the period were populated by legal fictions and self-constituted juridical mechanisms has been much underestimated. By fictions I mean suppositions as to the content of community or individual rights or powers that lawyers and courts would subsequently find to be erroneous. To those espousing them at the time, however, these were either genuine privileges, rights or powers – as real and material as any other species of legal rights – or they were legitimate manifestations of what the law ought to be, or what the true unrecognised law allegedly actually was.

In short, communities laid claims to powers that were in conflict with the views and traditions of the common law courts. Their claims were various but they substantially revolved around the right to exercise customary rights and sanction those who breached them, or to uphold understood principles of morality and chastise those who refused to conform to them. These were claims that contained, but went beyond, mere self-interest and they acknowledged not only legitimating but also limiting principles.

In such circumstances the actors were rarely disordered howling mobs, they rarely acted indiscriminately. Although facets of criminality will from time to time be observed among them, more often the parties involved had very clear ideas of what constituted a legitimate or illegitimate response to transgression. Similarly, many were not acting in their own immediate interests but in a spirit of solidarity, genuine indignation or altruism in performing acts that corresponded to their own legal construction of the world.

But were these acts really of any importance?

The contexts in which popular judgements were given and sanctions applied have often led to the significance of these acts being underestimated or trivialised. Informal justice was often delivered to very specific groups, often within festive time or festive space. For example, it was at the harvest supper that the conduct of delinquent harvesters was judged, during the Plough Monday celebrations that revenge was exacted upon village skinflints, and at the bonfire on 5 November that the conduct of contemporary malefactors was excoriated.

Outside observers – socially, geographically and psychologically distanced – have readily reduced this aspect of popular culture to the quaint and quixotic. Yet it was during celebrations that the community could be most readily gathered and constituted, and the power of shame in particular most easily harnessed as an instrument of social discipline. Lest 'festive' be thought to connote 'trivial' it is salutary to remember that Barry Faulk remarked that: 'To write a history of capital punishment in England is to write a history of festive life.'[1] Within their festive space, the

---

1 Barry Faulk, 'The Public Execution; Urban Rhetoric and Victorian Crowds', *Executions and the British Experience from the 17th to the 20th Century*, ed. William B. Thesig (Jefferson, N. Carolina: McFarland, 1990), pp. 77–91 at p. 77.

community paraded, performed and punished but remained for the most part within the constraints imposed by the limits of the festive calendar and festive tradition.

It is necessary to recover the humanity of those on the receiving end of festive judgement in order to comprehend what lay behind the whimsical descriptions of indulgent folklorists. True, a ducking can be a matter of a good-natured dunking in a river on a bucolic summer's day, accompanied by the feigned indignation that is expected as part of the play. Yet it can also be a matter of being stripped naked in front of the community and held down in a freezing torrent, possibly until one expires.

Receiving a fine is a trivial matter as long as one can afford to pay. If, in a rather atomised society, the power of social sanction escapes us, still it can be observed in the fate of those physically unharmed yet socially shamed who lost their homes and their situations and fled their communities.

In few of these cases, however, did the crowd seem to believe that it had exceeded its authority. Indeed when told that their activities had been unlawful they often reacted with genuine surprise, not knowing that they had strayed beyond the permissible. Sometimes, of course, they simply did not believe those who chastised them. It is not at all surprising that misapprehensions as to the contents of their powers and rights should be so frequently found within communities when the common law was imperfectly applied, and when it contained within itself a rhetoric that alleged that the common law was precisely founded upon customary practice.

Law in the Community

The first census in 1801 calculated that there were some 8.8 million people living in England and Wales; a modern estimation is that in England about two-thirds of this population was living in rural areas and only one-third in urban areas, defined as settlements of more than 2,500 people.[2] Not until 1851 did the numbers of town or city-dwellers match those in the villages and hamlets. It follows, then, that for many of these people the assize and the quarter sessions were but occasional events in a county town, which was itself a good long walk away. The local manorial court might be much more familiar. Predominantly, though, justice was delivered day-to-day by the justice of the peace (JP). He was guided by his clerk and by Burn's *Justice of the Peace*, a book that was to become the bible of magistrates. It was the lay-magistrate, then, who formed the interface between customary practice and common and statute law.

The JP was the local fount of the common law, though in some areas of law his reach might be constrained by the existence of other jurisdictions. He might be

---

2 P. Langford, *A Polite and Commercial People: England, 1727–1783* (Oxford: OUP, 1989), p. 418.

either zealous or lazy, ignorant or shrewd, but his was the task of reconciling local custom and the common law as expressed in his law books. How then might he react to the application of communal justice upon, for example, a village malefactor – an adulterer, a notorious gossip, a dishonest trader or other such? Much of this book concerns itself with the phenomenon of 'rough music', the practice of staging ritual shaming processions that were variously known as skimmingtons, stang ridings, ceffyl prens and the like. A JP's law books might tell him that in *Mason v Jennings* 1680,[3] it had been decided that to ride skimmington against someone was to defame them – although in that case the plaintiff had recovered nothing by his action. Yet this was a very old case and the very dearth of such cases in his law books might tell him that such activities were rarely proceeded against. How was he to act in the face of the unanimous assertion of the community that such activities were lawful provided they were carried on in three different places for three successive nights?

Claims of customary rights could be persuasive when the landscape was littered with different jurisdictions, ancient but sometimes almost moribund courts, manorial customs, feudal relics and special privileges allegedly based upon ancient charter. True, by the middle of the nineteenth century much of this had been swept away and magistrates were less permissive, with a clearer sense of their personal obligations and of what was lawful. By then, of course, magistrates could increasingly count on the assistance of sporadically zealous professional police forces. However, the impact of the arrival of the professional policeman should not be overstated – certainly not in the early years. Writing of the London police courts operating in the second half of the nineteenth century, Jennifer Davis noted that:

> The business of the courts demonstrates, in particular, that historians have underestimated the extent to which informal sanctions against wrongdoers applied within the community survived alongside official law enforcement as applied by the police and the courts at least until the end of the nineteenth century; while historians have similarly overestimated the extent to which the nineteenth century state was either able or willing to intervene in the everyday affairs of its subjects.[4]

Magistrates and clergymen remained limited in the forces at their disposal and limited too in respect of their knowledge. It seems very likely that they simply did not know whether the claims of right that informed many folkloric and punitive customs were valid or not. The general impression derived from the evidence from much of the period is that very few of the performers of skimmington rides, stangings, effigy burnings and other informal punishments were ever proceeded against, and where they

---

3 *Mason v Jennings* (1680) T Raym 401, 83 ER 209.
4 Jennifer Davis, 'A Poor Man's System of Justice: The London Police Courts in the Second Half of the Nineteenth Century', *Historical Journal* 27:2 (1984), pp. 309–35 at p. 314.

were convicted (typically of breaches of the peace) the penalties were often light. This is certainly true when compared to the harsh terms of imprisonment being imposed at the time for minor property offences. A sense of uncertainty regarding the law surely played its part in this.

One wonders of course whether the JP really cared about such things if there was no obvious challenge to his authority in evidence, or if there was no perceived threat to the social order as a whole. Where did his sympathies lie? The condescension displayed by contemporary newspaper editors catering for their somewhat exclusive audience, or by early folklorists collecting after the fact, should not dispose us to assume that the infliction of informal or extra-legal punishment was the sole prerogative of the lumpen labourer or ill-educated rustic. Whether it be a matter of the burial of an effigy of an officer by his disgruntled compatriots, the financing of political bonfires by well-heeled politicians or simply the participation of the middling sort in the rough music inaugurated by their less well-heeled neighbours, more classes were drawn into the system of shaming and symbolic sanctions than some of the commentaries would allow.

When it came to the harassment of a radical, the shaming of some alleged sexual deviant or simply the chastisement of a submissive husband, the magistrate did not always hasten to enforce the letter of the law. Indeed, when it came to measures against 'engrossers' and 'regraters' and the attempt to enforce price controls, many magistrates seem to have actively assisted in, as well as approved of, popular action. Whilst I shall argue that it was far from true that rough music rituals always reflected social conservatism, many did have that aspect and, as we shall see, such occurrences were much less likely to be punished, or punished severely, than those other acts of popular justice that could be viewed as attempts to disrupt the existing hierarchy of wealth and power.

A certain pragmatism was necessarily imposed upon legal officers by the limits of their coercive resources. Prior to the advent of professional policing a magistrate substantially depended upon lay-officers drawn from the community and presumably animated by community sentiments. He might have recourse to the goodwill of the respectable community as expressed through the *posse comitatus* or, as a last resort, call in military forces. Unfortunately, such forces were rather blunt in their application and on occasion represented a remedy that was worse than the disease. The inhabitants of Wantage and Abingdon complained in 1795 about the soldiers billeted upon them that 'such a sett of Villains never entered this Town before.'[5] In 1800 the inhabitants of Sunderland petitioned with the rector for the removal of troops since, 'Their principle aim is robbery.'[6]

---

5 Petition to Sir G. Young and C. Dundas, 6 April 1795 PRO WO 40/17.
6 Ibid.

Homely justice dispensed by cheery sympathetic JPs is not a picture one generally recognises when observing the aftermath of public disorder or the treatment of the itinerant poor! Nevertheless, however grudging, a degree of tolerance of local traditions, practices and beliefs was generally a politic course to pursue and this, to a degree, conditioned responses to the phenomena that will be under consideration here. In the eighteenth century, the cases that came before a magistrate depended substantially upon private complaints made in person (and intimidation was far from unknown) or upon the efforts of the local worthies, particularly the constables. A constable was, of course, a local man – a townsman or a villager steeped in its traditions and then raised up to oversee the community. Who living in a community in eighteenth-century England would believe that the annual perambulation to gather firewood and open paths, the riding of the stang to chasten the adulterer, the ploughing up of the gardens of the wealthy who were too miserly to provide the customary dole, were unlawful when, as so often the evidence suggests, the magistrate had winked at them and the constable had participated.

It was more than the fact of their continuing occurrence that argued for the legitimacy of such practices. The close association of such activity with the church calendar and with parish activities (such as beating the bounds) argued for their propriety as did their wide dispersal throughout the kingdom. Where this was insufficient, participants often anchored their claims in their own specific points of legal time, acknowledging that as a general practice a certain activity might not be permissible but in their own particular locality a particular grant or legal event did give it license. We might illustrate the point with a case of 'plough bullocking'. This was a somewhat rough-and-ready practice whereby the better houses within a rural community were visited on Plough Monday by gangs of men seeking as of right a customary dole of beer, food and/or coin. If the expected largesse failed to materialise the occupant would be abused and his property might be vandalised, but more specifically he was liable to have his garden or nearby crops grubbed up with the plough brought by the gang for that very purpose. A plough bullock in the 1880s, however, when asked if he was not afraid of being taken up by the police for such acts replied, 'They can stand by it and no law in the world can touch 'em, 'cause it's an old charter.'[7]

We may doubt that any royal charter ever legitimised this particular way of extorting money, and doubt that the speaker could give any further details of the charter in whose authority he claimed to be cloaked, but claims of ancient grants and charters were validated in other contexts sufficiently often to suggest to lay people that such claims had real legal foundation. As E. P. Thompson observed, during the dispute

---

7 R. Chambers, ed., *The Book of Days: A Miscellany of Popular Antiquities* (London, 1888), vol. 1., p. 95, cited in B. Bushaway, *By Rite, Custom, Ceremony and Community in England, 1700–1880*, 2nd edn (London: Breviary Stuff Publications, 2011), p. 5.

over rights in connection with Wigley Common in 1880 a copyholder appeared who had in his possession an old box known to the tenants as 'the monster' said to contain papers relating to the common. Sure enough, when the box was opened therein was an exemplification under the Great Seal of a decree in Chancery from 1591 declaring the tenants' rights.[8]

What one observes in the eighteenth century is a dense thicket of jurisdictions, privileges, grants, rights and anomalies, which in the nineteenth century were either steadily untangled by the judges or else largely administratively erased. This was a profoundly political process arbitrating between the interests of the strong and the weak, generally to the advantage of the former. In the meantime, however, in the dense undergrowth legal fictions were apt to bloom and indeed were often indistinguishable from the substance of 'the law'.

Under such circumstances the history of what was thought to be lawful (and that guided conduct accordingly), and the history of what was lawful according to the evolving doctrine of the common law, are rather different things. As for what the courts were actually doing at the time, there is no particular reason to suppose that the majority of the population understood or grasped the nuances of their judgements. As we shall see, mass trespasses and other collective activities could be inspired by a heady sense of rights allied to a misinterpretation of recent cases. There were, in short, strong reasons why the 'rule environment' governing day-to-day conduct and the 'legal environment' recognised by the courts were rather different things.

Some might suppose that what I am asserting is that the common population of England and Wales in the eighteenth and nineteenth centuries were astonishingly ignorant of the system governing them. I would not put it so. Rather, I would observe generally that ordinary people are not nearly as interested in the law as lawyers think that they should be, and life is lived as much in a world of legal fiction as legal fact. If we must speak of ignorance let us acknowledge it to be the general condition of mankind.

Misplaced legal beliefs have real political and social power and there is good reason to suppose that behaviours within eighteenth- and nineteenth-century society were every bit as informed by misapprehensions about the law and by false legal constructs as are behaviours observable within modern Britain. Such beliefs were not necessarily confined only to the ill-educated classes. Much of what was said in the eighteenth and nineteenth centuries about founding charters, strange bequests and visiting monarchs making grants was nonsense, but still it was nonsense that had indeed some legs.

Thompson made a great leap forward with his study of the moral authority of the crowd and this book could not have been written without him. However, I am not sure that the open invitation laid down by Thompson to move from the study of the moral authority of the crowd to the study of its claims of legal authority

---

8 E. P. Thompson, *Customs in Common* (Harmondsworth: Penguin, 1991), p. 159.

(however misplaced) has been made by many legal scholars. It seems to me that if we understood everything about the content and evolution of legal doctrine – if we were entirely aware of the way that the courts actually functioned and the manner in which magistrates, policemen, and jailers operated under their cloak of legal authority – without an understanding of the legal beliefs of the time there would still be a facet of the broader history of the law that was missing.

Beliefs, of course, are not likely to be of much interest to those seeking the 'true' history of contract, tort and other legal specialities; furthermore, they are not easy to come at. Certainly, when erroneous legal beliefs were documented in the past they were often presented as quixotic specimens, whimsical and trivial anecdotes collected by folklorists or gleefully offered by antiquarians to illustrate the stupidity of the uneducated for the general entertainment of the 'better sort'. Some of those beliefs seem somewhat bizarre. Taken together, though, such beliefs represented a powerful counterclaim to argument: in favour of the sole enjoyment of property rights; against those who believed in market pricing; in opposition to those who wanted to subdue public space and to suppress public festivity; and against attempts to reform traditional labour practices. It was the very essence of these counterclaims that they were anchored in the assertion that particular rights had had a long and uninterrupted enjoyment and that they had first been legitimised by an act in real legal time. Such claims were not always wrong; in the case of price regulation, the claims of the crowd could indeed be derived from moribund case law or statute that the contemporary judges and policy-makers had not yet explicitly disavowed.

There were many popular rights and privileges that judges and policy-makers of the eighteenth and nineteenth centuries wished to disavow and the right to disturb the peace in the cause of popular justice was one of them. However, many difficulties in dispersing fictitious views of the law, or in defeating claims based on genuine but now moribund claims of right and privilege, resulted from the fact that the views of the crowd were often derived from the sense of legal order that the judges and the lawyers had themselves created when asserting that the common law was founded in ancient custom.

Common Customary Law?

It is not clear whether the claim that common law was based upon custom was a very ancient one. Alan Cromartie points out that the earliest common law writers, 'were so far from admitting that common law might be a popular custom that they denied that its character was customary at all'.[9] The Glanvill and Bracton treatises made

---

9 A. Cromartie, 'The Idea of the Common Law as Custom', *The Nature of Customary Law*, ed. A. Perreau-Saussine and J. B. Murphy (Cambridge: CUP, 2007), pp. 203–27 at p. 204.

no attempt to argue popular *consuetudo* was as good as *lex*, they acknowledged the common law as unwritten law but emphasised the decisions of the higher courts and councillors derived from the power of the prince . . . they urged the 'usage of the judges of the king'. There was, however, an alternative tradition, one that had sprung up by the mid-fifteenth century when Sir John Fortescue claimed in *De Laudibus Legum Anglie* that the common law was rooted in the customs of the people unchanged from pre-Roman times, this view was expounded by William Fulbecke who declared in 1600 that 'the common law ariseth from the people and multitude but statute originally from the king'.[10]

The tensions between the sovereign and the common law judges led Lord Coke to subsequently try to strengthen the moral authority of the common law as against the unfettered power of the monarch, when he implied that the common law had actually been given to Britain by Brutus after he fled the Trojan War. Whether this tale of ancient origin was ever taken remotely seriously is hard to ascertain and Cromartie asserts that, in broad terms, there was a general indifference to the notion of popular consent amongst the Jacobeans. However, after the Civil War the notion of historical continuity and of a continuing vein of customary law and practice was advanced by constitutional royalists who 'paraded their attachment to determinate principles arrived at by consent'.[11] Matthew Hale in his *History of the Common Law* described the common law and custom of the realm as 'the great substratum that is to be maintained'. Sir William Blackstone subsequently referred to the common law as 'a collection of customs and maxims' and there were 'leges non scriptae, because their original institution and authority are not set down in writing, as Acts of Parliament are, but they receive their binding power, and force of laws, by long and immemorial usage, and by their universal reception throughout the kingdom'.[12] He too created his own mythical legal event in support of his premise asserting that the common law had its origins in an authoritative compilation of local customs undertaken by Alfred, but with a fresh compilation or new edition under Edward the Confessor.

Judges and jurists, then, were (and are) perfectly capable of constructing their own fictitious views of the origins of law. It was they who created what Hay refers to as: 'An extremely pervasive rhetorical tradition, with deep historical roots.'[13] The difficulty with creating myths to obscure realities is that sometimes people may indeed believe the myths and begin to assert them against the very institutions that it was hoped that they would uphold. In reality, contemporary scholars are agreed that

---

10 Ibid., p. 214.
11 Ibid., p. 221.
12 Sir Matthew Hale, *The History of the Common Law of England*, ed. C. M. Gray (Chicago, 1971), p. 45.
13 D. Hay, P. Linebaugh, J. G. Rule et al., *Albion's Fatal Tree: Crime and Society in 18C England* (London: Allen Lane, 1975), p. 35.

if common law was based upon custom it was not popular custom but rather legal custom as practised in the courts of justice: 'The common law was not developed in the community by the people but was developed in court by the artificial reason of judges.'[14] It was a synthesis of the legal culture of Westminster Hall, the Inns of Court and the pronouncements of judges as preserved in the Year Books. Common law, then, was customary lawyerly practice and true popular lay custom was, by the time of Bracton, seen as allowing only an occasional exception to the operation of common law:

> Sometimes consuetudo has its general meaning very close to lex, both standing alone and explicitly paired with lex, but it is far more common for it to refer to local customs contrary to the normal rules of the common law. There are examples of general statements of law being qualified by 'unless there is a custom to the contrary', be it the custom of a manor, a town, a county, or just simply custom without any further designation.[15]

Custom then both justified derogations from the common law and ran alongside it. At times it may have made the common law superfluous – as Sir John Salmond opined: 'Law is secondary and unessential... The administration of justice is perfectly possible without law at all.'[16]

However, it is probably a mistake to think of common law and custom as simply separate and contending systems of legal thinking. First, as James Murphy reminds us, because custom is not merely an alternative or a precursor to law but often rises up in consequence of law.[17] Second, because of the ability of common law lawyers and judges to dip into custom when necessary in order to secure the right verdict in the case before them: 'We cannot rule out the possibility that the custom was being created as a justification for reaching some desired decision and not as a disinterested exercise in formulating a general rule.'[18] We can talk of the common law courts as creating custom insofar as their occasional investigation of customary practice and determination upon it must have played an important role in recognising, fixing and propagating it. They would not have been able to do so, however, were it not for the manorial courts where local jurymen heard arguments about what indeed constituted local custom, adjudicated between rival traditions, and maintained the

---

14 M. Lobban, 'Custom, Common Law Reasoning and the Law of Nations in the Nineteenth Century', *The Nature of Customary Law*, ed. Perreau-Saussine and Murphy, pp. 256–78 at p. 258.
15 D. Ibbotsen, 'Custom in Medieval Law', *The Nature of Customary Law*, ed. Perreau-Saussine and Murphy, pp. 151–75 at p. 163.
16 Sir John Salmond, *Jurisprudence: Or the Theory of the Law* (London: Stevens and Haynes, 1902), p. 13.
17 J. Murphy, 'Habit and Convention at the Foundation of Custom', *The Nature of Customary Law*, ed. Perreau-Saussine and Murphy, pp. 53–78 at p. 67.
18 Ibbotsen, 'Custom in Medieval Law', p. 169.

routine transmission and enforcement of customary practice. It may perhaps be better to think of the manorial courts creating reservoirs of knowledge available to be exploited opportunistically by the common law courts rather than laying down local rules to which the higher courts felt obliged in local cases to demur. For Ibbotsen, 'Within the medieval legal tradition custom can be seen as a form of safety-valve enabling courts to derogate from the common law when there was sufficient pressure to do so.'[19] At best one could say, as Lobban does, that 'custom was assumed to be the foundation rather than the animating spirit of the law'.[20] There were, of course, rules for recognising custom, rules of certainty, reasonableness and uninterrupted enjoyment, to which we will return. However, custom was always vulnerable, as Ibbotsen suggests, to judicial manipulation or disavowal and was unlikely to survive long where its contents placed it in opposition to powerful political or economic interests.

In the period under consideration, faith in the power of custom was often to prove misplaced, but we can understand how that faith came about – for within the legal system custom did have its place, and in many localities and circumstances it did indeed guide the day-to-day rules of social and economic behaviour. More than that, though, the common law judges and the jurists had created a rhetoric of legitimacy around their own practice, which was based upon a kind of misdirection or a sleight of hand. One does not suppose that the Suffolk yeoman or Kentish saddler had any direct connection to Coke, Blackstone or their ilk but, as will be observed throughout this volume, English culture was a very legal culture. Ideas seeped, and artifice and imagery constructed a kind of fictive legal community accessible through aphorisms, invocations and emotional waymarks that were available for exploitation.

By the end of the eighteenth century a particular view of the legal community had become an important part of the patriotic discourse and a buttress against new radical ideas that threatened to question the existing order. Nowhere is this better exemplified than in Hannah More's *Village Politics*, published in 1792, which was constructed as a simple dialogue between two countrymen: Jack, the wise, true-blooded patriot, and Tom, a simple fellow, recently duped by the delusions peddled by Tom Paine. Tom naively reproduces the slogans he has picked up – only, of course, to have the supposed merits of the revolution in France systematically picked apart by Jack. The spearhead of Jack's attack is his assertion of the superiority of the English legal system before which everyone is equal: 'I may go to law with Sir John, at the great castle yonder, and he no more dares to lift his little finger against me than if I were his equal. A Lord is hanged for a hanging matter as thou or I should be.'[21] Heady stuff –

---

19 Ibid., p. 174.
20 Lobban, 'Custom, Common Law Reasoning and the Law of Nations', p. 258.
21 Hannah More, *Village Politics: Addressed to all Mechanics, Journeymen and Day Labourers in Great Britain by Will Chip, a Country Carpenter*, 5th edn (York: G. Walker, 1793), p. 5.

and when the scales of radicalism finally fell from Tom's eyes his first reaction was to burst into *O the roast beef of Old England*!, he then proposed to burn his copy of *The Rights of Man* and thereafter to make a bonfire – presumably to burn some effigy of Tom Paine himself.[22]

Important aspects of the way that the community was actually constructed and behaved in the eighteenth century were referenced by the responses of Tom. The significance of music in igniting collective solidarity, sentimentality or even savagery will be reiterated throughout this work. Here, the song conjured up the emotions and textures of the shared cultural values of England – which Jack had been trying to invoke from the first. A ritual repudiation of foreign-inspired nonsense was a logical next step, to be followed by a symbolic immolation of the works of the man whose ideas had so recently led Tom astray. If law played a very important part in Jack's mythologised patriotic construction, so did performance and festivity in Tom's response – it was not enough that he was persuaded by Jack's arguments, his first impulse was to manifest his new convictions with a song and a burning.

More, however, would not have it so. She and others were already responding to a perceived threat from the vibrant and disorderly popular culture that they feared might be radicalised and overbear the bounds set for it. Tom never got to build his bonfire, as Jack prevented him: 'If thou wouldst shew thy love to thy King and country, let's have no drinking, no riot, no bonfires; but put into practice this text which our parson preached on last Sunday, "Study to be quiet, work with your own hands and mind your own business".'[23] More left off on this salutary note, but one wonders what a real-life Tom would have felt upon receiving this advice; disappointment certainly, but also perhaps bewilderment. By the time of *Village Politics* a contradiction was beginning to emerge between the old politics of loyalty and the new expectations of obedience. On the one hand, social conservatives in their attempt to resist radicalism were appealing to one-nation principles, propounding fictional notions of equality, staging pageant patriotism and summing up idealised images of 'Old England'. On the other, however, deepening suspicion of popular culture made others less inclined to permit manifestations of communal sentiment, whether patriotic or otherwise. For More and her successors, the good subject was to be the passive subject, passive in the face of the operation of the free market, in the face of political controversy, passive in the face of food shortages and so on. More, via Jack, did not only wish to reverse the work of Tom Paine but to persuade her audience to reject the riotous festivity of yesteryear.

More's views, however, did not as yet prevail. Festivity and symbolic performance still served at the end of the eighteenth century as the media through which things

---

22 Ibid., p. 18.
23 Ibid., p. 18.

were done and feelings expressed. What happened within the wrapper of festivity, or through the medium of symbolic performance, will concern me greatly here – for whilst performance could indeed be simply festive or patriotic it was often also juridical. Whether it be in burning an effigy of Guy Fawkes, or of a Frenchman, or a peacemaker or a warmonger, whether it be in parading an image of a scold, ducking an informer or pelting a profiteer, communities gathered, celebrated and judged – and in judging became themselves. And this was not, for a very long time, much discouraged by social superiors. When we come to observe the burnings of the effigies of Tom Paine, of the Popes, of the Kaiser and so on, we shall see how powerful and useful ritualistic action was to the elites in constructing national society. Furthermore, criticism of the rumbustious popular culture was often nullified by the unprincipled opportunism of some of the critics themselves. There is scarcely any aspect of festive practice that was not condemned by educated commentators in the late eighteenth and early nineteenth centuries, and scarcely any aspect that was not encouraged and exploited by political elites in their struggles with each other.

Perhaps those elites had no choice other than to sit astride the engine of performance culture and attempt to steer it, for they had few other resources at their disposal. The state was rather weak during the eighteenth century and it was only gradually in the nineteenth that government became more formidable and authority became more centralised. Rule-based governance matched by a corresponding passivity on the part of the general populace became the aspiration of the better sort. One consequence of this was that, for good or ill, the juridical performances of the crowd became generally deprecated. Apologists for the process will prefer to concentrate on the development of calm and rule-based deliberation and the retreat from sometimes arbitrary and even morally repugnant acts of the unpacified mob. Cynics will observe that the retreat from popular justice involved elements of dispossession. They will observe that the process occurred during a time when the juridical power of the crowd had become less obviously focused upon the chastisement (real or symbolic) of the errant individual, and rather more engaged in passing judgement on the relationship between the orders themselves.

By the mid-Victorian period there was such a conflict between performance culture, popular festivity and all those Victorian virtues of morality, propriety and good governance, that it seemed to some contemporary commentators that two distinct cultural systems were in conflict. It was not so, however, and a wilful forgetfulness was being employed in the general omission to acknowledge that elite groups had, until very recently, been enthusiastically participating in many facets of the plebeian culture that they now so vigorously denounced. The facet of popular culture that interests me most here, that which sanctioned rough music and other justice rituals, had by this time become quite distinct from the operation of the formal legal process and as such was readily attacked. However, far from being the product of a distinct, separate, somewhat hidden counterculture, the performances that shamed and symbolically punished were in fact embedded within a framework of assumptions that had long informed the official justice visited upon criminal conduct. What by the end of the nineteenth century was appearing to educated commentators as quaint and absurd, was not the vestigial remains of an ignorant independent tradition antithetical to orthodox law enforcement, rather it represented a survival of the methodology by which England had for a very long time been governed. It is with the earlier systems of formal governance, then, that we begin.

1

Law, Symbolism and Punishment

Much of what was accounted in the nineteenth century as illegitimate and unwarranted popular punishment had its antecedents in the orthodox modes of chastisement observable in the seventeenth and eighteenth centuries; a time when, if communities did not own their justice systems, they nevertheless remained very interested shareholders. Given the rather vestigial nature of the government, some rough accommodation with general opinion was a necessity. William Paley warned in 1785:

> Let them, [civil governors] be admonished that the physical strength resides in the governed; that this strength wants only to be felt and roused, to lay prostrate the most ancient and confirmed dominion; that civil authority is founded in opinion; that general opinion ought therefore always to be treated with deference and managed with delicacy and circumspection.[1]

Nowhere, of course, was the need to reconcile general opinion to the operation of the legal system greater than in the area of criminal law, where the community had always played an important role in the identification and prosecution of offences. A reward system was in operation, but thief-taking and approving went into general decline following the disreputable career and final fall of Jonathan Wild in 1725. The system at the end of the eighteenth century was almost entirely dependent on the inclination of private prosecutors, the activities of private prosecution societies, or the vigour of the constables and their assistants in spying out and hauling malefactors before the magistrates. The resulting system was far from moribund. For example, there were at least 450 prosecution societies created in England between 1744 and 1856,[2] and Ruth

---

1 William Paley, *The Principles of Moral and Political Philosophy* (New York: B. and W. Collins, 1835 edn), Book VI Ch. 2.
2 A. Schubert, 'Private Initiative in Law Enforcement: Associations for the Prosecution of Felons, 1744–1856', *Policing and Punishment in Nineteenth Century Britain*, ed. Victor Bailey (New Brunswick, NJ: Rutgers University Press, 1981), pp. 25–41 at p. 27.

Paley has argued that in London, at least, the traditional mechanisms of law enforcement were not nearly as ineffectual as their opponents liked to claim.[3] Certainly, persons of lowly status had at least sufficient faith in the possibility of the system doing justice to bring their own prosecutions.[4] In certain circumstances, that is.

We cannot quantify the number of potential offences that were not pursued, not because of lack of evidence but because the putative prosecutors felt that a recourse to law was inappropriate. We can, however, observe that those who pursued criminal prosecutions with inappropriate malice, or who failed to exercise compassion by insisting that the full force of the often very harsh property laws be applied against defendants, were liable to excite social disapproval or even vengeance; also that the system was suffused with elements of reconciliation, compensation and arbitration – albeit not always visible. What remain most visible are the advertisements placed by malefactors: identifying their offence, begging pardon and expressing gratitude to the injured party for their magnanimity. It should also be noted that paying compensation to a victim as an alternative to being prosecuted was common, albeit unlawful in the case of a felony. Thus, when Richard Ainsworth stole from his master Nicholas Blundell in 1709 he agreed to work at repairing one of Blundell's houses in return for him agreeing not to prosecute.[5]

As for arbitration, the life of many a JP was bedevilled by the need to untangle complex petty disputes. Outhwaite remarks that the notebook of the Revd Edmund Tew, magistrate and rector of Boldon in county Durham, demonstrates that only a fraction of the disputes that came to the attention of an eighteenth-century magistrate were ever likely to come to court: 'Arbitration and summary justice, processes that leave no mark in formal records were far more common than trials.'[6] The nineteenth century was not so very different, Jennifer Davis has remarked that there was 'an important aspect to the nineteenth century police courts which has been largely overlooked by historians, and this was their utilisation by the poor as a source of advice, charity and adjudication in personal and neighbourhood disputes'.[7] Davis also noted that when the poor went so far as to prosecute they had very clear ideas of what they expected to be delivered by the courts.

---

3 See R. Paley, 'An Imperfect, Inadequate and Wretched System? Policing London before Peel', *Criminal Justice History* 10 (1989), pp. 95–130.

4 43 per cent of those who prosecuted for assault at the Essex quarter sessions between 1780 and 1789 were tradesmen or artisans and 24 per cent labourers. See P. King, 'Punishing Assault: The Transformation of Attitudes in the English Courts', *J. of Interdisciplinary History* 27 (1996), pp. 43–74 at p. 57, table 9.

5 N. Blundell, *Nicholas Blundell's Diary and Letter Book, 1702–1728*, ed. Margaret Blundell (Liverpool: Liverpool University Press, 1952), pp. 109–111.

6 R. B. Outhwaite, *The Rise and Fall of the English Ecclesiastical Courts, 1500–1860* (Cambridge: CUP, 2006), p. 102.

7 Davis, 'A Poor Man's System of Justice', pp. 309–35 at p. 315.

What one observes is certainly not a system of prosecution and judgement in which rich and poor were equally served but nonetheless a system that retained close connections to the mores of the broader community, and certainly one that allowed, in the eighteenth and early nineteenth centuries, interested parties to meaningfully influence the operation and outcome of the system. To say this is not to accept the unduly optimistic representation of a benign system offered by nineteenth-century apologists or to deny that the defendant was often profoundly disadvantaged, but to identify an attitude to the administration of justice that was characterised as much by a sense of independence as it was by subservience. People were prepared to bargain or compromise, they had strategies they could adopt to prevent prosecution or, to a degree, mitigate the consequences of conviction. Within the courtroom itself the well-educated, at least, might still get up from the audience and address the court, and the jurors were not afraid to question judges or return special verdicts.

It is necessary to point out that robust participation in the criminal justice process did not always have benign consequences. In the second half of the nineteenth century, judges were struggling to convince juries that self-induced intoxication did not amount to a defence to the charge of murder, and similarly that murder could not be excused if committed in consequence of minor provocation. Under particular scrutiny was the licence to do away with 'troublesome' wives. Martin Wiener has identified twelve cases of spousal killing in the 1860s in which jurors returned manslaughter verdicts in opposition to the instructions or clearly expressed views of the judge. Where the capital sentence was imposed, twenty-four recommendations of mercy were made by juries, only ten of which were supported by the judge. Jurors were prepared to assert their own views in the courtroom and in doing so presumably reflected the mores of the men of their communities. However, this did not necessarily result in justice being done on behalf of victims, or the protection of the law being fully extended to future potential victims.[8]

Most criminal cases did not, of course, proceed as far as an assize. Justice was instead administrated by local powers and applied close upon the commission of the offence. Justice was integrated into community space and community time and, for our purposes, it is important that justice time was also festive time, and justice space, festive space. This was true even of the assize, as illustrated by Martin Madan in 1785:

> Another cause of much evil is the trying prisoners after dinner; when, from the morning's adjournment, all parties have retired to a hearty meal; which, at assize-time, is commonly attended, among the middling and lower ranks of people, at least, with a good deal of drink. The symptoms of this vulgar species of festivity are usually too apparent,

---

8 Martin J. Wiener, 'Judges v Jurors: Courtroom Tensions in Murder Trials and the Law of Criminal Responsibility in Nineteenth Century England', *Law and History Review* 17:3 (1999), pp. 467–506 at p. 472.

when the court assembles in the afternoon – the noise, crowd, and confusion, which these occasion, seldom cost the Judge less than about an hour, before the court can be brought into any kind of order; and when this is done, drunkenness is too frequently apparent, where it ought of all things to be avoided, I mean, in jurymen and witnesses. The heat of the court, joined to the fumes of the liquor, has laid many an honest juryman into a calm and profound sleep, and sometimes it has been no small trouble for his fellows to jog him into the verdict – even where a wretch's life has depended on the event! – This I myself have seen – as also witnesses, by no means in a proper situation to give their evidence.[9]

Some of the barriers between recognised formal justice and informal community sanctions begin to break down once one (i) observes the festive qualities of judgement in the eighteenth and early nineteenth centuries; (ii) acknowledges the role often played in prosecution, process and punishment by local opinion; and (iii) conversely recognises the judicial quality innate in many of the contemporary popular festivities.

In December 1817, a 'trial of a novel description' took place in a public house at the village of Upstreet in Kent. The defendant was a young man who had allegedly tried to seduce a servant girl. A jury of villagers was convened and 'after a most patient investigation of his case' the defendant was found guilty. His sentence was to be forced to drink four pints of onion broth and to be hung upside down from a beam in the pub – a sentence which, despite his fierce resistance, was immediately carried out, 'to the no small amusement and gratification of the Company present'.[10] The newspaper report is humorous and the jurymen are described condescendingly as 'honest rustics'. Important elements, however, are likely to be missed if one simply regards the incident as a whimsical affair, a sort of good-natured event rather like that which sometimes occurs at a school fete where a teacher, protesting theatrically, agrees to be put in mock stocks and is pelted with wet sponges in order to raise money for the school. Here, the punishment imposed was unpleasant, humiliating and clearly accomplished with a degree of physical force. But this surely was not a juridical event – the participants cannot have thought that they were doing justice in a formal sense? Yet, in fact, the question is not as absurd as might at first be supposed. The public house was indeed a place for doing justice – justices operated out of them, coroners' juries sat over bodies in them, court-leets met in them and so on.[11] If the punishment was peculiar to itself, still, as we shall see, it fitted into that broad category of public

---

9 M. Madan, *Thoughts on Executive Justice, with Respect to our Criminal Laws, Particularly on the Circuits* (London: J. Dodsley, 1785), pp. 148–50.
10 *The Kentish Chronicle*, 9 December 1817.
11 In Salford, for example, Maurice Griffiths had operated out of, and committed offenders to prison from, the 'rival court' of the Crown and Thistle in opposition to the bench at the New Bayley Courthouse. See George Fisher, 'The Birth of the Prison Retold', *Yale Law Journal* 104: 6 (1995), pp. 1232–324 at p. 1241.

shaming punishments often inflicted upon those accused of sexual impropriety. If the people instigating and leading such proceedings were also men holding positions such as constable or sidesman, then might they not have been perceived of as having a quasi-official status?

If the rhetoric of law was often that of common ownership then one can also suppose that the claims of the crowd were in part substantiated by the employment of official sanctions that recognised that punishment was properly a matter of shame, as well as pain, and that the gaze of the public should provide at least one of the elements and sometimes both. It was in the performance of punishment rather than the adjudication of offences that the relationship between informal community justice and official sanction became most closely intertwined, for both employed a common language in constructing and signifying the shame that the malefactor was obliged to feel and endure.

The Tradition of Judicial Riding

As Martin Ingram has observed, the connections between official and unofficial punishments that were explicit in the medieval and early modern periods are probably most clearly exemplified by the processional punishments documented in respect of the City of London.[12] Offences that frequently invoked such judicial ridings were often connected to the use by retailers of unjust weights and measures or the vending of unfit produce, especially those falling under the assizes of bread and ale. A baker who produced an underweight loaf was dealt with thus:

> The first time let him be drawn upon a Hurdle from the Guildhall to his own house, through the great streets where there may be most people assembled, and through the great streets that are most dirty, with the faulty loaf hanging about his neck. If a second time he be found committing the same offence, let him be drawn through the great street of Chepe, in manner aforesaid, to the Pillory ... And the third time that the default be found, he shall be drawn, and the oven shall be pulled down, and the baker made to forswear the trade within the city forever.[13]

Bakers so exhibited were 'preceded by minstrelsy' and an image of just such a baker dragged on a hurdle with a loaf around his neck appears in the *Liber Albus*.[14]

---

12 See M. Ingram, 'Juridical Folklore in England Illustrated by Rough Music', *Communities and Courts in Britain, 1150–1900*, ed. C. W. Brooks and M. Lobban (London: Hambledon Press, 1997), pp. 61–82.
13 *The Articles of Usage of the City of London*, cited in L. Jewitt, 'The Pillory and Who They Put In It', *Reliquary* 1 (1861) pp. 209–24 at p. 212.
14 Calendar of the plea and memoranda rolls of the city of London: vol. 1: 1323–1364 (1926), pp. 1–10. Roll A 1a: April 1323–August 1326.

Being paraded to the pillory was also the punishment for the sale of other deficient commodities. In 1369 John Wastelle was convicted of having offered for sale five putrid snipe, two thrushes and a woodcock and was dragged to the pillory where the birds were burnt beneath him.[15] In 1374 three butchers convicted of selling rotten meat were pilloried and had their meat similarly burnt.[16] In the same year John atte Wode, a baker, was pilloried for having enticed one Robert de Cawode away from a market in order to buy up his grain secretly in the Church of the Friars Minors. He was convicted of an attempt to enhance the price of grain.[17]

We shall return to the assize of bread and other products later, for the moment it suffices to note that in the nineteenth century commentators became exasperated by the fact that the common people could not be induced to understand a free market in food and pricing, which fluctuated according to supply and demand. There was little acknowledgement that price-fixing and action against regraters, forestallers and others, had been the policy of the law for many preceding centuries.

The theatricality that frequently accompanied the journey to the pillory indicates that the procession was not merely designed to broadcast the fact of the offence but also to re-enact it, advertise its detection and anticipate its punishment. In 1517 the Court of Alderman had a tailor 'set there on horseback his face turned to the horsetail and holding the said horsetail in his hand with a paper on his head purporting the cause and title of this matter'.[18] A butcher selling rancid bacon was to be 'conveyed tomorrow throughout this city on horseback with his face towards the horsetail with a flitch of the said corrupt bacon cut into two pieces, whereof the one part shall be hanged before his breast and the other piece behind his back'.[19] Dishonest vending could take many forms. For example, a false pardoner was forced to ride through Cheapside seated the wrong way on his horse, with his forged indulgences hung around his neck and wearing a paper hat upon which his offences were written.

The procession allowed the populace to identify the perpetrator and follow him or her to the place of further torment. However, it may also have served to tell the malefactor how they should feel. William Ian Miller has claimed that expressions of individual emotion such as 'I feel sad' or 'I feel happy' were rarely used before the nineteenth century and that: 'One could hazard the claim that as late as the

---

15 Calendar of letter-books of the city of London: G: 1352–1374 (1905), pp. 258–63. Folios ccxli–ccli: Jan 1369–70.
16 Calendar of letter-books of the city of London: G: 1352–1374 (1905), pp. 327–34. Folios cccxxi–cccxxvi: May 1374.
17 Calendar of letter-books of the city of London: G: 1352–1374 (1905), pp. 169–78. Folios cxxx–cxl: September 1364.
18 Ingram, 'Juridical Folklore', p. 70.
19 Ibid., p. 71.

seventeenth century the self did not feel emotions at all; instead the emotions were borne almost as a quasi-juridical status or as allegorical personae that the subject put on mask like.'[20] The parade to the pillory, then, was a particularly apt punishment for those who had practised a form of deceit, who had concealed their natures from others. Their mask was stripped bare and they were forced to accept the shame and the estimation of themselves that was put upon them.

The ridings in London were not only associated with dishonest practice but also sexual impropriety or social deviance, and this was replicated elsewhere. Judicial riding was a widely distributed European phenomenon equipped with a common iconography. To give but one example, an illustration on the pictorial map of Seville from the *Civitates Orbis Terrarum* (1572–1617) shows just such an event. Three figures appear mounted on donkeys. The first is a woman who is stripped to the waist and is identified as a prostitute. The unfortunate woman is followed by a man who has two antlers protruding from his head, topped with flags and bells. A second woman follows him in a white robe and she appears to be whipping him. This is explained as 'execution de justicia de los cornudos patients', the judicial punishment of those who bear horns – that is, men who have allowed their wives to cuckold them. The three are being shepherded along by a man on horseback and two on foot; a group following behind is running to catch up with the procession.[21]

Processions in the City of London were rather elaborate. Prostitutes were forced to wear a gaily striped hood, scolds were obliged to parade carrying distaffs and each had their heads shaved.[22] Being a scold was an offence under law, a scold being 'a troublesome and angry woman who, by her brawling and wrangling amongst her neighbours, doth break the public peace and begat, cherish and increase public discord'.[23] One could be similarly punished for being an adulterer or a prostitute. In 1529, five licentious women were 'conveyed from the Counter [prison] to Newgate with minstrelsy, that is to say with pans and basins ringing before them and they to wear ray hoods and to have in their hands white rods in token of common bawds, strumpets and harlots'.[24] They were thereafter banished from the city. Although best attested in London, similar judicial ridings are also portrayed on fourteenth-century misericords from cathedrals in Bristol, Hereford and Wells.

---

20 W. I. Miller, *Humiliation And Other Essays on Honor, Social Discomfort, and Violence* (Ithaca: Cornell University Press: 1993) p. 177.
21 J. Simpson, *Folklore Society Newsletter*, June 2011, pp 15–16.
22 See H. T. Riley, ed., *Munimenta Gildhallae Londoniensis*, Rolls Series (3 vols in 4, London, 1859–62), i. pp. 457–60, cited in Ingram, 'Juridical Folklore', p. 69. See also, Thomas Walshingham, *Historia Anglicana*, ed. H. T. Riley, Rolls Series (2 vols, London, 1863–4), ii, p. 65.
23 Keith Thomas, *Religion and the Decline of Magic: Studies in Popular Beliefs in Sixteenth and Seventeenth Century England* (London: Weidenfeld and Nicholson, 1971), p. 528.
24 LMA COL/CC/01/01/013/ff. 141 v, 143, 27th May 1578–9 March 1529.

Throughout the medieval and early modern periods the issue of controlling women featured prominently in official local justice, and to the prostitute and the cuckold we must add the scold and the virago as likely targets for public humiliation. A fifteenth-century choir screen from Glasgow Cathedral shows a woman who has her husband on a leash; one of the sixteenth-century panels from Montecute House in Somerset shows a poor husband reduced to feeding the baby whilst his wife menaces him with her shoe. However, misericords also show the appropriate response. A triptych in Stratford-upon-Avon Church, for example, on the left has a scene with a woman sticking out her tongue insolently, in the middle she appears to be in some pain and on the right she has been fitted with a brank or scold's bridle. A bridled female head also features in a misericord from Ludlow dated to 1453.

However loose the definition, being a scold was an offence under law, so too was being an adulterer or a prostitute. There were already offences against social propriety that the law did not notice, but which the community might morally disapprove of. As we have seen, there was a general disapproval of tempestuous wives and unduly submissive husbands. Occasionally, such parties might be made the subject of official sanction. For example, it was decreed in 1572 that: 'Wodde's wife shall go about the town with a basin afore her and a sword a buckler on her shoulders, and her husband to follow her with a broom on his shoulder, which punishment is for biting away a piece of her husband's ear and for fighting with him and other using herself towards him.'[25]

Martin Ingram argues, however, that for the most part the law did not formerly recognise wifely viragos as offenders and so the community was left to take matters into their own hands. He notes two ridings from the diary of Henry Machyn (1550–1563), neither of which find their way into the records of the Court of Aldermen. The first, dated 1562, is described thus: 'on the 9 day of March, being Monday, one Tristram, a cook with Westmorland Place within Silver Street, rode upon a cowlstaff with a basket of grains before him, because that one of his neighbour['s] wife broke her husband['s] head, and cast grains upon the people.' Here, a neighbour appeared in the place of the benighted husband. John Stow in his *Survey of London* (1598) similarly describes an unofficial riding and Ingram believes that: 'These charivaresque customs were distinctively non-official, but they ran parallel to and in very close association with legal shame sanctions that were in regular and lively use.'[26]

As such one can readily imagine that informal justice might not always have been deprecated by the vicar, the constable or the magistrate. Complaint, on the part of the unfortunate recipients, might be a doubtful business. In 1708 a group of women were prosecuted in Kent by one Susannah Massingham for having 'rioted' against

---

25 See Graham Mayhew, *Tudor Rye* (Falmer: University of Sussex, 1987) p. 205.
26 Ingram, 'Juridical Folklore', p. 81.

her. However, the defendants were promptly acquitted by the quarter sessions and she herself was in return convicted both of being a scold and keeping a bawdy house.[27]

Characterising acts as belonging to the category of official punishment or informal community justice is not always easy today and may not always have been easy at the time. Joan Kent reports an interesting example from Burton-on-Trent in 1618. A mob broke into the house of one William Cripple, where a woman was cohabiting with him. He asserted that she was his wife but the mob did not believe it and dragged them out and along the street, 'with great noise and ringing of cow bells, basins, candlesticks, frying pans and with the sound of a drum, crying aloud, "A whore and a knave, a whore, a whore".'[28] The unfortunates were put in the stocks, mocked and pelted. Ostensibly, the event had all the facets of mob justice, save that the ringleader of the whole affair turned out to be the constable of Burton, Edward Lambe. According to Ingram:

> These were precisely the circumstances that, according to William Lambard and other legal commentators, justified a constable with the assistance of neighbours in invading the house to make an arrest; the officer also had the right to imprison the suspects in the stocks if they could not be taken immediately before a justice . . . In other words, this was not folk justice but – and historians of early modern England must be aware of the distinction – urban customary justice. Lambe may have stretched his authority a little, and it is certainly possible that the proceedings got out of hand and degenerated into gratuitous violence . . . But it is plain that what was done in Burton in this case was essentially similar to what was done by the authority of the magistrates in London.[29]

Stretching one's authority is a temptation of all times and all places. When systems become bureaucratised and more clearly rule-based, then perhaps the opportunities for ambiguous action become more circumscribed. The development of the Home Office, the emergence of professional policing, the tighter regulation of the magistracy and other legislative and judicial developments eventually swept away much that had hitherto been informal about the administration of justice, but it is not clear that the scope for manoeuvre offered to the JP, the constable, the headborough and other officials in a village in Staffordshire in 1800 would have been so very much less than that offered in 1618.

However, the decline of the use of judicial riding in the seventeenth century did more clearly expose the skimmingtons and stang ridings of popular culture as unofficial and possibly anti-authoritarian practices. Ingram identifies the abolition of Star

---

27 Kent A. O. Q/SI West Kent Mich. 1708 ff. 9, 12.
28 Joan R. Kent, '"Folk Justice" and Royal Justice in Early Seventeenth-Century England: A "Charivari" in the Midlands', *Midlands History* 8 (1983), pp. 70–85.
29 Ingram, 'Juridical Folklore', p. 73.

Chamber in 1641 as a significant step in the process, wherein the old civic punishments fell out of use. He writes of ridings that: 'The authorities' insistence on order and obedience in a period of rapid political, economic and social change did eventually lead to a hardening of attitudes to this popular arrogation of quasi-legal authority.'[30] He also suggests that whereas the middle classes participated in the urban ridings of the mid-sixteenth century, by the mid-eighteenth century they had become the preserve of the lower sort. I am not at all sure that this is correct. I hope that it will become clear over the course of this work that long into the nineteenth century there were some respectable people of property who supported the practice of popular ridings. Furthermore, it is not so certain that the authorities depreciated such practices to the extent that is sometimes suggested. Yes, there is evidence that in some places in the nineteenth century magistrates and police were very active in trying to suppress rough music but there were also places and cases in which the music was officially tolerated or even actively approved.

It has also to be said that whilst the particular species of judicial riding observable in the City of London did indeed disappear in the seventeenth century, there remained plenty within official sanction to encourage the belief that justice was an aspect of popular festivity to be claimed as a right. Parade, display and public punishment, both symbolic and actual, continued to inform the operation of the criminal law. Forms of ridings persisted in the sense that traitors continued to be dragged through crowds on hurdles,[31] and the Tyburn procession endured until 1783. Although not perhaps a formal riding, a trip to the pillory was often turned into such and the pillory endured as a punishment until 1837. Here, perhaps more than anywhere, was official punishment and community disapprobation most closely merged – or such, at least was the intent. Political pilloryings of authors and publishers were famously liable to backfire upon the authorities, as did the pillorying of Daniel Defoe in 1703. Political pillorying aside, it is significant that, as with rough music, it was sexual or social deviancy that was most likely to excite the crowd. Though half-hearted attempts might be made to offer some protection to the victim, especially as the pillory moved towards its eradication, nonetheless the criminal justice system often gave licence to the most feral instincts of the people. M. D'Archenholz spoke of the detestation of the English for sodomy, 'a certain unnatural crime' for which, he says: 'The punishment by law is imprisonment, and the pillory. With this accusation, it is, however, better to suffer death at once; for, on such an occasion, the fury of the populace is unbounded, and

---

30 Ingram, 'Juridical Folklore', p. 82.
31 By 1803 and the execution of Colonel Depard, however, the public exhibition of men upon hurdles had been dispensed with. Curiously, though, other elements were preserved – in what one suspects was a rather odd (perhaps even embarrassing) ritual, the colonel was drawn on a hurdle around the yard of Horsemonger Lane prison preceded by a procession of sheriff, clergy and constables with the prison keeper bearing a white wand and the executioner a drawn sword.

even the better sort of people have no compassion for the culprit.'[32] Many types of sexual misconduct invoked harsh retribution and it suffices to cite only a single example of the horrors that could be inflicted: Ann Marrow was blinded by an outraged mob in 1777 after she had allegedly impersonated a man and then married three women.[33]

The pillory was not the only method by which gender distinctions and social subordination were being enforced through pain and ridicule into the nineteenth century. There was still the possibility, albeit a remote one, that a scold might find herself exhibited, placed in the brank or 'scolds' bridle',[34] like that still in use in Lichfield in 1781.[35] The folklorist Georgina Jackson asserted that the 'brank' had been employed in Much Wenlock in Shropshire in 1840 and 1846, and Charlotte Burne claimed both that its last use had been imposed by the Mayorial Court of Shrewsbury upon a scold from Frankwell and that the woman was still living at the time of the publication of her collection of folklore in 1886. Nash and Kilday have perhaps more reliably identified a case from Scotland as late as 1858.[36] The brank or bridle seems always to have been more popular in Scotland than England, where ducking seems to have been more generally preferred. The longevity of this particular practice as an officially sanctioned punishment is difficult to ascertain. In 1809 Jenny Pipes was paraded through Leominster and immersed in the River Lugg by order of magistrates.[37] There may well be some scattered later examples.

As suggested above, the retreat from the festivity of public punishment was steady, albeit slow and contested. After 1817 women were no longer publicly whipped. The gibbet finally disappeared in 1834 and, as already mentioned, so did the pillory in

---

32 M. D'Archenholz, *A Picture of England: Containing a Description of the Laws, Customs and Manners of England. Interspersed with Curious and Interesting Anecdotes* (Dublin: P. Byrne, 1790), p. 197.
33 Place Papers BL.Add.MS 27826, fo.172.
34 See Thomas, *Religion and the Decline of Magic*, p. 528. For the use of these devices at a later period, see David Underdown, 'The Taming of the Scold: The Enforcement of Patriarchal Authority in Early Modern England', *Order and Disorder in Early Modern England*, ed. A. Fletcher and J. Stevenson (Cambridge: CUP, 1985), pp. 116–36.
35 See M. W. Greenslade, ed., *A History of the County of Stafford, Vol. 14: Lichfield* (Oxford: OUP, 1990), pp. 73–87. A scold's bridle was bought by the Conduit Lands Trustees in 1666–7 and one was apparently used in 1781. See D. 35/bailiffs' accts. 1704–94, p. 445 and D. 126/acct. bk. 1663 1805, acct. 1666 7. D. 35 Lichfield City Council records (Treasurer's Dept.) held at the Lichfield Joint Record Office.
36 NAS:JC 26/1031–1041 cited in D. Nash and A. Kilday, *Cultures of Shame: Exploring Crime and Morality in Britain, 1600–1900* (Basingstoke: Palgrave Macmillan, 2010), p. 35.
37 William S. Walsh, *Curiosities of Popular Customs and of Rites, Ceremonies, Observances, and Miscellaneous Antiquities* (London: J. B. Lippincott Company, 1914), p. 349. See also J. Piggott, 'Antiquities of Leominster: The Ducking Stool', *Notes and Queries*, 4th series, vol. 4 (17 July 1869), p. 61.

1837. The stocks seem to have disappeared from many towns by the 1830s,[38] but the minute book of the magistrates of the Borough of Wenlock shows that they sentenced one defendant to be placed in them in June 1852.[39] Men could still be publicly whipped but the incidence of this had declined dramatically in the 1830s, albeit the penalty remained available until 1862.

Another form of less corporeally painful but no less humiliating punishment had also disappeared by this time – that of being forced by the Church courts to do penance. There had been a general decline in the imposition of penance by the end of the seventeenth century. Outhwaite has shown, however, that the picture was rather mixed. Corrective presentments made by churchwardens and others, so called office prosecutions, actually increased in some areas between the end of the seventeenth and middle of the eighteenth centuries, notably in the deanery courts of Lancashire.[40] In 1789 at Salisbury, 'One Woodridge, a carpenter, at Petworth in this county, having married his late wife's sister, they both did penance together in the church at that place.'[41] Carrying out a penance while wearing a white sheet was still being performed at Much Wenlock in 1790. At Fritton Church, Suffolk in 1816, Hannah Freeman did penance 'for defaming the character of Mary Banham, spinster'.[42] John George Hall reports two penances around the same time in the East Riding of Yorkshire:

> A farmer's son, the father of an illegitimate child, came into the church at the time of Divine service on the Lord's day, covered with a sheet, having a white wand in his hand; he walked barefoot up the aisle, stood over against the desk where the prayers were read, and there repeated a confession at the dictation of the clergyman; after which he walked out of the church. The other was that of a young woman, 'who bore unhusbanded a mother's name.' She also came into the church barefoot, covered with a sheet, bearing a white wand, and went through the same ceremony. She had one advantage which the young man had not, her long hair so completely covered her face that not one feature could be seen . . . These appear to have been the last cases of the kind that occurred at Sancton. The sin was perpetuated, but the penalty ceased; my father [who died in 1829] observed that rich offenders evaded the law, and then the authorities could not for shame continue to inflict this penalty upon the labouring classes.[43]

---

38 For instance, the stocks had been removed from Blackpool by 1837. The Revd William Thornber, *The History of Blackpool and its Neighbourhood* (Poulton: Blackpool and Fylde Historical Society, 1837), p. 276.
39 Charlotte S. Burne, *Shropshire Folk-Lore: A Sheaf of Gleanings* (London: Trubner and Co., 1883) p. 467. The use of the stocks was finally abolished in 1872.
40 Outhwaite, *The Rise and Fall of the English Ecclesiastical Courts*, p. 83
41 *Salisbury Journal*, 28 December 1789.
42 A. Suckling, *The History and Antiquities of the County of Suffolk, with Genealogical Notices of Several Towns and Villages* (London: John Weale, 1846), vol. 1, pp. 352–9.
43 John George Hall, *A History of South Cave and of other Parishes in the East Riding of the County of York* (Hull: Edwin Ombler, 1892), p. 133.

Penance as a means of social correction was clearly becoming rather rare. In December 1839 a woman was forced to do penance at Walton Church, near Liverpool for defaming a neighbour. The *Liverpool Mercury* reported: 'It is many years since such an occurrence took place: the white sheet was not, however, enforced. This should be a warning to the fair sex who are troubled with an evil tongue.'[44] Ten years later, the vicar of Fen Ditton in Cambridgeshire caused a riot when he attempted to inflict a public penance on a woman who had allegedly defamed his wife. Three thousand people turned up, interrupted the proceedings and damaged the church.[45] A public penance was performed at Stonehouse in 1851,[46] but the ecclesiastical courts lost their final criminal jurisdiction in 1860.[47]

In short, it is the case that during the course of the nineteenth century, public humiliation was increasingly marginalised in the official punitive process. The fact remains, however, that for perhaps half the period under consideration here, the authorities were continuing to impose the sorts of punishments that would have been entirely familiar to the populace of two hundred years earlier. The relationship between official and popular justice throughout this time was often intimate and it was only in the second half of the nineteenth century that it was entirely broken asunder. The rise of imprisonment, the reformation of public space, a declining belief in the therapeutic and deterrent value of public exhibition, squeamishness, a preference for rule-based correction and a repudiation of arbitrary outcomes, these were but some of the reasons why the old punitive system was steadily abandoned. Some communities in the later nineteenth century were, however, still strongly advancing the claim that they were entitled to stage their own public shaming punishments. Whilst outside observers often parodied or treated with condescension such claims, the strength with which they were advanced must owe not a little to the fact that the instruments and language of the punishments proposed were donated from, or at the very least shared with, similar species of lawful activity that were still within the collective memory.

---

44 The *Liverpool Mercury* cited in *Freeman's Journal and Daily Commercial Advertiser* (Dublin, Ireland), Monday 17 December 1838.

45 A. F. Wareham and A. P. M. Wright, *A History of the County of Cambridge and the Isle of Ely: Volume 10: Cheveley, Flendish, Staine and Staploe Hundreds (north-eastern Cambridgeshire)* (London: Victorian County History Society, 2002), pp. 127–29.

46 F. S. Hockaday, 'The Consistory Court of the Diocese of Gloucester', *Transactions of the Bristol and Gloucestershire Archaeological Society* 46 (1924), pp.195–287 at p. 224.

47 The 1832 parliamentary report identified 372 Church courts in England, pp., 1831–2, xxiv, 552.

2

Localism, Justice and the Right to Judge

It is surely no coincidence that the places in the first half of the nineteenth century where we see the penitent still exhibited and the scold still ducked or bridled are those small market towns or parishes away from the babble of metropolitan politics and reform. These were also the places where rituals of popular justice were most firmly entrenched. Popular justice could only be delivered where it was possible to mobilise a crowd, where the offence was adjudged sufficiently egregious and where the participants were endowed with their own sense of entitlement. It was from a sometimes ferocious sense of local patriotism and a concern for communal reputation that the intuition that one was entitled to sit in judgement upon the acts of one's neighbours derived, although as we shall see this was not fostered by geography alone but often also bolstered amongst specific groups by a strong and additional sense of occupational affinity.

Local Patriotism

Parochial loyalty was highly developed in the early modern period but was likely getting stronger into the eighteenth and possibly even into the early nineteenth centuries. In part this was a consequence of the Poor Relief Act 1662, requiring parishes to offer relief to their own paupers but to remove paupers whose legal settlement was in another parish. Cash-strapped parishes were thereafter very keen to formalise the distinction generally acknowledged within the community, between those who genuinely belonged and those who did not. Suggett notes that, in Wales: 'By the mid-eighteenth century parish vestry books can on occasion reveal something approaching a siege mentality, with resolutions refusing to allow strangers to settle in the parish, condemning collections for "foreigners", and obliging migrant workers to carry "passports" noting their place of legal settlement.'[1] As the legal significance

---

1 R. Suggett, 'Festivals and Social Structure in Early Modern Wales', *Past and Present* 152:1 (1996), pp. 79–112 at p. 104.

of parish boundaries became even more formalised old rivalries were exacerbated. In Clwyd: 'Parish became opposed to parish, and whenever the young men belonging to the different parishes met they fought savagely, from no personal animosity, but from a mistaken notion that it was a duty incumbent upon them to settle in this way old parochial misunderstandings; or battles were fought because some feud of remote, unknown origin existed between one parish and another.'[2] Such parochial patriotism is evidenced from many parts of England and Wales. In Gloucestershire, for example, anyone who came to live in the village of Upton St Leonards 'was called a foreigner, especially applied to anyone living on the other side of the Severn. Some are said to have attended a nearby church and to have been told, "foreigners" were not wanted.'[3]

Whilst very real rights and privileges were at issue, hostility between parishes was enlivened by a sense of the otherness of the world beyond the parish. Snell observes the rich tradition of abuse between parishes predicated upon the assertion that the 'foreigners' were habitual drunkards, irremediably stupid, morally lapsed, physically deformed, invariably lazy and so on. Violence inevitably followed insult, and a person moving into a village 'was looked upon as a kind of foreigner or interloper, who had no right there. We have known persons both insulted and assaulted for a long time till they got initiated or naturalised.'[4] As E. P. Thompson put it: 'The communal economy was parochial and exclusive: if Weldon's rights were ours, then Brigstock men and women must be kept out.'[5] Bundled up with the parish were collections of customary economic rights that the parishioners were keen to protect.

However, economic activities sometimes transcended village boundaries and called into being larger loyalties – for the free miners of Forest of Dean, for example, their peculiar occupational situation probably transcended simple local loyalty. 'The Forest was "the country" and other places in England, especially the counties beyond Gloucestershire, were other "countries". People born outside of the Forest were "foreigners". That terminology contained a splendidly arrogant sense of election.'[6] Other occupational groups such as London's silk-weavers were organised in ways that also cut across parochial boundaries. Some of these occupation groups had been earlier formalised by guilds, charters and the 1563 Statute of Artificers, others had

---

2   E. Owen, *Old Stone Crosses of the Vale of Clwyd and Neighboring Parishes* (London: B. Quaritch, 1886), pp. 5–6.
3   Margaret Burne, 'Parish Gleanings from Upton St Leonard's, Glos', *Folklore* 22:2 (1911), pp. 236–9 at p. 237.
4   J. Lawson, *Progress in Pudsey* ([1887] Firle, 1978), p. 75 cited in K. D. M. Snell, *Parish and Belonging: Community, Identity and Welfare in England and Wales* (Cambridge: CUP, 2006), pp. 51–2.
5   Thompson, *Customs in Common*, p. 179.
6   C. Fisher, *Custom, Work and Market Capitalism: The Forest of Dean Colliers, 1788–1888* (London: Croom Helm, 1981), p. 104.

been collected together more recently in friendly societies and, in the late nineteenth century, nascent trade unions. Industry and craft remained generally localised, at best fostering regional rather than national identity.

For most in the eighteenth century, the conceptual unit through which the structures of the world were interpreted remained that of the parish. Aside from access to poor relief, to be settled within a parish meant being answerable to constables whose powers were constrained within its boundaries. It meant being liable to pay particular tithes, church and poor rates, and to hold specific rights of access to fuel or to commons. It meant being able to utilise certain rights of way, sometimes to indulge in very localised customs or receive the benefits of bequests or doles, even to pay allegiance to a particular family or magnate.[7] It also meant being a repository of legal testimony, a source of information out of which disputes as to boundaries with the neighbouring parishes might be resolved. So for instance, the practice of defining the boundaries of the parish by an annual perambulation, which often took place on Rogation Days or Rogation Sunday, was much more than merely a token celebratory affair, it was rather a procedure that 'provided the community with a mental map of the parish . . . this mental map was the collective memory of the community'.[8] The Church, whose interests were just as invested as the general community, led the way in defining the borders of parish authority. Aside from accompanying the perambulations, the local clergyman was often entrusted with the creation of a written record that observed the proper placements of the boundary marks and the extent of the parish in places where no visible marks were discernible. The perambulation at Diss in Norfolk in 1825 involved a circuit of seventeen miles and required the reverend and thirty-nine parishioners; that at Fersfield involved the clergyman, the churchwardens, overseers, constables, surveyors and older inhabitants (whose memory might be called upon at disputed points on the boundary).[9] In many places the educative function of these occasions was reinforced by impressing upon the accompanying youth the location of important waymarks upon the perambulation, both carrot and stick being employed – the carrot being the opportunity to scramble for prizes or coins at these waymarks, the stick being the administration of a whipping at the selected spot in order to impress it upon the memory.

Memory could nonetheless be imperfect, Robert Studley Vidal remembered the consequences in late eighteenth-century Devon:

> These boundaries are very tenaciously kept: in so much that I well remember my having, when a child, been present at some desperate conflicts between the commonality of neighbouring parishes who happened to clash in their perambulations or chanced

---

7 Snell, *Parish and Belonging*, p. 37.
8 Bushaway, *By Rite: Custom, Ceremony and Community in England 1700–1880*, p. 54.
9 Ibid., p. 55.

perhaps to meet on a spot that from the uncertainty of the district to which it belonged was regarded as debatable land.[10]

Conflicts between organised bands of young men from neighbouring parishes, or even regions, were by no means infrequent, and Stevenson has gathered together an impressive list of confrontations such as the fights between the villages of Bruton and Balcombe in Somerset, between Llechryd and Cardigan in Wales, Clovelly and Appledore in Devon, and 'up' and 'down' constituencies in many small towns throughout the land. David Harris (who died in 1904 aged ninety-four), from Upton St Leonards in Gloucestershire, remembered that as a young man it would happen that men from Brockroth and Waddon 'came to attack we. We met them with our fists and with sticks, and the blood did flow; it was like Waterloo in Upton. Some constables were there, but they was no good.'[11] Often these conflicts worked themselves out in the context of annual competitions such as the football match between the parishes of All Saint's and St Peter's in Derby, or the stick-fighting competitions between St Anne's and St Giles in London.[12] Within festive culture they also manifested themselves in the competition between groups of celebrants who disagreed over territory and the revenues to be gleaned therefrom. For example, there was endemic fighting between rival gangs of pace-eggers in Blackburn (Lancashire) into the 1840s, though it seems that these activities were suppressed after a fatality.[13]

According to Cobbett, 'every man and woman and child old enough to understand anything, looks upon his parish as being partly his'.[14] Given the importance of the parish as an economic unit, as a repository of privileges and rights, as a psychological horizon and as a cultural home, it is no surprise that the inhabitants of the parish should also conceive of it as a juridical unit within which they were entitled to scrutinise the conduct of their neighbours. There is no reason to suppose, though, that everyone received equal attention – and every reason to imagine that, given the intense parochial patriotism, newcomers were subject to special examination.[15]

---

10 Letter from Robert Studley Vidal to John Brand dated Cornborough, 31 July 1805. British Library Additional Manuscripts 41313 ff. 3–4. Cited in Bushaway *By Rite: Custom, Ceremony and Community in England 1700–1880*, p. 56.
11 Burne, 'Parish Gleanings from Upton St Leonard's, Gloucestershire', pp. 236–9 at p. 236.
12 J. Stevenson, *Popular Disturbances in England, 1700–1870* (London: Longman, 1979), pp. 51–2 cited in Snell, *Parish and Belonging*, p. 57.
13 J. Harland and T. Wilkinson, *Lancashire Folk-Lore, : Illustrative of the Superstitious Beliefs and Practices, Local Customs and Usages of the People of the County Palatine* (London: Frederick Warne, 1867), pp. 228–30.
14 W. Cobbett, *Political Register* (20 February 1834), pp. 241–2.
15 In 1969 my family moved from Nottingham to the village of Ticknall in Derbyshire. Our cottage abutted the main road and faced another house on the opposite side. However, we were shielded from view by a long and luxuriant hedge. My father recalls that he was astounded to come home

George Ewart Evans explained that with foreigners from other parishes, 'Ordinary commerce was sometimes inevitable, but any intimacy was frowned upon: to be married to one of them was almost a crime.'[16] Young men who tried to court girls from other parishes were often very roughly handled by the local youth who resented trespass on their domain. Such hostility likely goes a long way to explain the findings of Snell's research: that a rising proportion of rural marriages in the eighteenth and early nineteenth centuries were between partners who were both parochially resident, though after the mid-nineteenth century economic changes, a flight from the countryside, railways and the bicycle were to slowly erode parochial identity.[17] That erosion, though, took a very long time indeed. Gareth Williams recounts an anecdote from the beginning of the twentieth century concerning a Welsh tenant in the Vale of Aeron who was asked by a Major Lewis where his son was living – 'on the continent' came the reply. Somewhat surprised, the major asked where exactly, and was told 'Tonypandy'.[18]

However, as the above anecdote also suggests, life in the village was never entirely sclerotic. Men and women came awhile, never intending to stay and then moved on; some came in the cause of commerce; some followed the paths of seasonal labour (though much conflict might thereby be occasioned with the locals). Some also came to settle as servants, tradesmen and skilled labourers, and almost one-third of marriages involved one of the parties becoming settled in a new parish. Whatever the inhabitants might wish for, parish boundaries were porous. However, an acute awareness of the difference of these newcomers seems to have been maintained.

When in the next chapter we come to the species of 'rough music' or charivari that will occupy an important part of this book, I will have occasion to observe that whilst the ostensible reasons advanced for the performance of punitive popular rituals show a certain consistency, what is rarely explained is why one particular wife-beater is selected for punishment as opposed to any other. One sees though, in the context of these tightly bound parish units, that 'otherness' was a quality that was likely to inspire critical inspection, otherness being signified by being outside the parish, or being in an uncertain social situation or maintaining different life habits or religious

---

from work one day to find that a 'window' had been cut in the hedge perhaps 3ft deep and 15ft or 20ft feet long. We were now in full view. The tenant of the opposing cottage cheerfully came over to explain that he had cut our hedge because his wife 'liked to see what was going on'.

16 G. E. Evans, *Ask the Fellows Who Cut The Hay* (London: Faber, 1956), p. 239 cited in Snell, *Parish and Belonging*, p. 61.
17 From a survey of sixty-nine rural parishes distributed throughout England and Wales, Snell found that by the 1830s some 70 per cent of all marriages were parochially endogamous. See *Parish and Belonging*, p. 200.
18 Ben A. Jones, *Y Byd O Ben Trichrug* (Aberystwyth, 1958), pp. 10–11, cited in G. W. Williams, 'The Disenchantment of the World: Innovation, Crisis and Change in Cardiganshire c.1880–1910', *Ceredigion* 9:4 (1983), pp. 303–21 at pp. 309–10.

conscience. There was, for example, what Snell describes as: 'A long tradition of impugning the sexual purity of women from the other side or place.'[19] As I proceed I will note many occasions upon which those who came into communities from outside became the victims of rough music. One simply cannot tell what proportion of all those subjected to rough music overall were outsiders, or in some other way stood apart from their fellows, but there is enough evidence to suggest – and what our common observation of mankind would lead us to suppose – that those embedded within a community often subjected a stranger to a higher moral standard than they did to one of their own.

Youth Delivering Justice

The identity of at least some of those who set themselves up as judges of conduct will be explored shortly. For the moment, though, it should be observed that in actual application of sanctions against malefactors a recurrent theme in the sources is the predominant role played by young men and adolescents. The same is observable in respect of the charivaris in medieval and early modern France, as studied by Natalie Zemon Davis.[20] By way of explanation Davis points out that the young Frenchmen in rural communities from the fifteenth until the end of the seventeenth centuries were unable to marry until they reached their mid-twenties. One of the ways in which the large numbers of single, and somewhat rootless, young Frenchmen occupied themselves in the meantime was by forming into 'Abbayes de la Jeunesse' who in turn elected a king or abbot from amongst themselves at Christmas or Lent. These abbeys then took upon themselves a wide jurisdiction within their communities and, in particular, in respect to sexual matters. They might either fight or fine outsiders coming to court village girls, might stigmatise girls whose chastity was suspect, and exercise taxing or levying rights by intruding upon weddings and demanding customary dues from the newlyweds. More surprisingly perhaps, they claimed the right to regulate marital relations between those older than themselves. Thus, according to Davis, it was they who organised duckings, instigated parades and ridings backwards upon an ass for cuckolds and adulterers: 'The masked youth with their pots, tambourines, bells, rattles and horns might make their clamour for a week outside of the house of their victims, unless they settled and paid a fine. Others in the village might join them, but it was the young men who took the initiative.'[21] Youth abbeys were to be found throughout rural Europe in Switzerland, Germany, Italy, Hungary, Romania and, Davis speculates, probably in England and Scotland as well.

---

19 Snell, *Parish and Belonging*, p. 47.
20 Natalie Zemon Davis, 'The Reasons of Misrule: Youth Groups and Charivaris in Sixteenth-Century France', *Past and Present* 50:1 (1971), pp. 41–75.
21 Ibid., pp. 52–3.

Nothing so elaborate is actually documented in respect of England or Wales, but we do get a sense of how adolescents and young men might have organised themselves in the seventeenth century through Capp's study of the chapbook, *The Pindar of Wakefield*.[22] Its hero, George a Greene, is a young man holding a minor manorial office as a pinder or pinner, an impounder of stray animals. Endowed with this authority he forms his friends (who are described as a taberer, a cobbler, a tailor, a thresher, a miller and a smith) into a kind of quasi-official body, aping military rank with a colour bearer, a drummer, sergeants and a lieutenant. The group resolve to police their community for the general good and set themselves up to do so by the adoption of a set of rules. These are posted up at both ends of the town so that all are aware of them. They include promises to challenge anyone who 'gives them the lie' to a bout of cudgels or to levy a fine upon them, to fine anyone who breaks the hedges or tramples the corn, to force outsiders to submit to their authority, to take the part of any injured party and to avoid drunken brawls. The rules are accepted on oath and the group meets every Monday at the local tavern. Outsiders are treated with suspicion and they skirmish with the servants of two clothiers who refuse to accept their authority. Observing that there is in the town a 'rank scold' who hits her husband with a ladle and who, 'After hunny moon was past began to call him Rogue and Rascal instead of Lord and Master', they resolve to punish them both. They:

> Put a Boy drest in womens apparel like the woman, and a man like her husband, and put them both on a horse: All in the Town and the Countries thereabouts having notice of this new iest, came to see it. Thorow the Towne thus they rid, the woman beating the man, and scolding at him terribly, the poore man wringing his hands spinning with a Distaffe, Tom the Taberer with his Taber and Pipe playing before them, others playing on Gridirons, Tongs, Bagpipes, tinging on brasse Ketles, other some with paring Shouels, Pitch-forkes, Broomes, Mops, Spits and such rablement, and all the people running and hooting after them.[23]

The group engaged in other activities; they defeated a gang of housebreakers and dealt with a 'troublesome Knave'. Capp notes that, 'the protection of the values, interests and prestige of the community is an essential part of its function, and secure it a respectable position within the town. Throughout the chapbook there are repeated assurances of the group's popularity with the inhabitants at large.'[24] This popularity

---

22 *The Pindar of Wakefield: Being the Merry History of George a Greene, the Lusty Pindar of the North* (London, 1632, S. T. C. 12213). See B. Capp, 'English Youth Groups and the Pindar of Wakefield', *Past and Present* 76 (1977), pp. 127–33. References are to the modern edition *The Pindar of Wakefield*, ed. E. A. Horsman (Liverpool: English reprints ser., xii, 1956).
23 *The Pindar of Wakefield*, pp. 13–17, cited by Capp, 'English Youth Groups', p. 131.
24 Ibid.

seemingly extends to the local magistrate, who jests with George when he is brought before him on a false charge. Capp argues that 'the chapbook points at least to the strong probability, then or earlier, of organised adolescent groups with a measure of formal recognition, acting as guardians of social morality'.[25]

George a Greene's followers, it may be noted, were not drawn from unskilled agricultural labour but from the skilled and artisan elements within the community. The activities in which they were engaged involved the acquisition of a horse, a cart, upon one occasion the construction of an effigy, the occasional distribution of handbills, the arrangement of 'crying' in different parishes and, all in all, evidenced a high degree of organisation. All this and more can be found in communities in the eighteenth and nineteenth centuries. Their spirit seems to echo in the activities of the 'Bonfire Boys' and the 'Skeleton Army' active on the South Coast two hundred years later and is further testimony to the territoriality of youth groups – their potential hostility to those seen as outsiders and their capacity to respond to those who commit offences within their perceived area of jurisdiction. Simple thuggery could sometimes ensue as a consequence of this sense of territoriality. George a Greene was no mere hoodlum, however. He stood for values that were normative within his community and was seemingly in good standing with the local sources of authority.

The Gentlemen Behind the Scenes

There is no warrant for supposing that the local patriotism exhibited by Greene and his followers did not also influence those higher up the social scale who in some senses might feel an even greater responsibility for the morals of their locality. Later on I will refer to the employment of rough music practices in the context of political contest and economic rivalry. Suffice it to say for the moment that gentlemen far beyond the situation of George a Greene can be observed to have employed rough music as a tool of social discipline in the seventeenth and eighteenth centuries. In 1643 Henry Oxinden, a gentleman from Barham, Kent instigated the mockery of a woman who had responded in an unseemly fashion to her drunken husband. Oxinden had 'dressed a man in woman's apparel' and was accused of having acted 'obscenely to hang your servant's smock on a pole'.[26] In 1672 a riding was seemingly proposed by a Lady Haslewood after a drunken smallholder, Antony Cable from Northamptonshire, was knocked down by his wife.[27] The local squire, Sir William Haslewood JP, intervened to prevent it because Cable had rendered good service in the past. Given that

---

25 Capp, 'English Youth Groups', p. 133.
26 Brit. Lib., Add. MS. 21800, fos. 281, 284.
27 *The Diary of Thomas Islam of Lamport, 1658–81*, trans. Norman Marlow, ed. Sir Gyles Isham (Farnborough, 1971), pp. 155–7, cited in Capp, 'English Youth Groups', p. 133.

skimmingtons and stangings were public affairs carried out on successive nights, the comparatively few occasions before the mid-nineteenth century upon which justices of the peace intervened to prevent their performance, may suggest the inadequacy of the instruments at their disposal before the deployment of a paid police force, but it may also suggest that they were sympathetic to such performances or, at the least, extended to them a tolerant indulgence. Henry Oxinden defended his conduct by claiming that such things were 'a harmlesse pastime, which according to the opinion of honest divines is not only lawfull but in some sort necessarie'.[28]

The most revealing study of the complexities of a village performance comes from David Rollison's scrutiny of an event that took place in the Gloucestershire village of Westonbirt in 1716.[29] The affair began when a 'foreigner', Walter Lingsey, a tenant from another parish, confided to two day-labourers that he had been sodomised by George Andrews, the bailiff of Sir Richard Holford. The main instigator in what followed was one Isaac Humphries, who although a tenant of another of the local gentry, Sir Thomas Estcourt, was the largest employer in the locality and clearly a man of some importance. With his encouragement, the community of Westonbirt decided to hold a 'mock groaning' a piece of street theatre in which the comical pretence would be adopted that George Andrews's act had resulted in the fathering of a child. Organising the event took some time. A collection was held to purchase meat for the festivities, a fiddler was hired from another parish and, interestingly, a churchwarden, Walter Watts, was persuaded by his landlord, who happened to be Isaac Humphries, to put his house (which was at the centre of the village and next to the church) at the disposal of the crowd. Walter Lingsey, the supposed victim of the alleged assault, was to play the pregnant woman in the performance and Watt's wife provided him with a petticoat, apron and bonnet. On the day in question, Lingsey acted his part outside the church and delivered a child, a manikin made of straw and dressed in children's clothing. A company of some one hundred or more assembled for the occasion, from seven neighbouring parishes, and drank copiously to the health of the child. The manikin was then taken into the churchyard and one of the company appointed as parson. He recited the service of baptism – as well as he could remember it – and the manikin was then baptised 'George Buggarer' and assigned godparents. The assembled company then drank until the barrel of beer they had brought with them was empty, then they staggered home.

That Humphries was the prime mover is evidenced in several ways. After the affair, Sir Richard Holford ordered the local rector, John Jackson, to investigate the matter and Jackson concluded that the beer supplied to the crowd had actually been brewed

---

28 Brit. Lib., Add. MS. 21800, fos. 281, 284v. cited in Capp, 'English Youth Groups', p. 133.
29 D. Rollison, 'Property, Ideology and Popular Culture in a Gloucestershire Village 1660–1740', *Past and Present* 93 (1981), pp. 70–97.

by Watts at Humphries's instruction. On the day in question the revellers were 'entertained with ale at Walter Watts, where farmer Humphries was and received them as his guests'. Humphries was discrete though, and although 'he was seen to look on the divercons' he did not leave Watts's house during the performance. What we have, then, is a local man of substance sponsoring a performance against the bailiff of an absentee squire. It is fairly clear that there was more to the affair than simply outrage over the alleged offence, which may or may not actually have occurred. Humphries likely had a grudge against Sir Richard Holford insofar as he had previously been Sir Richard's tenant but had been displaced in 1710 in favour of a man who just happened to be the father of George Andrews. He had in addition also quarrelled with the parson, Holford's nominee, Mr Jackson, over church tithes.

One would like to know more about the views of Sir Thomas Estcourt from whom Humphries now held his tenancy. Perhaps the very fact that Humphries gained a tenancy from Sir Thomas after having lost his tenancy with Sir Richard is indicative of some friction between the two great men. Both men were Masters in Chancery; and Rollison detects in Holford's correspondence evidence of professional and political tensions between the two of them. This is not to suggest that Sir Thomas necessarily colluded in the affair, merely that Humphries may have calculated that his landlord would not have been too displeased with the outcome. It is a salutary lesson, for when we come to try to identify the reasons why species of shaming performances were held, without the chance survival of Holford's correspondence we would have a very impoverished understanding of the whole event.

In the aftermath, Mr Jackson conducted his own investigations and listed all those linked to the affair. Given the rather small population of the surrounding parishes Rollison concludes that at least one-quarter of the local population attended. Furthermore, 'No occupational groupings likely to have been represented in the neighbourhood – farmers, tradesmen and labourers – are missing. People from all ranks of local society – characterised throughout the Cotswolds by a lack of a resident gentry, and hence by a foreshortened hierarchy – participated.'[30] Ultimately, the solidarity of the neighbourhood ensured that no one was prosecuted for the groaning. Not the least of its offences was the sacrilege that had been committed during the mock baptism, but John Jackson begged Sir Richard not to force him to proceed, 'for should I prosecute it as for myself, not only my parish, but the whole countery around me would be upon me'; a prosecution, he went on, would 'not only endanger my own safety, but greatly prejudice me amongst my parishioners'.[31]

The Westonbirt groaning was a complex affair. On one level it was a traditional, sanctioned response to an accusation of immoral conduct, on another it was the

---

30 Ibid., p. 92.
31 Ibid.

consequence of a personal grudge between an absentee landlord and a disgruntled former tenant. It may well have been the state of relation between Sir Richard and Sir Thomas that enabled the groaning to be actually carried through. However, it was also made possible by the solidarity of the district in the face of perceived outsiders, a solidarity that rallied the populous to attend, and continued in such a way as to turn aside potential retribution. One doubts whether any of them had any apprehension of having done anything 'wrong' – for tradition, local patriotism and activism surely informed them of the opinion that the community itself had always acted as, and was entitled to continue to be, a juridical unit.

The Juridical Community

In the previous chapter I referred to a 'mock trial' at Upstreet in Kent. At the end of the eighteenth century informal tribunals and mock courts, of wildly varying degrees of sophistication, were to be found widely distributed through occupational groups and amongst smaller communities. In them, defendants were purportedly 'tried' and verdicts reached under the guidance of a so-called judge or magistrate who embodied the community desire to penalise the complained-of conduct. When describing the operation of what might otherwise be called 'meetings', 'assemblies', 'tribunals' and the like, I generally prefer to use the term 'court', not because I wish to endow them with any bogus authority or necessarily imply a court-like formalism but simply because 'court' is the term most often used by the contemporary reporters themselves. The origins of these 'courts' are often unknown but we can observe that some were embedded in popular festive traditions and practices; some mocked official courts in the sense of consciously ridiculing them, with the actors being aware that they had no true legal authority; and some aped official proceedings, seemingly in the sincere belief that they were repositories of genuine authority and legal authenticity.

I have suggested that the vigour and supposed legitimacy of rough music and popular punishment in the later period owed much to its inheritance of the earlier law tradition of chastisement. Similarly, I would argue that the deep episteme of juridical knowledge that can be observed in lowly groups within English and Welsh society owed much to the plethora of minor courts and plural legal systems still distributed throughout the land. It is true that these were very much in decline, yet it would be a mistake to underestimate the degree of legal pluralism still apparent at the end of the eighteenth century, or to dismiss as irrelevant the systems of social judging that served to guide, govern and penalise conduct but which operated in their own petty jurisdictions outside the purview of the higher courts of common law.

When Holdsworth claimed that, 'With the exception of the petty criminal business entrusted to the justices of the peace, practically all of the judicial work of the country was done by the judges of the common law courts, the Lord Chancellor or the Master of the Rolls, and the judge of the court of the Admiralty',[32] he was expressing a very crabbed and narrow view of the judicial function. It repeated the all-too-common view that only high-end offences or substantial civil actions were (or are) of any importance. Viewed from the bottom up, however, authority over many aspects of daily life at the end of the eighteenth century still remained vested in manorial courts, hundred courts and the like. It was they who declared rights and adjudicated the disputes over boundaries, privileges and other issues that were so important to the well-being of those beneath the notice of the higher courts. It was they who, through a combination of festivity and ceremonial, defined the community and maintained its ancient privileges. Thus the court-leet books of Tiverton report that in 1774:

> The Portreeve and Free Suitors having adjoined, the Court Baron processed from the Church House with the Bailiff, the children of the Charity School, the water bailiffs, the Free Suitors, Portreeve, the steward, other gentlemen, the Common Cryer of the Hundred Manor to the Market Cross and there at Coggan's Well where the Cryer declared that 'by order of the Lords of this Hundred, Manor and Borough of Tiverton, and on behalf of the inhabitants of this town and parish, the Portreeve and inhabitants now here assembled, publicly proclaim this stream of water for the sole use and benefit of the inhabitants of the town of Tiverton.' All parties then dined at the local inn and the boys were given money for attending the procession.[33]

It is true that many other customary courts such as the verderers' courts, swainmotes, were in decline or simple abeyance by the start of the nineteenth century. Courts that had once been powerful centres of local legal authority, such as the stannary courts, were being divested.[34] The process, however, was slow and uneven. William Marshall observed in 1818 that: 'Manor courts are pretty generally held, even where the copyhold tenure is extinct, and their utility is experienced on many occasions, as the settlement of boundaries and preventing of litigations, appointment of constables etc.'[35] There were still about three hundred active local or particular courts operating in 1831 and they were still dealing with more cases than the Westminster Courts.[36]

---

32 William Holdsworth, *History of English Law* (London: Methuen, 1964), vol. 1, p. 188.
33 F. J. Snell, *The Customs of Old England* (London: Methuen & Co., 1919), pp. 207–8.
34 For example, the stannaries were reorganised by the Stannaries Act 1836 (6 & 7 Will IV, c.106) and their business finally transferred to the county court in 1896 by the Stannary Court (Abolition) Act 1896, (59 & 60 Vict., c.45).
35 William Marshall, 'The Review and Abstract of the County Reports to the Board of Agriculture: Vol. IV, Midlands Department' (York, 1818), p. 215, cited in Bushaway, *By Rite, Custom, Ceremony and Community in England, 1700–1880*, p. 59, fn. 10.
36 According to the 'Fourth Report of the Commissioners Appointed to Enquire into the Practice and Proceedings of the Superior Courts of Common Law no 239 (1832) Appendix 1, part V', there were 250,000 civil cases started in the forty-seven largest local courts alone in 1830 as opposed to 90,000 in the Westminster courts.

Manorial courts continued to supervise market activities and, throughout most of the nineteenth century, one could find occupational courts such as that of the marblers of Purbeck continuing to exercise powers under ancient statutes and charters.

Well into the first half of the nineteenth century, then, there were plenty of men who had sat on manorial juries, attended occupational courts, held minor manorial and ecclesiastical offices such as pinner or sidesman, or who perhaps had served as the local constable. Higher up the social scale, officers will have sat on court martials, academics in university courts, and so on. In addition, many a farmer or craftsman was, in a sense, a magistrate in the eyes of his labourers or apprentices and the wide latitude allowed him under the common law to discipline his workforce did nothing to disabuse anyone of that notion.

All this was in addition to the very active tradition of ordinary people bringing cases before the summary courts. Peter King's study of one of the 'hundred' divisions in the county of Essex – that of Winstree – showed that: 'The great majority of Winstree households in 1792 must have had at least one member who had directly experienced a summary hearing in the last four years.'[37] This is not to say that there were an extraordinary number of convictions since, 'A huge variety of minor disputes – illegally detained property, inter-personal violence, insults, wages, poor relief, dangerous driving, swearing, etc. etc. were all resolved by these magistrates without recourse to jury trial or summary punishment.'[38] King's work in establishing that ordinary people readily resorted to the magistrates adds substance to my argument that popular justice traditions were not the result of a distinct counter-culture that had evolved separately from, and was intuitively hostile to, the official justice mechanisms. Rather, in a society that did not expect uniformity, that was largely indifferent to the ideas of process efficiency, and which had never known anything other than legal pluralism, different strategies and different institutions were employed according to the nuances of place and context. The dominant theme was not one of subservience. As Jennifer Davis observes in respect of the later London police courts:

> Although the working class brought a significant number of criminal prosecutions to the courts and sought the magistrate's arbitration in their personal disputes, to a large extent their conflicts continued to be resolved, as in the eighteenth century, informally in the neighbourhood. Furthermore, even though the working class took their problems to the court in large numbers they appear to have done so with clear expectations as to what constituted a just resolution to those problems. If they failed to achieve that outcome, or if the agencies of law enforcement intervened in their activities in ways they

---

37 P. King, 'The Summary Courts and Social Relations in Eighteenth Century England', *Past and Present* 183 (2004), pp. 125–72 at p. 132.
38 Ibid., p. 148.

had not themselves initiated, then they were likely to perceive the law as oppressive and even to oppose its application.[39]

One might also add that if they knew that they would not, or could not, achieve a desired outcome through an official channel then they were perfectly capable of substituting mechanisms of their own.

Under modern conditions the distinction between the activities of the highly centralised court system operated by the state and any illegitimate tribunals delivering rough vigilante justice would be obvious. Under the conditions of the late eighteenth century the distinction was not so readily apparent. Localism, regionalism, the persistence of customary practice, the slew of jurisdictions and unresolved claims relating to them complicated the picture. Legitimate local courts animated by customary practice, acknowledged (to a degree) by the higher courts and making reference to very ancient traditions (sometimes of dubious validity), could not but suggest that independent judicial enterprises also claiming similar foundations might also be empowered with authentic judicial power. This is not for a moment to suppose that any circuit judge ever believed that a coolstrin court in Wales had any legal foundation, or that the pronouncements of a mock mayor had any legal force but to suggest that for many people further from the sources of legal knowledge and further down the social ladder there were, in addition to the petty sessions, quarter sessions and so on, other forms of judicial enterprise to which they submitted and whose authority they habitually upheld.

The spirit of enterprise that evidently animated these sources of extra-legal authority is hardly to be wondered at when one considers the degree to which the official justice system was itself predicated on self-help. Negotiation and arbitration were the very stuff of legal disputes (as they are today, of course), and in the eighteenth and early nineteenth centuries these were joined, in the case of criminal law, by the compounding of offences.

Remaining with criminal law for a moment, whilst the prosecution societies that emerged in the eighteenth century were intended to improve the effectiveness and deterrent value of prosecution under the legitimate criminal justice system, still we can see that in the way that they were foundered and operated they had much in common with older festive practice. Prosecution societies commissioned regalia, took subscriptions, invented titles, elected officials and bound themselves to common purposes. Little and Sheffield, who have studied six such societies in the Halifax area, note that three of them equipped themselves with intimidating charters that were witnessed and sealed – one signed by some 140 witnesses. A hierarchy and formal ceremonial procedure were signified in one society by the possession of five

---

39 Davis, 'A Poor Man's System of Justice', pp 309–35 at p. 310.

maces while another, the Skircoat Society, spent subscriptions on a chain of office for the president. All seem to have taken part in annual processions, one of which, the Heptonstall Prosecution Society, was still taking place at the end of the nineteenth century.[40]

None of these attributes and activities, however, actually distinguishes the several hundred societies from the activities of groups promoting traditional activities or performances – who also took subscriptions, invented often grandiose titles, selected officials and endowed them with regalia and so on.[41] Such festivities often contained within them judgemental episodes whereas, conversely, many prosecution societies seem to have been social and celebratory as much as prosecutorial. However, the social status of the members of prosecution societies was fairly high; the key and obvious difference between prosecution societies and popular courts lies in the fact that: 'There is no evidence that the prosecution societies ever sought frequently or systematically to usurp the power of the official courts. The rule of law was not in question.'[42]

One wonders, though. In the records of the Skircoat Society, Little and Sheffield found one case in which a suspect was called before the society's committee, admitted to having stolen a key and then paid a fine in lieu of prosecution. Malcolm Tyson of one of the last surviving societies, the Ambleside Bond for the Prosecution of Felons, believed that in the nineteenth century wrongdoers were taken before the Bond Committee in order for them to decide what punishment should be given. Ambleside was somewhat unusual in the nineteenth century, it being inaccessible for much of the winter and a magistrate visiting only every three or four months. Under such circumstances the Bond Committee would offer summary justice or allow the perpetrator to await the next visitation.[43] The evidence is far too slender to suggest that such societies may have regularly usurped judicial functions, but the societies are a reminder of the vestigial nature of the state at this time and of the way in which such organisations could constitute themselves and, having newly come into being, how they might attempt to acquire social capital and thereby authority.

Prosecution societies, of course, did not have antiquity to lean upon. Those seeking to legitimise 'customary' modes of adjudication, or to claim that calendric customs granted them special licence to set up courts or tribunals, routinely claimed that their activities had been practised since time immemorial. They wilfully or genuinely forgot

---

40 C. B. Little and C. P. Sheffield, 'Frontiers and Criminal Justice: English Private Prosecution Societies and American Vigilantism in the Eighteenth and Nineteen Centuries', *American Sociological Review*, 48:6 (1983), pp. 796–808 at p. 800.
41 At least 450 such societies came into being between 1744 and 1856, ibid., p. 798.
42 Ibid., p. 801.
43 Interview with Malcolm Tyson (b.1929) on 8 January 1998. Ambleside Oral History Group, Ambleside Public Library.

recent innovations and their claims of great antiquity have therefore to be treated with great caution. Keith Chandler, commenting on the supposedly 'time honoured' election of a 'mock mayor' at Ock Street in Abingdon, Oxfordshire, observed that there is no evidence that it existed before 1869 and that such epithets 'will be familiar to students of folk culture generally as ones invoked (often by tradition bearers themselves and increasingly so as the activity becomes subjected to disapproval from those higher up the social hierarchy) to legitimate the continuation of custom and belief'.[44] E. C. Cawte observed that the May Day custom of dressing up a 'Jack-in-the-Green' is not attested before 1790 but a century or so later it was being referred to as a survival of druidic sacrifice![45] Skimmingtons, stangings and related punitive processions are well-attested in the medieval period, and questions as to their antiquity need not trouble us greatly here. In respect of 'traditional' courts and their judges, however, if I use the word 'traditional' to describe them it is rather more in the spirit of describing how contemporaries thought about them than a confident assertion that the courts themselves, or their officials, were necessarily of any great antiquity.

However, some of the most common sources of extra-legal popular authority in the countryside may indeed have been of very ancient foundation, if Bob Bushaway is right in arguing that they descended from the old Norman ripreeves.[46] The 'King of the Harvest', the 'Lord of the Mowers', or the 'Captain of the Shearers' were just some of the titles granted to those under whom men and women placed themselves for the duration of their labour and whose judgement they agreed to be bound by:

> To him all the rest were required to give precedence, and to leave all transactions respecting their work. He made terms with the farmers for mowing, for reaping, and for all the rest of the harvest work: he took the lead with the scythe, with the sickle, and on the 'carrying days' he was to be first to eat, and the first to drink at all their refreshments, his mandate was to be law to all the rest who were bound to address him as 'my lord', to show him all due honour and respect. Disobedience in any of these particulars was punished by imposing fines according to a scale previously agreed on by the 'lord' and all his vassals. In some instances if any of his men swore or told a lie in his presence, a fine was imposed.[47]

The most important function of such a 'lord' was to negotiate terms and conditions under which his men would work – a negotiation that required a careful survey

---

44 K. Chandler, 'The Abingdon Morris and the Election of the Mayor of Ock Street', *Aspects of British Calendar Customs*, ed. Theresa Buckland and Juliette Woods (London: Folklore Society: 1983), pp. 119–36 at p. 122.
45 E. C. Cawte, 'It's An Ancient Custom But How Ancient?' in Buckland and Woods, *Calendar Customs*, p. 39.
46 Bushway, *By Rite, Custom, Ceremony and Community in England, 1700–1880*, p. 72.
47 Chambers, ed., *The Book of Days*, vol. ii, p. 376.

of the task in hand and hard bargaining with a farmer who knew his land and the difficulties thereupon. The skills of the lord may have actually grown more important (for a time) as the nineteenth century progressed and as seasonal labour slowly began to give way to the employment of permanent farm servants, and the gradual spread of farm machinery reduced the amount of labour that was required. The limitations of machinery meant, however, that mechanical mowers and harvesters could only cope with certain types of crop. Furthermore, where a crop had been flattened or the ground was poor, mechanical mowers or reapers could not be employed. By the second half of the nineteenth century, farmers still needed some seasonal labourers but they knew that they could deploy machinery more economically on certain crops and on the better land. Seasonal labour had no interest, of course, in only being partially employed on marginal pieces and was not backward in trying to preserve its interests. In the 1880s at Stubble Farm in Berkshire, for example, the farmer purchased a combined harvesting and reaping machine but was told, 'Well master, you wants us to go and cut all them meadows where the grass is laid, and you're going to cut all the uplands with that there machine, and we don't think it jestly right. Them as cuts the one ought to cut the other.'[48] The farmer refused to employ them to do all the work and the men moved on to another farm. Sometime later the machine was vandalised. When the corn harvest came the men returned but struck a hard bargain, demanding four shillings per day and refusing to work into the evening without payment of overtime.[49]

Group solidarity was obviously important in maintaining bargaining power, although overall the position of seasonal workers was in decline:

> Well, when harvest was getting close, the 'lord' 'Id call his team together and goo an'argue it out with the farmer. They'd run over all the fields that had got to be harvested and wukk it out at so much the acre. If same as there was a field badly laid with the wather, of course the 'lord' would ask a higher price for that. 'Now there's Penny Fields', he'd say – or maybe Gilbert's Field – or whatever it was; 'that's laid something terrible', he'd say. 'What about that, farmer?' And when the price was named he would talk it over with his team to see whether they'd agree. The argument was washed down with plenty of beer . . .' Now I'll bind you', the farmer 'id say, and give each man a shilling.[50]

There was obviously a delicate balance of calculation between the need of the farmer to get the harvest in and the need of the harvester for wages. Calculations on both

---

48 Anon, *Stubble Farm, or Three Generations of English Farmers by the author of Earnest Struggles* (H. Simmons) pp. 209–11, cited in D. H. Morgan, 'The Place of Harvesters in Nineteenth Century Village Life', *Village Life and Labour*, ed. R. Samuel (London: Kegan Paul, 1975), pp. 29–72 at p. 64.
49 Ibid., p. 65.
50 C. H. Warren, *Happy Countryman* (London: Geoffrey Bles, 1939), p. 119.

sides were informed by an estimate of the ability of the farmer to get other labour should negotiations fail. The establishment of a large harvesting company may have precluded the possibility of such labour being sourced locally and it may have prevented outside labour from entry. So, for example, in the Aldingbourne area of Sussex in 1831 the workforce tried to 'set up a resolution that no out parishioners at all should be employed however this may protract the Harvest, and that instead of 8s. an Acre for which the Farmers can get the wheat reaping done, they will have 14s'.[51]

Notwithstanding the hard negotiation, dealing with harvesting companies obviously had certain advantages for a farmer. The job was done at a fixed price within an agreed time. In addition, the responsibility for the discipline and management of a large number of men, women and children was assigned to the head of the company. Binding the company was accomplished by rituals of authority, the use of titles and rites of initiation. The lord 'would have a halter and take it and put it over the head of all the new men. The lady, that is the lady of the harvest, who mowed next in line to the lord, would then take a small hammer, like the foot of the new hand and tap him on the sole of his foot and he would call beer. Then they would read the harvest rules . . .'[52] It was characteristic of these seasonal companies that rules of behaviour were written down and read to the company; the rules may perhaps have been customary but the company did not rely upon customary practice alone. These were bodies conditioned by legal thinking, even though their practices themselves may not have always been legally enforceable. The agreement made to regulate a company of sheepshearers drafted at the Swan Inn in Sussex on 21 May 1828 is a case in point. This specified that all the men 'must be at the place they are going to work at seven o'clock in the morning'. Precise regulations were laid down as to the quantity of food and beer the men were to have and the payment to be given for each sheep or lamb sheared. Fines might be levied for deviation from the agreement and these were to be distributed to those shearers thought most deserving. Furthermore, it was said that, 'The Captain shall have full power to discharge any shearers not acting up to these regulations.'[53]

Gleaning, which might be thought an individual entrepreneurial exercise, was similarly bound by common rules and placed under the authority of a mock sovereign – in most cases a woman. At the proclaiming of the 'Queen of the Gleaners' at Rempstone in Nottingham in October 1860:

---

51 Letter of William Tyler to Lord Egremont, 27 July 1831, WSRO, Petworth Archive cited in M. Reed, 'The Peasantry of Nineteenth Century England: A Neglected Class?', *History Workshop* 18:1 (1984), pp. 53–76 at p. 63.
52 Lilias Rider Haggard, ed., *I Walked by Night: The Life of the King of Poachers* (London: Nicholson and Watson, 1935), pp. 91–2.
53 *Sussex Notes and Queries: A Quarterly Journal of the Sussex Archaeological Society*, vol. ii, (1929), pp. 4–5 cited in Bushaway, *By Rite, Custom, Ceremony and Community in England, 1700–1880*, p. 72.

The village crier having 'proclaimed the Queen', nearly 100 gleaners assembled at the end of the village ... [A] royal salute was shouted by the boys, and the crown brought out of its temporary depository. This part of the regalia was of simple make; its basis consisted of straw-coloured cloth surrounded with wheat, barley and oats of the present year... The ceremony of crowning was now performed; after which the Queen, enthroned in an armchair decorated with flowers and branches, moved ... [to] the first field to be gleaned.[54]

As with many other customary entitlements, the legitimacy of gleaning gained much from its apparent patronage by the Church. Bells were rung to sound out the moment at which the gleaning could begin and when it must end.[55] Thus, 'from the Parish church itself came a formal recognition – even celebration of the annual suspension of property rights. In gleaning, the final stage of the harvest, one sees the clearest expression of the psychological advantage which the village labourer and his family enjoyed in the few brief weeks of the harvest.'[56]

One would like to know, though, what the participants really felt and thought when they invested a 'Queen of the Gleaners', particularly as in this case the 'office' was actually being revived after having become defunct. It seems that such proceedings were not mock, in the sense of the participants being aware that their actions were ridiculous. Nor, were the proceedings being performed in order to mock other parties. There were no such parties to mock.

What, then, did the participants think they were doing? Did they think that they were re-enacting time-honoured ritual and reclaiming ancient hallowed authority? I see no reason why not – given the loud assertions of right that we shall observe throughout this book. Even if we assert that such practices were not of any great antiquity in our own time, with a far freer access to the 'true' records of the past, are there not groups who reconstruct that past and in all seriousness re-enact ancient rituals, such as druidic practices, for example? They seem to believe in what they are doing and are happy to remain ignorant of the fact that a modicum of research would reveal their practices to be the creation of the wild imagination of Victorians pandering to the credulous or the incurably romantic! Furthermore, what ritual means to the performer is notoriously difficult to ascertain – especially during periods of transition. The transition from ritual that is interiorised by the subject to ritual that is merely performed by the subject is a gradual and uncertain one. For example, at what point does the African dancer cease to feel the emotional call of music and tradition

---

54 R. F. Sketchley, 'Coronation and Proclamation of the Queen of the Gleaners', *Notes and Queries*, 2nd series, vol. 10 (13 October 1860), p. 285.
55 Gleaning bells were still being rung in many parishes in Leicestershire and Rutland into the 1880s; see Bushaway, *By Rite, Custom, Ceremony and Community in England, 1700*–1880, p. 35.
56 Morgan, 'The Place of Harvesters in Nineteenth Century Village Life', p. 61.

that goes back, so far as he believes, into time immemorial and instead dispassionately observes himself as a man who has temporarily shed his jeans and put on a costume to go through the motions of a ritual, largely for the edification of uncomprehending tourists on safari? No doubt these latter disenchanting types of sentiment became more established in English communities as their folk tradition became indeed more 'folksy' and less meaningful. The speed of the process can be exaggerated, however, or the very existence of an original kernel of meaning be readily ignored by those observing from a position outside of the affective reach of the phenomenon itself. Whilst there may have been some degree of self-consciousness about the investiture of 'lords' or 'queens', nevertheless the affective nature of the process was sufficient to invest them with an authority that – although time limited, although less durable than any authority likely to be recognised in any textbook on legal history – was yet as real a factor in the life of the harvester as the authority of the constable or the clergyman.

Some of the punishments that might be meted out under this authority have been observed. At one end of the spectrum there were fines: if a man was away from work for a day it might cost him ten shillings, but only two shillings and sixpence if he could plead illness, or five shillings if his absence had been due to drink.[57] For harvesters, shearers and the like, dismissal was the severest sanction. Gleaners who disobeyed the accepted practices by starting too early were punished by having their gatherings thrown back onto the fields.[58] Why, one wonders, was their produce simply not confiscated and given to others? The answer, I suggest, is that the community was animated by more than a desire to give all the gleaners an equal chance at acquisition. Rather, the gleanings had been improperly obtained and there was a sense that the property in the harvest still lay with the farmer and that his land should not be touched until the due time. Conversely, once the harvest was completed and the due time had passed, the gleaners claimed the leavings as an entitlement not a privilege. In short, gleaning was a rule-based activity.

It should not by now surprise us that in addition to fines, confiscations and expulsion, corporal punishments were also employed as sanctions against misdemeanour: 'When any one has misconducted himself in the field during harvest, he is subjected to a mock trial at the harvest home festival and condemned to be booted.'[59] Booting seems to have been a generic term for punishments of some variation. For example, a booting was awarded for spilling a load of corn:

---

57 Rider Haggard, ed., *I Walked by Night*, p. 91.
58 Enid Porter, *Cambridgeshire Customs and Folklore* (London: Routledge, 1969), p. 124.
59 A E. Baker, *Glossary of Northamptonshire Words and Phrases* (London: J. R. Smith, 1854), entry under 'Booting' cited in Bushaway, *By Rite, Custom, Ceremony and Community in England, 1700–1880*, pp. 73–4.

At the harvest supper during the evening the delinquent was laid face downwards on the table and one of the leaders of the festival administered some blows with one of the master's boots, while holding the boot in a peculiar manner. As a physical chastisement it was of no account; but it was probably intended as a degradation in the face of the blunderer's fellow-workers.[60]

Can one really speak of 'lords of harvest' having a kind of judicial power, when punishments such as that described above seem so trivial when compared to the punishments that 'real' judges had the power to impose? I think we can – if we are interested in the lives of the majority (the 'poor') as they were lived and in those kinds of authority that actually governed their lives. Richard Ireland in his *A Want of Order and Good Discipline* began with a sound critique of the tendency for the history of criminal justice and criminal law to become the history of serious crime and correspondingly 'serious' punishment. For Ireland, this shows an inadequate attention to the realities of social relations, and perhaps also an inadequate empathy for the situation of the subject: 'A "minor" financial penalty or a few days imprisonment, which could tarnish "character" (which was conceived of as given by others, not intrinsic to the self) and therefore jeopardize earning capacity, might make the difference between financial survival and the institutionalisation of an entire family in the Union workhouse.'[61]

The presence and authority of these harvest lords within the seasonal companies is not as remarkable as would have been their absence – for wherever one looks in the eighteenth and nineteenth centuries one finds examples of men and women who came together to work collectively and who bound themselves under systems of regulation that made them liable to sanctions that were, for the most part, outside the vision or beneath the notice of the criminal justice system. Some, perhaps most, of these sanctions were unlawful but they were rarely complained of. Whilst no one, for example, doubted the right of a master to beat his apprentice (within reason), a harvester booted on the instructions of a harvest lord could technically argue that he or she had been the victim of a battery. If such men and women did complain, however, the offences were too trivial to leave any trace in the records. It is more likely, though, that a complaint was rarely a real social possibility. The labourer who was hauled over a table and booted presumably knew that any remedy in law would be doubtful, of negligible value and would simply lead on to unemployment with all its attendant consequences. Booting, as Bushaway points out, was to be found

---

60 Joseph Stevens, *A Parochial History of St. Mary Bourne: with an Account of the Manor of Hurstbourne Priors, Hants.* (London: Whiting & Co. 1888), p. 338, cited in Bushaway, *By Rite, Custom, Ceremony and Community in England, 1700–1880*, p. 74.

61 R. Ireland, *'A Want of Order and Good Discipline': Rules, Discretion and the Victorian Prison* (Cardiff: University of Wales Press, 2007), p. 4.

in many other occupations besides the agricultural; for example, in the regulations of eighteenth- and early nineteenth-century printing chapels, where the flouting of the rules led to the offender being laid across the correcting board and beaten eleven times: 'Similar customary forms were more widely distributed throughout English society during the eighteenth and early nineteenth centuries than is usually thought. It was not that printers took part in local harvests, or that Suffolk harvestmen worked in printing chapels . . . but that, for much of the period, a common language of ritual linked many different areas of the experience of work.'[62]

Wherever authority was absent, inadequate, untrustworthy, indifferent or corrupt, then groups brokered common agreements and set up different kinds of juridical mechanisms in order to enforce them. The consequence was the appearance of 'courts' in some surprising locations:

> They choose a lord chief justice, and a certain number of judges, who assemble once a week, and decide controversies. In this court they terminate all quarrels, make laws concerning the police, hear all complaints, and pronounce final judgement: in a word, every thing is equally attended to as in a well governed community. Every one has a right to attend and plead his own cause. Those who are not able to express themselves with propriety in public, such as women, for example, employ others to relate their complaints, or defend their interests . . . A colonel on half pay, who possessed great eloquence and abilities, for many years presided in this court, which he governed with the greatest propriety and decorum.[63]

This description by D'Archenholz, of the court of the debtors in King's Bench Prison is, like so much of his work, idealised. Both King's Bench and the Fleet were, he claimed, 'Two republics existing in the bosom of the metropolis and entirely independent of it.'[64] The level of social organisation that he alleged was achieved within these rather peculiar communities was, if we accept his word, impressive. Watchmen were appointed to secure the peripheries, rules were displayed, regulations promulgated and everyone had the right to lay their complaints before the court. D'Archenholz knew that: 'These proceedings may appear laughable to my readers; they are not, however, so to those who incur the displeasure of the judges.'[65] Enforcement was robust but judgement was (allegedly) not partial: 'Twelve jurymen being empanelled, as in the national courts, they give a verdict, after having made the necessary inquiries.' Deprived of any further powers of incarceration, the court employed traditional measures to deal with criminality, 'the culprit, with a paper stuck to his breast describing his crime, is obliged to walk through every street,

---

62 Bushaway, *By Rite, Custom, Ceremony and Community in England, 1700–1880*, p. 75.
63 D'Archenholz, *A Picture of England*, p. 170.
64 Ibid., p. 164.
65 Ibid., p. 170.

preceded by a herald, who with a loud voice assigns the reason of the punishment, and tells the inhabitants to beware of the delinquent'.[66] As an observer, D'Archenholz was, on occasion, shrewd and careful and, at other times, frankly witless. However, such courts are attested later both at Newgate where judge and jury were constituted in order to try prisoners,[67] and at Coldbath Fields. At Coldbath Fields by the 1850s, shame had been replaced by more brutal measures; conviction of an offence against the prisoners' own code might mean being forced to run the gauntlet through prisoners armed with knotted ropes.[68]

One can readily understand why prisoners and debtors might be unable or unwilling to resort to formal complaints to properly constituted authority. However, it should not be supposed that such informal proceedings were necessarily the consequence of the groups in question being too lowly to have recourse to the legal system. Self-regulation was a preference expressed throughout society, and even at the highest levels the rules established amongst equals were not always trumped by the operation of the 'real' law. A case in point was that of the officers' mess in the army or navy, which often met to discuss the conduct of members found wanting. These meetings had a powerful influence over the careers of alleged reprobates. One area in which they were particularly prominent was in interpreting the so-called 'laws of honour' and in calling to account those who had violated them. The duelling that arose in consequence of honour culture endured in Britain into the 1840s and a significant proportion of such duellists were army officers who felt impelled to duel in consequence of the decisions of their officers' mess.[69] To give but two examples, an officers' mess sent a Captain Bulkley to Coventry in 1785 for having made a formal complaint against another officer and they would not accept him back amongst them until he had duelled with the other party.[70] Another mess forced a Mr Cunningham to duel with a Mr Riddell and the death of the latter was the consequence.[71] Now, under the common law, to issue a challenge to a duel was of itself a misdemeanour; to kill in the course of a duel was a felony. Military law was fully cognisant of this fact and duelling was explicitly prohibited in the Articles of War. Nonetheless, messes continued to incite or compel their members to commit these offences.

---

66 Ibid., p. 171.
67 Arthur Griffith, *Chronicles of Newgate* (London, 1884) p. 354 cited in U. R. Q. Henriques, 'The Rise and Decline of the Separate System of Prison Discipline', *Past and Present* 54 (1972), pp. 61–93 at p. 62.
68 G. L. Chesterton, *Revelations of Prison Life*, 2 vols (London: Hurst and Blackett, 1856), i., p. 47.
69 See S. Banks, *A Polite Exchange of Bullets: The Duel and the English Gentleman, 1750–1850* (Woodbridge: Boydell, 2010).
70 *The Times*, 3 February 1785, p. 3, col. a.
71 John. G. Millingen, *The History of Duelling: Including Narratives Of The Most Remarkable Personal Encounters That Have Taken Place From The Earliest Periods To The Present Time*, 2 vols (London: Richard Bentley, 1841), ii, pp. 116–17.

One tends to assume that within state institutions rules of law will trump what one might call customary practice, but it was not so in the army in the eighteenth and early nineteenth centuries, where officers were effectively penalised by tribunals for refusing to break both military and common law. Thus in 1766 a Captain Beilby was court martialled and suspended from his commission for a year for refusing to commit a misdemeanour, that is to say for failing to issue a challenge to another officer and accepting 'language unbecoming the character of an officer and a gentleman without taking proper notice of it'.[72] The Judge Advocate did intervene in this case, pointing out the irony of the situation: 'I do not conceive that the sentence of a Court of Justice can at any rate be supported which awards a punishment for neglecting to seek a method of redress forbidden as well by the military as the common law.'[73] However, army officers who refused to duel continued to lose their commissions under the so-called 'Devil's Article' for conduct unbecoming an officer. Lord Hardinge eventually intervened to enforce the Articles of War, and cashier officers who duelled and deprived widows of those killed in duels of their pensions.[74] This did not, of course, emasculate the messes who continued in other areas to sit in judgement upon the lives of their members.

Thus far, I have referred to what might be termed occupational groups, harvesters, gleaners, prisoners and officers. In rural areas tribunals or courts are often to be found associated with those festive occasions accompanied by the election of a mock sovereign. One of the functions of the election was the dispensation of justice. For example, the celebration on Halgaver Moor near Bodmin involved dancing, gurning and a good deal of drinking, but at the same time: 'There is also a mock court held here at this time, whose president is then called the Mayor of Halgaver, and where persons found guilty of infringement upon the rules of the place, etc., are punished by being rendered ridiculous in appearance, as being obliged to ride woman-wise through the place, have their clothes turned inside out, etc. etc.'[75] Here the administration of justice seems to have been not so very different from that administered by the harvest 'lord' at the time of the harvest supper.

Other courts seem mainly to have been associated with initiation or registration and mark the passage of an outsider into the group. Variations of pie poudre courts, for example, were still carrying out initiations at some fairs. At Weyhill, the process of allowing a new member to join the community of traders was known as 'horning the

---

72 W.O. 71/50 cited in A. N. Gilbert, 'Law and Honour Amongst Eighteenth Century British Army Officers', *Historical Journal* 19 (1976), pp. 75–87 at p. 80.
73 W.O. 81/111 cited in Gilbert, 'Law and Honour Amongst Eighteenth Century British Army Officers', p. 81.
74 Banks, *A Polite Exchange of Bullets,* pp. 231–2.
75 *Western County Magazine,* 3 (1789), p. 245.

colt'.[76] At Stourbridge the newcomer was known as an 'infidel' until he was presented to the court for initiation.[77] When Purbeck apprentices – who 'by their laws' had to be the sons of existing quarrymen – reached the age of twenty-one they were required to present themselves 'in court' at Corfe with a pint of beer in one hand, a loaf in the other and eight shillings and sixpence in their pocket, with which to be entered onto the list of free men of the marbler's company.[78] This marked the conclusion of a merry day, which included a game of football between the new members and the right, for a day, to kiss any woman (married or unmarried) in Corfe.

Some courts, I profess I simply do not know what to make of; for example, the 'lawless court' held by the manor of Rochford. This court was said to derive from a conspiracy against the manorial lord by his tenants:

> As a punishment he ordered all tenants should ever afterwards assemble at a certain hour of the night, on the same spot where the conspirators met and do homage for their lands. The court is held in the open air on King's Hill, on the midnight of the first Wednesday after Michaelmas day; and all business is transacted in whispers, the minutes being made with a coal instead of a pen and ink. The steward opens the court in as low a voice as possible; yet those tenants who neglect to answer are deeply fined and every absentee forfeits double his rent in every hour's absence.[79]

Whether official or unofficial, these courts in all their forms were repositories of varying degrees of social power, ranging from the utterly frivolous to the deadly serious, but generally able to apply a wide range of lesser but important sanctions against misdemeanour. They created of themselves a sense of juridical entitlement, which sometimes expressed itself in surprisingly elaborate forms.

A case in point is that of the coolstrin court in the Vale of Glamorgan, which was called into being when a husband was suspected of being subjugated by his wife. The court was held in a churchyard and presided over by an old man acting as judge. He wore the collarbone of a horse mounted on his hat and was attended both by attendants bearing white wands and by a guard of men with pitchforks. According to Redwood, the court would open with a declaration by the town crier of the offence complained of, whereupon the court would adjourn for seven days in order to summon witnesses and give the defendant a chance to compose her defence (in Redwood's account this appears to be a court only for wives). On the day of the trial,

---

76 William Hone, *The Year Book of Daily Recreation and Information* (London: Thomas Tegg, 1864), pp. 772–3, cited in Bushaway, *By Rite, Custom, Ceremony and Community in England, 1700–1880*, p. 119.
77 Ibid.
78 O. W. Farrer, 'The Marblers of Purbeck', in *Papers Read Before the Purbeck Society, 1855* (Wareham: C. Groves, 1856), pp. 191–204 at pp. 193–4.
79 C. Kenny, 'The Lawless Court of Essex', *Columbia Law Review* 5:7 (1905), pp. 529–36 at pp. 531–2.

advocates would be appointed to argue out the matter and the affair would be concluded by the judge making a speech upon the subject of the tyranny of women (one presumes that the defendant was always guilty as charged!). An opportune day would then be appointed for a riding and, on that day, a procession would set out through all the villages of the vale led by the judge, the wand bearers and a group of musicians. Following behind would be two standard bearers, one bearing a pole decorated with a petticoat and one a pole decorated with an upside-down pair of breeches, and behind them two men impersonating the husband and wife complained of. The procession would finally terminate at the home of the culprits and the poles would be set outside and pelted with mud.[80]

It is not entirely clear, however, how far into the nineteenth century this elaborate ritual survived. David Williams believed that the process of mock trial was abandoned well before mid-century, in which case the incident described by Redwood may have been the last one.[81] Evans reported a mock trial in 1843,[82] and a somewhat similar court operated at Cynwyl Elfed in Carmarthenshire until 1865. The court met by a large white stone at the centre of the village, above which stood an oak tree. A villager would climb the tree to act as the judge or 'Voice from Above', whilst an effigy of the accused was placed on the stone. A prosecutor would begin the proceedings by shouting 'Who has sinned?' – at which the judge would name the culprit. A dialogue would ensue between the prosecutor, the judge and the witnesses called forth to testify. At the end of the testimony the judge would give his verdict and ask the audience of villagers to consider a suitable punishment, which was invariably the burning of the effigy of the accused.[83]

In Cardiganshire a species of punitive parade – the ceffyl pren or 'wooden horse' – was often employed against malefactors. I shall return to the ceffyl pren in a subsequent chapter, but for the moment what interests is that the actual punishment itself was frequently preceded by some form of tribunal, demonstrating what Rosemary Jones calls 'the structured, quasi-institutionalised nature of the Ceffyl Pren in that area':[84]

> A Society has been formed in this town, for the suppression of vice, but more especially for the total abolition of Matrimonial infidelity. No sooner is any one suspected of this

---

80 C. Redwood, *The Vale of Glamorgan: Scenes and Tales amongst the Welsh* (London: Saunders and Otley 1839), p 274.
81 D. Williams, *The Rebecca Riots: A Study in Agrarian Discontent* (Cardiff: University of Wales Press, 1955), p. 191.
82 Evans, *Ask the Fellows Who Cut the Hay*.
83 I. C. Peate, 'A People's Court', *Folklore*, 56:2 (1945), pp. 273–4.
84 R. N. Jones. 'Popular Culture, Policing, and the 'Disappearance' of the Ceffyl Pren in Cardigan, 1837–1850', *Ceredigion: Journal of the Cardiganshire Antiquarian Society* 11:1 (1988/89), pp. 19–39 at p. 25.

crime, than a meeting of the members of this society is convened, and the subject is maturely debated. The debate generally ends in a large machine being ordered, technically called, 'Ceffyl Pren'. On some appointed night, this machine is carried through the principal streets, accompanied by some hundreds of persons, singing and hooting. They then halt near the suspected person's house, and one of the members mounts the 'Ceffyl Pren', and harangues the assembly at great length, stating the reasons they had for their proceedings . . .[85]

All of these proceedings in Wales were somewhat more formal than the irregularly constituted proceedings in which individuals were dragged before others and supposedly judged. For example, in 1845 William Kendrick complained at Ledbury Petty Sessions about the conduct of four men after he had impounded a horse belonging to one of them because it had strayed into Cutley Rye Meadow, 'for which grave offence the defendants arraigned him before themselves at the bar of the Bell Inn, Bosbury, Cole acting as judge, and condemned him to the stocks for six hours! He was accordingly placed in the stocks, but liberated before the time allotted expired.'[86] For their offence each of the men was fined varying sums of a little over £1. It is of course significant that the affair took place during Bosbury Wakes, when drink and festivity granted licence for revenge upon the over-officious. Unfortunately, one does not know how the village of Bosbury reacted to the victim's decision to make a formal complaint.

In some of the above examples the defendant appeared *in personam* and was liable to a variety of immediate forms of sanction. In others, such as the court at Cynwyl Elfed, trial and penalisation involved only the effigy of the malefactor. Broadly speaking these effigies might be characterised as being of two types. First, effigies of people who were within the physical, psychological and social reach of the community who tried and immolated them. The adulterer in the village might not be immediately affected when the community gathered to try or burn his effigy, but one can be sure that there were all sorts of ancillary consequences. He might not gain employment and may not be spoken to in the street or be welcomed at community celebrations and so on. Second, there were trials and burnings of persons so far outside the reach of the community in question that the 'victim' can never have had any personal knowledge of that community or connection with them, indeed they might never learn of the acts that had been done. Trying an effigy had long been embedded within the broader tradition of charivari. Few mock trials in England, though, seem to have been as elaborate as those observable in the French charivaric tradition. For example, at Turgon in the commune of Druillat in 1867:

---

85 *Cambrian*, 6 April 1839, cited in Jones 'Popular Culture, Policing, and the 'Disappearance' of the Ceffyl Pren in Cardigan, 1837–1850' p. 25.
86 *Worcester Herald*, 7 June 1845, cited in Bushaway, *By Rite, Custom, Ceremony and Community in England, 1700–1880*, p. 75.

On 22nd January a large mob met together. Upon a large cart whereto a pair of horses were harnessed sat sundry individuals representing a court of justice, all in appropriate costumes: a president in a toque and a red gown, five judges in robes made of women's dresses or window-curtains, an officer of the public ministry dubbed Procureur de la Cornaillerie, two lawyers, a jury, two policemen, and two witnesses. Before the solemn tribunal came a husband and wife represented by two other persons. The first was accused of having received, the second of having given, sundry blows from a broomstick. In front of a cart was a float whereon was the effigy of an ass, and on this ass, seated with his face to the tail, was a man bearing on his head the horns of a stag and in his hands a distaff which he was pretending to spin.[87]

Judgement was never given because a spoilsport group of real policemen appeared and arrested the protagonists, who ended up being fined forty sous each. In the next chapter and thereafter I will be returning to the subject of effigy so for the moment I will only observe that there were many occasions in England upon which effigies were 'tried' and sentence pronounced upon them. For instance, in the case of Thomas Paine, the many burnings of his effigy were sometimes preceded by trials. At Castle Donington he was given 'a fair and candid hearing' after which, of course, his effigy was destroyed.[88]

The word 'mock' is often employed in nineteenth-century folklorist material for a wide variety of judgemental activities, sometimes it is used as an expression of disdain for proceedings that, to the unfortunate victim, would have appeared anything but frivolous. On one interpretation what makes a true mock trial is not so much the place where the court is constituted, the authority under which it operates, the background or qualification of the officials present or, strictly, the procedure followed, but rather the impossibility of the accused securing his or her acquittal. If a debtor could be dragged before the judges and fellow debtors in the prisoner's court in King's Bench prison and clear himself of a charge laid against him then, in that sense, the 'court' was not a mock court. The harvest lord was a judge properly titled if he could hear a complaint laid against a harvester and conclude that the man was not to blame. In some of the instances cited above, this may have been a real possibility. In others, the process was but a precursor to inevitable punitive action.

Punitive action, it has to be said, is much better documented in the sources than the informal tribunals alluded to in this chapter. For example, how often the coolstrin court or the court at Cynwyl Elfed met is quite unknown. The state of the record leads one to suppose that they were not very often convened. By contrast, the ceffyl

---

87 Walsh, *Curiosities of Popular Customs and of Rites, Ceremonies, Observances, and Miscellaneous Antiquities*, pp. 210–11, citing *Courier de l'Ain*, 1867.
88 *Leicester Journal*, 9 November 1792. For a similar case from Wollaston see *Northampton Mercury*, 22 December 1792.

pren seems to have appeared (in various forms) rather regularly throughout Wales in the early nineteenth century. However, we really have no way of knowing how many instances of 'rough music', to which I shall turn in the next chapter, were preceded by some sort of enquiry or discussion that purported to weigh the case against the putative target. What we can say is that when such instances occurred they seem to have been quite often informed by an awareness of procedural forms. These legal forms were copied without any awareness that, in the context at hand, they were absurd. Judgement, however unfair, was not supposedly arbitrary and, as we shall see in the next chapter, when judgement passed on to the infliction of punishment conduct was generally (but not always) rule-based. This was perhaps not, one suspects, so much in the interests of the victim, as in furtherance of the claim that the community was exercising an entitlement, one which like the common law itself was legitimated by long practice and upheld by the observance of customary norms.

3

The Forms of Rough Music

This chapter and much that follows thereafter concerns itself with the phenomenon widely distributed throughout European society into the twentieth century and known broadly as charivari in France, katzenmusik in Germany or shivaree in North America. In Britain the broadest term employed was 'rough music', the essence of which was the staging of a shaming procession through a community in response to some alleged turpitude. The term 'rough music' derived from the hullabaloo made by the participating crowd on pots and pans and anything else that came to hand. These processions had close affinities with earlier judicial ridings – indeed the term 'rough music' was employed in describing the behaviour of the crowd during both activities. There were two important differences, however. First, the popular practices of 'rough music' were not formally sanctioned; second, these parades did not necessarily involve, and by the later period only rarely, the parading of the actual wrongdoer. Sometimes a substitute was employed in his or her stead to mimic and declare the offence, though more often the effigy of the offending party (or parties) was employed. Whatever the form of the procession, many of these affairs terminated with the additional burning of the effigy of the miscreant. There seem to have been some occasions upon which a bonfire and burning alone sufficed, but the fact that a parade is not reported in a (usually brief) account of such an event is not reliable evidence that one was not staged. It seems to have been the burning that was deemed most worthy of notice by reporters and, in truth, parades and immolations were intermixed such that it is often difficult to categorise them as different species of act.

Although rough music is and was employed as a general labelling, most contemporary observers described such events using one of the many regional terms in popular usage. Broadly, in the north of England the recipient of the crowd's attention was said to have been 'stanged' or made to 'ride the stang'. The stang was originally a pole carried between two men and was used to carry a water vessel – but it was readily adapted to mount a victim or his substitute, hence the name. Stanging could also encompass carrying someone in a basket, parading them tied to a ladder and so on. In the south of England the victim was more often said to have been the subject of a 'skimmington' or a 'skimmity ride', a reference to the importance of rough music in the medieval and early modern periods in chastising scolds and rumbustious wives. The term is said to derive from a species of large ladle with which a henpecked husband might be belaboured by his spouse. In Wales the victim, or again, his substitute, might be said to have been made to ride a wooden horse, a ceffyl pren. At a more local level, a bewildering variety of names were also employed, sometimes interchangeably. In Berkshire, for example, a malefactor was often said to be the victim of a 'hussitting', in Warwickshire he might endure a 'lewbelling' or 'lowbelling', in Shropshire the victim might experience a 'ran tanning'; elsewhere he might be on the receiving end of 'skymmetry' or a 'tin-panning', a 'nominey' or a 'wooset'. One commonality amongst all these activities was that they could hardly be staged without an enthusiastic constituency of support. Rough music activities were species of entertainment as well as punitive endeavours and it will therefore be useful to start by exploring the relationship, sometimes difficult to interpret, between rough music and popular festivity.

Popular Custom, Shame and Opportunism

A noisy parade can, of course, be a matter of congratulation as well as of condemnation, and many of the forms common to what I shall call for the moment 'rough music proper' were also employed upon occasions that appear at first sight to have been wholly celebratory. Thus rough music construed at its broadest was used 'indiscriminately to express either approval or disapproval . . . in workshops and factories in the towns . . . in the days of apprenticeships the completion of indentures was sometimes heralded in this manner, and was the summons to the payment of the footing the ex-apprentice was expected to provide on attaining his freedom.'[1] According to Hislop: 'Among the pitmen of former times it was customary to make a man ride the stang as a triumph. The bridegroom was thus borne aloft by fellow pitmen.'[2] Incoming apprentices in Coventry and Birmingham were sometimes treated to rough music and so were girls who were decorated on the day that they left to get married.[3]

There is a temptation, then, to suppose that this is a case where two completely different types of group practice, distinguished by quite different purposes, have rather inaccurately and unfortunately been lumped together through the employment of a misleading common terminology. Indeed some types of predominantly celebratory activity do employ their own terms such as 'lifting', 'heaving' or 'chairing'. The posi-

---

[1] R. Palmer, *Folklore of Warwickshire* (Gloucester, Tempus Stroud, 2004), p. 60.
[2] R. O. Hislop, *Northumberland Words. A Glossary of the Words used in the County of Northumberland and on the Tyneside* (London: English Dialect Society, 1892), p. 577.
[3] Palmer, *Folklore of Warwickshire*, p. 97.

tion, however, is rather more complicated. What was contained within many of the celebratory forms of music was a claim that some particular event or season entitled the participants to demand some species of benefit from the objects of their action. Celebration, then, called for reciprocal generosity. The punitive performance was at its most vigorous when staged to penalise some previous wrongdoing by the person it was intended to target. Yet punitive performances also occurred in celebratory contexts, where the object of the crowd's attentions failed to respond as he or she should have done to the aforementioned claim: thus one could move very quickly from a mood of celebration to a determination to punish. This can be seen in particular in the case of the observation of calendric customs wherein it was believed that a period of festivity entitled the participants to demand doles from the better off, or to exercise types of licence that were at other times barred to them. If the attempt to exercise these rights was first couched in terms of a good-natured or jocular request, denial of the same was often accompanied thereafter by punitive responses, by species of rough music.

One facet of popular justice, then, was the penalisation of those who failed to respond appropriately to community ritual practice. To give a specific example, John Lawson described one such stanging custom in Wetheral c.1870 wherein an armchair was fixed to the stang pole and decorated with ribbons. It was then carried through the streets led by a man with a flag and followed by a band. A victim would be forced into the chair and carried until a sum of money was extracted from him (or her) whereupon he or she would be 'given a drink'. The proceeds would be recorded in a book (perhaps to stop the victim being stanged twice) and eventually spent in the local pub.[4] This kind of stanging – until money, beer or even a kiss were bestowed – was a widely distributed phenomenon. In Shropshire men 'heaved' women in chairs decorated with flowers on Easter Monday – and the women returned the compliment the day after. The custom was particularly strong in colliery areas but declined during the second half of the nineteenth century.[5] Bushaway argues that it is a misunderstanding to view this only as a picturesque custom as 'the undertones of sexual threat are evident and strong in the ceremony as it occurred on Easter Tuesday', there was a 'sense of sexual aggression' inherent in the custom 'as when women lifted men' and this was 'particularly threatening to middle class genteel male society'.[6] In 1827, the *Westmorland Gazette* condemned the custom of stang riding at New Year as 'being used as a means of extorting money under circumstances which we think very disgraceful'.[7]

---

4 M. Rowling, *The Folklore of the Lake District* (London: B. T. Batsford, 1976), p. 135.
5 S. Burne, *Shropshire Folk-Lore: A Sheaf of Gleanings* (London: Trubner and Co., 1883), pp. 296–8.
6 Bushaway, *By Rite*, pp. 117–18.
7 Rowling, *The Folklore of the Lake District*, p. 135.

It should be noted at this point that this species of extortion was not confined to the labouring classes alone. For example, during the Ad Montem celebrations, held since the sixteenth century, the schoolboys of Eton expected a customary exaction. Ad Montem was first held annually, then biennially and finally triennially on Whit Tuesday. One part of the festivity involved yet another species of procession up the Salt Hill, and until 1778 this concluded with one unfortunate boy being ceremoniously kicked down it. Meanwhile, two senior boys, the 'salt bearers', attended by their twelve servitors, blocked the bridges over the Thames and levied 'salt money', in effect their own toll, for which they issued a receipt. During a typical Ad Montem a substantial sum would be collected, and the salt bearers would pass a bounty of between £600 and £1,200 to the Captain of Montem.[8]

Interestingly, the boys are said to have carried staves and issued receipts bearing legends such as '*Mos Pro Lege*' (custom for law). Ad Montem was finally abolished in 1847, but until then it displayed many of the facets of other humbler customs. It was governed by a strong sense of entitlement, reinforced by custom and the assumption of an elaborate hierarchical structure that gave its officers an assumed and temporarily acknowledged authority. Ritualistic and symbolic violence seems to have lain at the heart of the Salt Hill procession, but where expectations were denied, actual violence followed – the schoolboys of Eton were not above hiring toughs and roughing up those who refused to pay their dues.

No doubt the boys of Eton could have managed without their dues. One reason that the poor responded so vigorously to the failure to acknowledge traditional festivity was that the licence and opportunities allowed for such festivity permitted waypoints of pleasure in lives frequently blighted by extreme poverty and uncertainty. Successful doling or levying activities allowed for a very modest distribution of resources within communities. A refusal to provide the expected munificence signified both contempt for the traditions of the locality and a refusal to ameliorate the harsh state of power relations between the orders. The festival or celebration then served as a way of remembering and claiming rights, repudiation of which was fiercely resisted.

Many folk customs contained within them, then, the real possibility of violence. The earliest full text of a mummers' play, the *Revesby (Lincolnshire) Play* of 1779, started by asking, if not demanding, 'for bread and beer . . . and something out of your purse'.[9] Large quantities of drink and a rare sense of licence were, of course, the very essence of such events and the mummers with their blackened faces were not

---

8 T. A. J. Burnett, *The Rise and Fall of a Regency Dandy: The Life and Times of Scrope Beardmore Davies* (London: John Murray, 1981), pp. 24–5.
9 E. K. Chambers, *The Medieval Stage*, 2 vols. (Oxford: OUP, 1903), vol. i, p. 105, cited in G. Seal, 'Tradition and Agrarian Protest in Nineteenth-Century England and Wales', *Folklore* 99: 2 (1988), pp. 146–69 at p. 150.

above exacting revenge if their demands for largess were unfulfilled. In Cornwall, Christmas 'guise dancers' disguised behind their masks were notorious for their violence.[10] 'Meggies' or 'kitties' in Flintshire equipped themselves with cudgels and beat spectators on 5 November until they received a suitable token of appreciation. In Herefordshire, Shropshire and Worcestershire, men in women's clothes with blackened faces accompanied the roving Morris dancers, demanding money.

In many districts these entrepreneurial activities were particularly focused upon Plough Monday. This was the first Monday after Twelfth Night and marked the end of the land workers' Christmas holiday and the traditional opening of the plough season of the new year. It was one of those occasions upon which agricultural labourers expected to receive contributions from farmers, which were collected by the plough bullocks. The legitimacy of the proceedings was established by first blessing the plough in the parish church: 'This was followed by a procession of ploughmen and farm labourers who hauled a plough from door-to-door in the parish and collected contributions for rustic festivities, merry-making, and refreshment which were enjoyed until late at night.'[11] The plough, called in some places 'the fool plough', was generally decorated with ribbons and drawn by farm labourers dressed up and, 'in some cases ochred and ruddled ... Merry mummers sometimes performed a traditional play, and never failed to go round with the traditional money-box.'[12]

In Lincolnshire in 1821 it was said that, 'The excesses of these persons have arrived at such a pitch that it is impossible to bear them any longer, and it would be well if the country and the farmers in particular, would second the endeavours of the magistrates...'[13] In 1845 a correspondent in Nottinghamshire declared that he was 'pleased to learn that this vulgar and demoralising festival of the lower grades of our community has, through the exertions of the police, supported by the magistrates and influential private individuals, passed over this year in the villages round about us generally, with fewer outrages on public decency than on almost any former occasion'.[14] Another misanthrope, complaining about Plough Monday, remarked that it had brought to Lincoln:

> The annual fooleries of the morris-dancers, and two or three bands of scarmouches were performing in various parts of the city, and levying 'black mail' upon the inhabitants without interruption. After one band a train of two or three hundred boys followed, shouting and bawling at 'Moll with the broom'. Other beggars, who are a far less nuisance, are taken up and punished.[15]

---

10 M. A. Courtney, *Cornish Feasts and Folk-Lore* (Penzance: Beare and Son, 1890), pp. 10–11.
11 *Nottingham Evening News*, 15 January 1945.
12 *Nottinghamshire Guardian*, 19 January 1929.
13 *Lincoln, Rutland & Stamford Mercury*, 26 January 1821.
14 *Nottinghamshire Guardian*, 16 January 1851.
15 *Lincoln, Rutland & Stamford Mercury*, 17 January 1845.

To the performers themselves, however, they were not beggars at all. William Howitt complained about the attitude of Plough Bullocks in 1841 and expressed the relief that the tradition had declined: 'They visited every house of any account and solicited a contribution in no very humble terms . . . In some places I have known them enter houses, whence they could only be ejected by the main power of the collected neighbours . . . Nobody regrets the discontinuance of this usage . . .'[16] However, in Derbyshire in 1851 'plough bullocks' were occasionally seen, young men yoked to a plough, preceded by a musical band and accompanied by 'a fool and Bessy . . . When anything is given, a cry of largess is raised, and a dance performed around the plough; but if refusal to their application for money is made, they not infrequently plough up the pathway, door stone, or any other portion of the premises that happen to be near.'[17]

The traditions of Plough Monday were a long time dying. In 1897 the *Lincoln, Rutland and Stamford Mercury* reported that the 'old mummeries and mendicancy of Plough Monday' were still 'happily dying out'. That year, though, no revels were held in Stamford, whereas formerly the streets 'were invaded by men and hobbledehoys from the rural district . . . who were pernicious in their demands for beer money, and who often forced themselves into houses to gain their objects'.[18] Oswald P. Scott, however, in the same decade remembered an altogether more vibrant Plough Monday at Cropwell Butler in Nottinghamshire:

> Plough Monday we lads spent a week going round the farms doing charades – Tom the Fool, the Soldier, the Lady Dame Jane, Beelzebub and the Doctor. I can still remember every word. The farmers supplied us with beef and ale, and after we had finished the village we spent a whole night at Wyverton Hall, four miles away and residence of the Chaworth Musters family, entertaining the ladies and gentlemen who had come down for the hunting season. More ale and cheese and seven shillings and sixpence each, which, in those days, were riches.[19]

Scott offers a more congenial picture than that advanced by the letter-writing misanthropes, one in which both farmers and local gentry freely and enthusiastically indulge in the festive traditions. It was not simply the threat of violence or property damage that induced the more reluctant to cough up but also the desire to avoid the shame that would accompany a refusal. A somewhat similar tradition to plough bullocking

---

16 W. Howitt, *The Rural Life of England*, 2 vols (London: Longman, 1840), i, p. 218.
17 F. W. Lewellyn Jewitt, 'On Ancient Customs and Sports of the County of Derby' *Journal of the British Archaeological Society* 7 (1851), pp. 201–2.
18 *Lincoln, Rutland and Stamford Mercury*, 10 January 1897.
19 Oswald P. Scott, 'Memories of a Villager', *Nottinghamshire Countryside* 21:4 (1960/1961), pp. 20–3.

was that of 'lent crocking'. This practice involved youths going from house to house soliciting pancakes, money or other food or drink. If nothing was forthcoming at an address then the front door was subjected to a shower of broken pottery, 'designed to show that the owner was a person so inhospitable, so destitute of common charity, as to refuse even a Pancake to the Poor on Shrove Tuesday'. The householder had to endure 'the notion of scandal and disgrace which the Common people annex to anyone's having Potsherds thrown at his Door at this particular Season'.[20]

A festive season is, of course, only festive if a significant proportion of the community participates – and there is every likelihood that the little free time enjoyed by labour was under considerable pressure from masters seeking to cajole or tempt hired hands to work during such periods. We can, then, possibly detect an early form of labour solidarity in the fact that rough music ridings were sometimes staged to penalise those who failed to acknowledge the existence of a traditional holiday. The levying of a fine upon such a person both served as a disincentive to labour over such a period and, of course, fuelled the festivities themselves.

In 1791 *The Gentleman's Magazine* remarked that: 'Early on the morning on the first of January, the Faex Populi assemble together, carrying stangs and baskets. Any inhabitant, stranger, or whoever joins not this ruffian tribe in sacrificing to their favourite saint day, if unfortunate enough to be met by any of their rank, is immediately mounted across the stang (if a woman she is basketed), and carried shoulder high to the nearest public house, where the payment of six pence liberates the prisoner.'[21] At Langwathby, near Edenhall in the Lake District, anyone found working during the Langwathby Rounds festival might be stanged –unless they paid a forfeit instead. The *Westmorland Gazette* of 1827 deplored the staging of ridings on New Year's Day, 'being used as a means of extorting money under circumstances which we think very disgraceful'.

In Conway, Easter Monday was celebrated in a particularly elaborate and peculiar fashion with 'stocksing'. As so often happened, young men and youths led and enforced the festivities. On Easter Sunday a crowd of them would gather and declare that men under the age of twenty were not permitted to go to bed at all that evening, men over twenty but under forty could do so but had to be up and in the street by 4.00a.m. the next morning and those over forty but under sixty had to make their appearance by 6.00a.m. Presumably, those over sixty had earned their right to a lie-in. In the morning, stocks would be set up in the main street and a party with a fife and drum would set off with a cart to find all who had overslept. The party would not hesitate to force its way into houses and drag out culprits, who were placed in carts and

---

20 BL Add. Mss 41313. F.80 Letter from Robert Studley Vidal to John Brand dated 10 July 1805. Cited in Bushaway, *By Rite, Custom, Ceremony and Community in England, 1700–1880*, p. 115.
21 *The Gentleman's Magazine*, 1791, p. 1169.

taken to the stocks. There they were incarcerated and pelted with mud.[22] Enforced participation in communal celebration was a common phenomenon. According to J. S. Leicester, ridings were commonly staged against those who 'followed their occupations on Christmas Day, New Year's Day or any other general holiday, or at prohibited times when there was a strike among workmen, they ran a great risk of having to go through the same ignominious ordeal'.[23] By 1887 *All The Year Round* was reporting this as a once popular but now redundant practice in Cumberland and Westmorland, where it had once been 'quite common for people to assemble early in the morning with baskets and stangs, and whoever did not join them, whether inhabitant or stranger, was immediately mounted across the stang and carried shoulder high to the next public house, where sixpence was demanded for the liberation of the prisoner'.[24]

The boldness of the populace upon such occasions was much enhanced by the widespread assertion that festive time existed outside of normal legal space and time. In 1810 a group of Plough Monday bullocks ploughed up the land of a Bakewell farmer who had refused them food and money. They were subsequently summonsed by him before Derby assizes. However, they boldly declared to the court that, 'whatever they might do on that day the Law could not take hold of them for it'. No doubt they were disabused of that notion, but the sympathies of the court are nevertheless apparent as the farmer had asked for a guinea compensation and in the event was awarded only one shilling.[25]

It is noteworthy, however, that the claims of licence so often advanced on such occasions also contained within them their own sense of limitation. It was equally important that if there was an expectation of what would be given and how, there was also an expectation of what could be asked and when. Departures from the traditional practices were discomforting, invited disapproval or, at the least, required explanation. According to George Roberts, the inhabitants of Lyme Regis objected in 1827 to the arrival in early December of a group of 'waits' (performers) from the countryside. The traditional day for their appearance was Christmas Eve and such objections were raised to their untimely performances that 'the party was near being put into the watch-house'.[26] On another occasion, when Cecil Sharp stayed at Old Headington, a group of Morris men knocked at the door: 'The men apologised for

---

22 Robert Williams, *History and Antiquities of the Town of Aberconwy* (Denbigh: T. Gee, 1835), pp. 108–10 and *Cambrian Quarterly Magazine*, III, p. 366 for an account dated 1831.
23 J. S. Leicester, 'Riding the Stang', *Monthly Chronicle of North-Country Lore and Legend* 1:3 (1887), pp. 122–6 at pp. 122–3.
24 *All The Year Round*, 31 December 1887.
25 Derby Central Library, Derbyshire Deeds vol. x, ms 3555, Brief for the Plaintiff, 11 August 1810.
26 G. Roberts, *The History and Antiquities of the Borough of Lyme Regis and Charmouth* (London: Samuel Bagster, 1834), p. 257.

being out at Christmas ('they knew that Whitsun was the proper time'), but work was slack and they thought there would be no harm in earning an honest penny.'[27]

Celebration, then, could move on to punishment but the reverse could also be the case. Punitive endeavour could become transposed into purely celebratory activity – if the recipient of the crowd's attentions had not committed too egregious an offence and if they were prepared to acknowledge their fault and 'play ball' by making some appropriate restitution to the crowd. This could mean pledging not to repeat the complained-of conduct, but frequently also required the offering of money or drink to the multitude. When James Tuckfield ignored a strike in 1826 by his fellow shipwrights in Bristol and attempted to go to work he ended up being mounted on a pole and carried about the city. However, when he promised to rejoin the shipwrights' club and rejoin the strikers they drank beer with him in a public house and then allowed him to go home. James Tuckfield seemingly parted on equable terms with his captors but his case illustrates that attempts to induce the victim to legitimise the proceedings were not always successful. Tuckfield subsequently made a complaint against his captors and had them hauled before the quarter sessions.[28]

As we shall see, there were many occasions when the crowd was not mollified and the victim could not or would not attempt it. The crowd might still enjoy the punishment, however, and there were good practical reasons why they might choose to stage a 'serious' stanging or skimmington during a festive season. It was during such time that one might reasonably expect to receive donations that would enable the putting-on of a good show – if one wants to burn someone in effigy one might well wait until 5 November when the resources were available to do the whole thing properly.

One particular nuance, observable on occasions in England, was the attempt to get the victim or victims themselves to pay for the performance. On one occasion, c.1850, when two married men and a woman living near Barnsley were found to have been 'guilty of incontinence', their neighbours:

> perambulated the three townships of Hurworth, Hurworth Place and Neasham, on three successive nights, loudly proclaiming the gross delinquency of the parties in set terms, and the third evening carrying with them in a farmer's cart the effigies of the trio, which were finally burnt in front of one of their houses. And then to crown the whole, the parties were asked to pay fifteen pence, the costs of the performance, which, if they had not done, a worse thing would doubtless have come to them.[29]

---

27 R. Samuel, '"Quarry Roughs": Life and Labour in Headington Quarry, 1860–1920. An Essay in Oral History', *Village Life and Labour*, ed. R. Samuel (London: Kegan Paul, 1975), pp. 139–263 at p. 187.
28 M. Gorsky, 'James Tuckfield's "Ride": Combination and Social Drama in Early Nineteenth-Century Bristol', *Social History* 19:3 (1994), pp. 319–38.
29 Leicester, 'Riding the Stang', p. 123.

When in 1883 the effigy of a wife-beater was paraded on a cart through Welburn, Yorkshire and burnt, the man in question was also required to pay up.[30] No doubt the money was converted into beer at the earliest opportunity, as the date of the performance was 21 June, Midsummer's day.

It was rather more usual for these occasions to be financed by the participants or staged on the basis of objects (and also consumables) donated by interested parties. Sometimes the hat would go round at the event itself. Charlotte Burne describes one such occasion near Shrewsbury in 1884. A 'mawkin' or effigy was carried around the village until it came to the culprit's house: 'The doggerel acte d'accusation was shrieked out amid a horrible uproar of shouting, whistling, and clattering pans . . . a bonfire was lighted and the mawkin was burnt upon it.' The display was not, however, offered gratuitously, 'The getters-up of this ritual expected money from the bystanders as a reward for their efforts in the cause of order.'[31]

One observes in rough music practice a wide range of behaviours nuanced according to context and sometimes according to the very particular predilections of the crowd. What is rarely absent entirely is a sense of enjoyment, of festivity and excess. Unfortunately, antiquarians and reporters interested in the carnivalesque and oftentimes comedic quality of such affairs – and generally rather condescending to groups with whom they had little in common socially, geographically and educationally – have often trivialised popular justice performances. Newspapers, in particular, tended to report skimmingtons and stangings in the fashion of whimsical anecdotes designed to lighten the mood before returning to the more serious business of the day. 'Guess what those silly rustics have done now!' might aptly head many a snippet. The outward comic appearance of certain activities has undoubtedly aided us – why else would we know that the village of Ilsington on Dartmoor punished an allegedly immoral woman c.1860 by compelling her to sit on a goat and ride around the village?[32] However, the temper of the crowd was frequently volatile upon such occasions; outcomes were hard to predict and, for the victim or victims, the punitive element was real enough. Notwithstanding the fact that many rough music activities were contained within a wrapper of festivity, it is rarely safe to dismiss even the milder of such activities as mere horseplay.

Performing the Music

Some indications of the way that rough music might be performed have already been given above. Such performances usually commenced with the arrival of a noisy crowd

---

30 Reported by I. Taylor, Settrington Rectory, *Folklore Journal* 1 (1883), pp. 298–9.
31 Burne, *Shropshire Folk-Lore*, p. 295.
32 T. Brown, 'A Further Note on the "Stag Hunt" in Devon', *Folklore* 90:1 (1979), pp. 18–21 at p. 19.

at the home of a malefactor (sometimes at his or her workplace) and thereafter three broad possibilities presented themselves. Sometimes the wrongdoer was dragged out and forced to participate in a parade through the community, during which he or she was subjected to all the indignities that the crowd might choose to impose. On other occasions, a volunteer was called upon to impersonate the wrongdoer: he would periodically announce the name of the person he was portraying as he was carried around the village or neighbourhood and would proclaim the offence that had caused the particular event to be staged. These two options appear to have been mutually exclusive, but a final shaming strategy – the construction of and parading of an effigy of the wrongdoer – could either be employed on its own instead of the two aforementioned procedures or it could be combined with either one of them. The effigy could be abused much more vigorously than would be proper with the actual malefactor or his surrogate and, as aforementioned, was normally enthusiastically burnt at the conclusion of the proceedings. All these activities required the procurement of certain materials and as such were very rarely the result of spontaneous eruptions of popular resentment. Furthermore, for the most part they were not arbitrary in their executions but tended to be planned with a very clear idea of just what was required in order to make a stanging or skimmington valid and meaningful.

If we begin with the first and most indiscriminate form of rough music when a person was actually dragged from their home, significant physical harm usually resulted. One gets the sense that as the nineteenth century progressed such occurrences became steadily less common and that it was the most egregious offences that were likely to inspire them. Beatings and peltings commonly accompanied such occasions and the preferred terminus to the day was a ducking in a local river or pond. Ducking, in some of the contemporary accounts and in our modern usage, has rather light-hearted connotation, though *Chambers Edinburgh Journal* gives a sense of the violence and terror of such proceedings:

> The person (a shoemaker) so dreadfully denounced had barely time to lock and barricade himself from the threatened vengeance. In vain. The windows and doors were smashed and battered in, and a violent tumult took place in the interior. Within two minutes the culprit was dragged out, pale and trembling and supplicating for mercy ... The ministers of public justice were inexorable – his sentence was pronounced, his doom sealed. The portentous pitchfork was immediately laid horizontally from the shoulder of one to the shoulder of another of the ablest of the executioners, who thus stood, front and rear with the stang between them ... The unmanly fellow who had provoked this fate showed by his terrors that he was just one of those cowards who could ill-treat the creature who had the right to his protection and had not fortitude to endure an evil himself. He howled for compassion, appealed by name to his indignant escort, and prayed and promised ... [he was taken to a pond about a mill wear and thrown in] he went over head and ears and rose again, by no means 'like a giant refreshed' and no sooner did he reappear, than a powerful grasp was laid upon him and down again he was plunged and

replunged, with unrelenting perseverance. The screams of his distracted wife fortunately attracted the attention of a magistrate (my revered father) whose garden shelved down to the edge of the stream and he hastened to intervene. Had he not done so, life might probably have been lost, for the ruffian was execrated by his fellow-man.[33]

The victim in the above case was a wife-beater and it was rather unusual for such offenders to be penalised in so severe a fashion. There were particular activities that were likely to invite such retribution – in Chapter 5 we shall see the vigour with which criminal gangs responded to the activities of informers. One alleged offence, which I wish to notice here, was that of witchcraft. This was no longer an offence after the Witchcraft Act 1736, but the subsequent history is worth visiting briefly here because it serves to illustrate points that will be important throughout the study: that a high degree of self-help was being exercised in communities that for a long time were not obviously conscious that they were acting beyond the law and that traditional beliefs and punishments persisted in the quiet places of the kingdom long after they had ostensibly been eradicated.

In 1751 Ruth Osborne was famously drowned at Tring. The Osborne affair had begun six years earlier in 1745 when Ruth Osborne had been turned away by a farmer, a Mr Butterworth, from whom she had begged milk. She had allegedly declared that 'she hoped the Pretender would soon be at Tring and take away Butterworth's cattle' – and from that point onwards the farmer suffered a number of misfortunes. Interestingly, his first response was to engage a white witch to try and neutralise Ruth's baleful influence but when that failed and his misfortunes continued, 'he had it declared by the town criers of Hemel Hempstead, Leighton Buzzard and Winslow, "This is to give notice that on Monday next a man and a woman are to be publicly ducked at Tring, in this county for their wicked crimes".'[34] Ruth and her husband were to be dealt with within the rubric of traditional justice, there was nothing covert about the affair, and indeed the declaration of intent in three parishes was widely held to legitimate popular justice practice. The officials of the local workhouse in which the Osbornes were residing were more au fait with the actual state of the law. They 'privately removed the old couple, in the dead time of night, to a place of safety'. However, they seem to have been surprised by the fervour of the crowd that assembled and attacked the workhouse. The mob dragged the governor down to a stream and threatened to drown him and fire the town if the wretches were not given up. They were, and thereafter both were battered and ducked. Her husband survived but Ruth died, and twenty-nine people were subsequently indicted for murder. Only one, Thomas Colley, was selected for an exemplary hanging and to affect it the authorities

---

33 *Chambers Edinburgh Journal* 78 (28 June 1845), p. 416.
34 *Northampton Mercury*, 6 May 1751.

staged a counterdemonstration of their own. Colley was paraded in a carriage from St Albans through Berkhamsted and Tring to the gallows at Gubbclutt Cross where he remained on a gibbet thereafter. The authorities had no doubt where the sympathies of the crowd lay – a strong company of cavalry was deployed to prevent any attempts to rescue him.[35]

Belief in witchcraft and the right to put suspects to trial was not, however, so easily subdued. In 1770 another woman suspected of causing the death of cattle, this time from Slapton in Buckinghamshire, was taken to a mill to be swum: 'The Miller, recollecting the fatal consequences of a similar Affair about eighteen years ago declined performing it before so great a Concourse of Spectators, but promised he would do so in private the first Opportunity.'[36] On 7 May 1808 Anne Izzard, an elderly woman of Great Paxton in Huntingdonshire, was dragged from her bed by several men and stripped in the yard outside, where three women lacerated her with pins and other implements. The assault was repeated the following day and the assailants were subsequently called to appear at Huntingdonshire assizes. Some weeks before, Anne had been accused of witchcraft and, 'the poor in general of the parishes of Great and Little Paxton, some of the farmers also, really believe she is actually a witch'.[37] The nature of the assault presumably reflected an old belief that if the blood of a witch was drawn her powers were weakened. A similar case occurred at Weymouth in 1845, where a man attacked his mother-in-law and scarred her face with a thorn because, so he alleged, she had bewitched him and only drawing her blood would break the spell.[38] As late as 1876, Margaret 'Peg' Grover of Newport found herself suspected of witchcraft after the sudden death of a girl in her village. She was seized, tied with rope and dunked in a river but rescued by some of the more sympathetic locals.[39] The same edition of the *Illustrated Police News* also reported that Anne Tennant from Long Compton in Warwickshire had recently been murdered by a labourer, James Haywood, who had stabbed her with a pitchfork believing her to be a witch. Haywood was eventually found not guilty by reason of insanity but 'fully a third of the village were said to share his belief'.

By the time that Margaret Grover was seized the temper of the times was less extreme and the expansion of professional policing had, to a degree, controlled disorder. Whilst the authorities often either tolerated rough music rituals that merely punished a malefactor symbolically, or else found the law rather inadequate to deal with them, they had a ready arsenal of criminal offences available to employ against those who had actually committed a battery on a complainant.

---

35 *Northampton Mercury*, 2 September 1751.
36 *Northampton Mercury*, 2 July 1770.
37 *Northampton Mercury*, 28 May 1808.
38 *Worcester Herald*, 12 April 1845.
39 *Illustrated Police News*, 1 July 1876.

The second type of rough music involved the employment of a substitute in place of the miscreant and was at all times a safer strategy for the crowd. It was also one that in its own way was equally entertaining. The substitute gave voice to the mocking rhymes composed to entertain the crowd that had gathered to humiliate the wrong-doer. It is fair to say that stangings and skimmingtons conducted in this manner were much more controlled than the instances of direct physical assault. It seems that there were men within communities who specialised at being the master of ceremonies at such events, and even 'stang bands' hired themselves out for such occasions. Verses (sometimes ribald) were composed to honour the miscreant, verses which nonetheless acknowledged local lyrical traditions that were seemingly transmitted down the generations. According to William Henderson, stangings in counties in northern England in the 1870s began with the mounting of a young man upon a ladder who would declaim, 'Hey derry! Hey derrydan! Tis neither for my cause nor your cause that I ride the stang, but tis for . . .'[40] At Beverley, Yorkshire, the declaration was, 'With a ran, dan, dan, at the sign of the old tin can, For neither your case nor my case do I ride the stang.'[41] These opening verses seem to have served as a kind of safety mechanism, the reciter affirming that he is not the one who is being shamed and that the abuse of the crowd should thus be properly directed elsewhere. What followed thereafter was usually descriptive of the fault of the offender and not infrequently threatening as to the consequences if he or she did not mend their ways. A verse from South Stoke in the Cotswolds ran as follows:

> There is a man in our town who often beats his wife;
> And any man who beats his wife deserves to lose his life.
> So if he does it any more
> We'll pull his nose right out before.
> Holler boys, holler boys,
> Make the bells ring.
> Holler boys, holler boys
> God save the King![42]

In the instances above, the perambulation of a young man upon a pole or ladder served as a substitute for the employment of an effigy. At a procession in Holderness in the East Riding, however, both were employed. The procession commenced at the home of the malefactor and went on to the churchyard. There, a young man was carried seven times around the church, stopping each time at the principle door

---

40 W. Henderson, *Notes on the Folklore of the Northern Counties of England and the Borders* (London: Folklore Society, 1879), p. 30.
41 Mrs Gutch, *Country Folklore vol. iv. Examples of Printed Folk-lore concerning the East Riding of Yorkshire, collected and edited by Mrs Gutch* (London: Folklore Society, 1912), pp. 130–1.
42 Katharine M. Briggs, *The Folklore of the Cotswolds* (London: B. T. Batsford, 1974), p. 115.

whilst the admonitory verses were proclaimed, 'With a ran dan at the sign of awd tin can and much ageean his ease does X ride stang' and so on. This ritual was performed for seven days but on the seventh an effigy was produced, which was burnt in front of the malefactor's door.[43] The offender was allegedly 'frightened out of his wits and took to his bed for some days thereafter'.[44]

It seems that the third species of rough music, the one that involved the mere employment of an effigy, was by the time of the period under consideration much more common than either of the other forms considered above. Edwin Grey offers a very vivid picture of such music in a Hertfordshire village in the 1860s:

> When it became known that so-and-so were to be given the rough music on a certain night at a certain time, the news spread like magic; by whose authority the night and the time for the demonstration was fixed no one knew, but somehow everybody did know it, so that at the appointed time one might have seen a very mixed up gang, composed of men, youths, and women, gathered outside the offender's house, each member of the gang carrying some sort of article whereby he or she could make discordant noises; old kettles with stones inside, old tea-trays and sticks, bells, whistles, clackers etc. At a given signal all would get in procession and march to and fro past the house, rattling the kettles, banging the tea trays, clanging the bells, twirling the clackers etc. as they paraded up and down, thus making a most terrific and ear-splitting din, for about an hour or so, and this for three successive nights sometimes, but generally one or two nights were sufficient for letting off steam . . . they carried an effigy or effigies of the offending person or persons, which effigies, after the rough music parades were over, were taken on to the Common and burnt; here on the Common, the music makers were able to give vent to their feelings and shower abuse on the effigy to their heart's content.[45]

The vehemence of the crowd in this account is palpable, but what real harm could such rough music actually do to the victim? Thomas Hardy's *The Mayor of Casterbridge* suggests that it could do a great deal. In the novel, Farfrae's wife Lucetta collapses upon seeing her effigy paraded for a skimmington and thereafter dies after miscarrying her child. Of itself this might be dismissed as a mere literary device, but there is a great deal of evidence that the performance of such music could amount to a profound assault upon the reputation, self-image and psychological stability of the victim.

William Henderson described the experience of rough music in general as 'a

---

43 Anon. *Holderness and the Holdernessians: A few Notes on the History, Topography, Dialect, Manners and Customs of the District by a Fellow of the Royal Historical Society* (London: Trubner and Co., 1878), pp. 77–8.
44 Ibid.
45 E. Grey, *Cottage Life in a Hertfordshire Village: How the Agricultural Labourer Lived and Fared in the Late 60s and 70s* (St Albans: Fisher Knight, 1935), pp. 160–3.

horrible ordeal' and this was the case whether one was physically molested or not.[46] At Edmondstone near Edinburgh in 1736 a wife-beater, George Porteous Smith, was found hanged the day after a crowd had treated him to a dose of rough music. The *Caledonian Mercury* speculated, however, as to whether he had done away with himself or whether he had been murdered.[47] In Northamptonshire in 1853 villagers responded to the news that a married man, Samuel Peekover, had got another girl pregnant, by 'lowbelling' him outside of his cottage during which 'all the old pots and kettles in the village were put into requisition'. The consequence was that Peekover tried to commit suicide by swallowing a draft of mercury.[48] Others were made of sterner stuff such as the cottager at Burford who determined upon frontal assault: he burst from his house armed with a pitchfork and thrust his effigy and several members of the crowd into the river.[49]

It would be a mistake, I think, to suppose that crowds were ignorant of the harms that their actions might cause. There is no warrant for supposing that they were more often merely thoughtless than actually malicious. As we shall see, there were instances where mere unthinking horseplay went too far. However, on many occasions the intentions of the crowd were clearly both punitive and very vindictive, even though their abuse of the victim's effigy was merely symbolic. They can hardly have been unaware that a common consequence of rough music was that the victims were thereafter forced, or felt impelled, to flee their communities – with all that that meant at the time. This indeed was often the intention of the performance. When Francis Hole, a 'sporting gentleman of small fortune', made himself obnoxious to the residents of a small Essex village in 1838, the inhabitants convened in the Shepherd and Dog and planned rough music, with the 'clear intention of forcing the complainant out of the village'.[50] James Higson in a letter to *Notes and Queries* noted the performance of stang ridings around Manchester and observed that, 'As a rule, the guilty parties could not endure the odium cast upon them but made a "moonlight flit" i.e. left the neighbourhood clandestinely.'[51] It was said in 1887 that at the least the victims 'very seldom recovered their character in the opinion of their neighbours'.[52] In 1893 the editor of a Dorset journal described rough music as 'the strongest expression of outraged public opinion that a country district is capable of conveying'.[53]

---

46 Henderson, *Notes on the Folk-lore of the Northern Counties of England and the Borders*, p. 29.
47 *Caledonian Mercury*, 29 March 1736.
48 *Northampton Herald*, 16 April 1853.
49 Briggs, *The Folklore of the Cotswolds*, p. 116.
50 *The Times*, 29 October 1838, p. 6 col. e.
51 J. Higson, 'Riding the Stang', *Notes and Queries* 5th series vol. 5 (25 March 1876), p. 253.
52 Leicester, 'Riding the Stang', pp. 122–6 at p. 122.
53 *Dorset Natural History and Antiquarian Field Club* 14 (1893), p. 182.

Well into the twentieth century rough music practices were capable of driving men and women to abandon their homes and livelihoods. However, the full effect of such practices, in instances where no actual physical violence was involved, is a little difficult for us to comprehend. We can imagine the terror of being dragged from one's bed, beaten and half-drowned. Similarly, intellectually we know that the rich performative culture of the eighteenth and nineteenth centuries was able to inspire powerful affective responses in both its participants and its victims. Shaming rituals in the past were potent, nuanced and often succeeded in casting individuals emotionally and psychologically beyond the boundaries of their community, with consequences that were barely or not at all tolerable. However, the truth is that community approval or disapproval has much less sway over the psychological well-being of most individuals in modern Britain than it did in the preceding centuries. Shame as a term in itself has been very much downgraded and its very ubiquity in conversation deprives it of its real meaning – 'it is a shame that our team didn't win the match'. Phrases such as these have hardly any content left and, similarly, for the most part, acts such as the burning of the Guy on 5 November now have a limited affective depth. We can hardly imagine, then, the awful weight of the shame within which a victim was enveloped when his or her effigy was consigned to the flames. To the victim, that act was a malignant one that forced him to confront the detestation in which he was now held and made the ill-will around him palpable. In the face of such a clear and strong manifestation of hatred given by one's neighbours, workmates, superiors, inferiors and even perhaps one's former friends only a very strong-minded victim could remain unmoved.

There was, then, something of a very ancient cruelty and malice about the burning of an effigy by one's community. Whether such an act was justified or not is another question. Dr Jasper Porter of Little Dean in Gloucestershire clearly thought his particular targets fully merited their fate when he made a rather remarkable will that survives in the Somerset County Archives. Within it there is a most peculiar bequest:

> In consequences of being defrauded of my birthright and paternal estate by the cruel and unnatural will of my father in 1779 who was effected by the Villainy and Artifice of my Sister, to aggrandize her fortune and become his Executrix, I would stigmatize their memory to latest posterity and exhibit a picture of them in full length that I may deter the vicious from acts of injustice which disgrace humanity and assure the world that the memory of bad actions can be only effaced by public marks of detestation and abhorrence. Wherefore my will is that £10 be deposited in the hands of the Overseers of the Parish of Enmore, that they shall distribute equally amongst ten of the oldest men paupers of the said Parish, on condition that on the 5th day of November, they make two effigies, representing a man and a woman who shall be fixed on two stakes and a copy of my father's will shall be affixed thereto with a label in large characters of these words

'To expiate the crimes of fraud and perfidy and make some atonement to the manes of the Testator we commit this effigy to the flames at the request and in consideration of our Benefactor.'

The ten men shall assemble at the Castle Inn at Enmore and 'walk in slow procession' at the beat of the drum through the village and carry the above effigies with my Father's will affixed thereto, as far as the great [?] on the crossings near the Church where a Bonfire shall be provided for the purpose of burning the effigies – The oldest of the ten men on arriving at the place shall then commit the said effigies to the flames and in a solemn and audible voice first repeat these words, 'To expiate the frauds and perfidy and make some atonement to the manes of the Testator we commit these effigies to the flames at the request and in commendation of our benefactor.' After performing the ceremony the men shall repair to the Castle Inn at dinner and there receive the £10 divided amongst them, agreeable to the words of my Will on the 5th day of Nov. every year provided that they perform the ceremony of burning the said Effigies in the manner above recited.

14th Feb 1795[54]

I began this book by observing that in ancient belief to write something down or indeed to make a representation of something was to bring that thing into the real world, to make a connection with that thing, to actuate its power or to express one's own power upon it. The sentiments and beliefs that seem to have accompanied Dr Porter's bequest would not be unfamiliar to anyone who has studied the Mesopotamian curse tablets or the many forms of their successors. What we do not know, unfortunately, is whether Dr Porter's sister was still alive at the time that he drafted the will. Did he anticipate that she would learn of the intended performance? Whilst the circumstances of the will are more than a little unusual, the burning of the effigy itself places it within a by now well-evidenced tradition, but the proposed annual repetition (and we do not know if the proceedings were ever in fact carried out) is suggestive of a particular malice.

It should be said that the signification and activation of malice was not the only purpose of effigy burnings and their like. The circumstances and offence described above were very particular to Dr Porter himself. For the most part, though, one of the purposes of gathering together the crowd was to consolidate a common view of the subject – to establish a world view in which the victim was discredited and placed in his appropriate position in human regard, whether his offence be adultery or free thinking. The ritual involved in this social placing (or expelling) often depended upon the employment of behaviours and demeanours that replicated other social

---

54 Somerset County Archives, DD\X\Port/1.

situations, mimicking not in the sense of mocking but rather in the sense of taking upon themselves the affective content of other forms of social experience but turning it to other ends.

So, for example, whilst burning an effigy was a powerful statement of disapprobation, an even more acute psychological assault upon the victim seems to have been occasioned by the conduct of their mock funeral. Thus, Thompson observes: 'The symbolism of public execution irradiated popular culture in the eighteenth century and contributed much to the vocabulary of rough music ... To burn, bury or read the funeral service over someone still living was a terrible community judgment in which the victim was made into an outcast, one considered to be already dead. It was the ultimate in excommunication.'[55] As such, mock burial seems to have been a rare phenomenon – or perhaps it is better to say that it was rarely reported. In 1905 a Cornish miner, Louis Higman, petitioned for divorce. A local builder, Richard Jacob, gave evidence during the proceedings that the behaviour of the respondent and co-respondent had long been the source of scandal in the village of Bugle where they lived. The villagers had been so much incensed that in 1898 they had buried them in effigy. Jacob had been present and reported that a person had conducted a funeral service dressed as a clergyman and there had been a choir, mourners and an undertaker.[56] According to the *Morning Post*, the whole proceedings had been 'carried out with the great decorum, and although there was an enormous attendance there was no sign of rowdyism, but solemn silence was maintained, the only voice heard, beside the lamentations of the "mourners" being those of the "clergymen" and the "choir" and those who chose to join in the "service". The police were present but their services were not required.'[57] The 1905 report seems to have sparked a brief interest in the phenomenon for, not to be outdone, the *Daily Telegraph* reported the mock burial at Colchester of an unpopular senior officer by other officers of the Essex Volunteer Brigade: 'After dinner some thirty officers turned out, attired in long black cloaks, and each carrying a lighted lantern. In front was borne a deck chair, covered in a Union Jack and supposed to bear the corpse of the officer referred to. The procession passed around the officers lines, and a mock internment was conducted, after which the assembled officers sang a song, and indulged in quadrilles and a cake-walk, the proceedings closing with the National Anthem.'[58]

The position of the detested officer in the Volunteer Brigade was probably untenable thereafter. Life for a social outcast in the small village of Bugle must have been very hard indeed. However, having tried to suggest something of the power of such

---

55 E. P. Thompson, 'Rough Music Reconsidered', *Folklore* 103:1 (1992), pp. 3–26 at p. 7.
56 M. Peacock, 'Burial in Effigy', *Folklore* 16:4 (1905), pp. 463–4.
57 *Morning Post*, 16 May 1905.
58 *Daily Telegraph*, 10 August 1905.

malignant demonstrations, there remains a contrary point to be made. Such acts were most effective when the victim was himself caught up within the value system of the perpetrators themselves. Common sense informs us that there are forms of distance that make such exhibitions likely to be less effectual. I am more likely to be affected by acts done by perpetrators I know than by those I don't. If I am that sort of person I may be more affected by the acts of social equals or superiors than by those whom I perceive to be social inferiors. Upon a practical level I may well be more deeply troubled by the sentiments of those who can in addition reach out to materially harm me than by the sentiments of those who cannot. Perhaps most importantly, I am more likely to be disturbed by the actions of those with whom I share a concurrent life view than by those whose world is constructed upon the basis of quite different sets of assumptions. With whom I associate myself may make an enormous difference to the way that I interpret acts. If I were to be burnt in effigy by certain members of higher education's increasingly bean-counting and vacuous bureaucracy then I should, save for mundane practical reasons, be not the slightest bit disturbed. Indeed I should feel it something of a compliment. Were the same act to be performed by my students, however, I feel sure that I would be deeply troubled.

Attempts to 'reach' the subject of rough music rituals were then of varying effect. Sometimes they sufficed to drive the victim to absolute despair, sometimes they entirely failed to ruffle the feathers of their target. Robert Peel was presumably one of the latter when after being immolated in 1842 he coolly wrote to Thomas Assheton Smith that, 'I cannot regret being burned in effigy when the flames excited so gratifying a demonstration in my favour.'[59] Politicians in the early nineteenth century were very robust creatures indeed, and political life was replete with instances in which contending interests sought to bind constituencies and express solidarity by theatrical endeavours that not infrequently terminated in the symbolic destruction of their opponents. I doubt Robert Peel felt much congruence with the mob.

However, in between the two extremes there were obviously a variety of positions. Even victims of effigy burnings who were not entrapped within their communities, who were articulate and socially separate, may not always have been as indifferent to such proceedings as it may have been in their interests to profess. As the will of Dr Porter suggests, the well-to-do were also caught up in the values of performative culture. Amongst the gentlemanly classes, character and honour remained for a very long time a matter of public performance, it mattered very much how one represented oneself and how one was represented by others. It does not follow that these demonstrations operated to no effect at all merely because the more socially powerful were able to publicly respond to them with apparent indifference.

---

59 Somerset County Archives, DD\WHb/A/86. Letter marked 1842 but otherwise undated.

For 'ordinary people' the experience of rough music had the potential to be very traumatic indeed, and so in the next chapter I will move on to consider in more detail the types of behaviour that were most likely to expose them to the risk of its performance.

4

Sex, Gender and Moral Policing

The examples of rough music already cited have probably already indicated to the reader that such practices were often inspired by irregular gender behaviour or sexual practice and it is these offences that I intend to explore here. Before pursuing the causes of the music, however, it is appropriate to first say something further about the performance itself insofar as gender symbolism and gender reversal seem to have themselves played an important part in the punitive enterprise.

The 1744 edition of Samuel Butler's *Hudibras* contains a depiction of a skimmington (by William Hogarth) that contains two interesting gender elements. Two figures are mounted upon a donkey. One, the object of the crowd's attention, faces backwards. Sitting in front of him on the donkey but facing forwards is a fearsome creature who upon inspection turns out to be a man in women's clothes. This virago is half turned, however, so that she/he can belabour the victim with a ladle. Amidst the tumultuous crowd two motifs are apparent, the display of horns (a traditional sign of the cuckold) and the display upon long poles of womens' apparel. The victim is clearly a henpecked husband punished for his failure to subdue his wife. A hundred years later the people of the Wiltshire villages of Burbage (1835) and Ogborne St George (1840) were still using a similar procedure to penalise their submissive husbands. While they now employed a stuffed effigy on a horse, this figure nevertheless continued to be enthusiastically belaboured with a ladle by a man in women's clothes.[1]

Feminine or transgender elements are found within a wide variety of rough music and more general folkloric elements. As employed against the downtrodden husband, the display of female garments performs the fairly obvious function of challenging the masculinity of the victim. However, there were other ways of placing the miscreant within the wrong gender categorisation and, furthermore, the targets were not always those who had abrogated their appropriate role within the household – other offences could inspire such mockery. So, for example, the mock mayor of Halgaver

---

1 B. H. Cunningham, 'Moonrake Medley', *Wiltshire Archaeological Magazine* 50 (1943), pp. 278–80.

Moor punished those who offended him by forcing them to ride 'woman wise' and to be otherwise ridiculed by having their clothes turned inside out.[2] Into the 1920s and 1930s the practice of 'white shirting' was used in mining communities to disgrace those who had broken ranks and gone to work during an industrial dispute. The power of the performance lay in the fact that the shaming was done by groups of women, as well as the fact that during the proceedings female apparel was waved in front of the offender.[3]

The voluntary appearance of men in women's clothes was of a broader significance and a common feature of mummers' plays, molly dancing and the like. For example, the plough on Plough Monday was 'accompanied by a fool and Bessy; the fool being dressed in the skin of a calf... and Bessy, generally a young man in female attire, covered with a profusion of ribbons'.[4] The donning of women's clothes signalled the entry into a transgressive time and space in which normal rules of social behaviour and social categorisation were suspended. It liberated the carnivalesque. Invoking justice and invoking festivity being, as we have seen, so interconnected, the adoption of transgender behaviour could signify the entry into that transformative space in which power belonged to the powerless and judgement to the judged. It was during that time that wrongs could be recognised, punished or amended so that paradoxically the community could return to the equilibrium from which it had been displaced. Allied to Girard's concept then of mimetic violence we can add a concept of mimetic judging.[5] Mimetic judging did not return the community to an idealised existence but, as it ran its course, it served to define and proclaim what the community's normative values should be.

This chapter is mainly about the particular penalisation of deviant individuals for violations of general moral codes. As we proceed further, however, we shall see that folkloric and sometimes more specifically rough music practices were employed in order to mobilise communities against specific threats to their interests. In constructing a language of resistance, recourse was very often made to the familiar, to those ritualistic endeavours during which the community self-evidently came most into being. The community had to be constituted in order for it to be mobilised; once constituted it was most effective when its actions were legitimated by being embedded in empowering and anti-hierarchical time and space. Protest, then, could be made into a kind of folk event in part actuated and carried through by transgender behaviour.

---

2 *The Western County Magazine*, 1789, p. 245.
3 Jaclyn J. Gier-Viskovatoff and Abigail Porter, 'Women of the British Coalfields on Strike in 1926 and 1984: Documenting Lives Using Oral History and Photography', *Frontiers: A Journal of Women Studies* 19:2 (1998), pp. 199–230 at p. 200.
4 Jewitt, 'On Ancient Customs and Sports of the County of Derby', pp. 201–2.
5 René Girard, *Violence and the Sacred* (Baltimore: Johns Hopkins University Press, 1977).

Many examples will become apparent as we proceed so I shall give but a few here. In the seventeenth century resistance to enclosures in the Forest of Dean had been led by a 'Lady Skimmington' and her lieutenants had indeed been disguised as women. During food riots at Bellamarsh in Devon in 1795 a crowd assembled to demolish a mill that had been exporting biscuits to the navy and, 'from the great number of petticoats, it is generally supposed that several men were dressed in female attire'.[6] During the 'Scotch Cattle' activities in South Wales between 1820 and 1835 blacklegs and working miners were visited by masked gangs blowing horns, making rough music and wearing women's clothes.[7] Finally, a march into Bradninch, Devon in 1867 to set food prices was led by a man dressed as a woman.[8] The appearance of such a man signalled that something important, transgressive, threatening and yet often also potentially normalising was about to occur.

Sex, Marriage and Social Expectation

As a phenomenon rough music was a practice that admitted of much variation in its severity, ranging from the light-hearted to the almost murderous. As already mentioned, marital improprieties, inappropriate gender behaviour or sexual malpractice were commonly advanced as reasons for rough music. These too admitted of degrees in their impropriety. Logically enough there is a considerable connection between the behaviour of the crowd and the severity of the conduct complained of. The correlation was not, however, absolute. Even at what one might call the light-hearted end of the spectrum things could, and occasionally did, go horribly wrong – especially when the victim refused to respond in the appropriate manner. Furthermore, whilst I shall be considering the reasons articulated for the performance of the music it will become clear that upon occasion there were other underlying issues in play, such that the behaviour of the crowd at the time may not always be explained by the nature and severity of their avowed complaint.

Beginning with the generally less threatening end of rough music activity one observes occasions upon which the crowd was not really complaining at the conduct of persons so much as signalling that an event had occurred that inspired a compensatory expectation. This was rather similar to the calendric doling customs, except that here a particular person or persons was expected to provide largess in consequence of something that had happened to them personally rather than because of their social standing and the time of the year. In particular, weddings were expected to be

---

6 *London Chronicle*, 18 April 1795.
7 D. J. V. Jones, 'The Scotch Cattle and their Black Domain', *Welsh History Review* 5:3 (1971), pp. 220–49 at p. 238.
8 D. Storch, 'Popular Festivity and Consumer Protest: Food Price Disturbance in the Southwest and Oxfordshire in 1867', *Albion* 14:3 (1998), pp. 209–34 at p. 219.

times of generosity to one's neighbours such that the couple became participants in a broader communal celebration. Those couples (or their parents) who did not share their good fortune might be charged with meanness and thus lay themselves open to a certain degree of chastisement. Judicious hustling ensured that many an uninvited crowd or band turned up at a wedding. In 1864 a Mr H. E. R. remembered in *Notes and Queries* that on the occasion of his own wedding in 1815 he had received a card upon his return from church inviting a donation to the local musicians. The sender had claimed that he had 'Books of Presidents [precedents] to show'. According to the groom, 'There was also an intimation that the marrow-bones and cleavers were in readiness, and would play if required. Few persons refused the gratuity (about five shillings) in order to escape what would have been an annoyance to themselves and neighbours.'[9] William Bernhard Smith remembered in 1864 the activities of itinerant or opportunistic musicians who attempted to extort money at a wedding in Marylebone c.1850:

> It was a serious annoyance; a party of fellows with their bones and cleavers came to the door; they produced a book containing the names of those on whom their blackmail had been levied: the sums marked were probably fictitious, and perhaps some of the names as well; but this I know, that in my capacity as best man, I once paid a sovereign to allay the fears of the bride's mother, who shrank from the idea of the 'rough music' threatened by her unwelcome visitors.[10]

The above examples seem indeed to be but examples of barefaced cheek. However, requests could become forthright demands if there was some facet of the wedding that led the crowd to suppose that it was entitled to some particular restitution. If we look at the French cultural context for the moment, there forms of charivari were often associated with the remarriage of widows. Violet Alford in her study of the medieval and early modern periods observed that: 'Out of 250 examples under my hand I find 77 are for the remarriage of widows, 49 for husband-beating, 35 for adultery, 89 for other causes, 24 of which are in a special group directed at newly-married couples as a communal warning and prophylactic treatment.'[11] Allan Greer has observed of Lower Canada that, prior to 1837, charivaris there were almost always directed at newly married couples in which one of the parties had been widowed or where there was a significant difference of age or social status between bride and groom. The emphasis, though, was rather more on compensation than penalisation; the fines levied in such cases by charivari crowds:

---

9 Mr H. E. R., *Notes and Queries*, 3rd series, vol. 1 (25 June 1864), p. 524.
10 W. J. Bernhard Smith, *Notes and Queries*, 3rd series, vol. 6 (20 August 1864), p. 158.
11 V. Alford, 'Rough Music or Charivari', *Folklore* 70:4 (1959), pp. 505–18 at p. 506.

Acted as a token of agreement signifying the establishment of peace between the targets and perpetrators of ritual attack. In offering money, the newly married couple signified, however reluctantly, their submission to the judgment of their neighbours. Moreover, this forced gift implied a recognition – purely at the level of outward acts of course – of the legitimacy of the charivari itself. The subjects were needled, nagged, annoyed and threatened until they made a gesture signifying acceptance of the charivari, until they themselves became participants in the proceedings.[12]

In the English and Welsh context of the eighteenth and nineteenth centuries, there is much less evidence of the pursuit of widows per se. However, Thomas Hardy suggests that remarriage could arouse disapprobation if it was perceived as being unduly hasty. His ballad, *The Fire at Tranter Sweatley's*, gives an example of what might happen if a decent period of mourning was not observed. A girl, Barbara, is forced to marry a drunken tranter, but he sets fire to the house on their wedding night and dies in the flames. A longstanding admirer then carries her away to his mother's house but the neighbourhood is shocked:

> There was skimmity-riding with rout, shout and flare,
> In Weatherbury, Stokeham, and Windleton, ere
> They had proof of old Sweatley's decay:
> The Mellstock and Yalbury folk stood in a stare
> The tranter owned houses and garden-ground there,
> But little did Sim or his Barbara care
> For he took her to church the next day.[13]

It does seem to have been the case that, as again with Lower Canada, where there was a significant age disparity between bride and groom or a difference of social expectation then an unwelcome visit was more likely. When George Ball of Lew Down married in 1892 he had a good inkling that a good many unwelcome guests would try to attend the wedding – he was seventy years old and his wife about forty-five. In order to forestall any demonstration of popular feeling, 'He therefore made arrangements with the rector for the wedding to be on Monday morning last at 8 o'clock. In his best clothes he went alone across the fields to the church and Joanna came from her house to the church alone. A grocer living nearby acted as witness.' Word got out, however, and, 'In the evening a number of young men met to give the "happy pair" what they call "a good kettle band" ... George, being annoyed at the proceedings, tried to drench them with water.'[14]

---

12 Allan Greer, 'From Folklore to Revolution: Charivaris and the Lower Canadian Rebellion of 1837', *Social History* 15:1(1990), pp. 25–43 at p. 31.
13 J. Proffatt, 'The Fire at Tranter Sweatley's: A Wessex Ballad by Thomas Hardy', *Appleton's Journal* 14 (1875), p. 594.
14 *Devon and Exeter Gazette*, 24 May 1892.

George was perhaps imprudent. As with the doling customs, provocation by either party sometimes meant that even these apparently rather benign activities could get out of hand. In 1879 Robert Barnes of Newport on the Isle of Wight, the father of a new bride, ended up prosecuting six seamen friends of his son-in-law. The complaint at the petty sessions was occasioned by the decision of his daughter and her husband to spend their wedding night at his house. Barnes had anticipated that someone might appear in the night in order to interrupt their marital bliss. He had accordingly set a pail full of water above the gate. At about 10.00p.m. a party of twenty to thirty men, one imagines somewhat inebriated, had appeared and had paraded outside the house with a banjo and melodeon. Some of them had got drenched when they tried to open the gate and unfortunately they had not responded with good humour. They 'broke through a hedge, trampled his shrubs and threw stones through his windows. The magistrates concluded that the damage had been done after great provocation and the case was dismissed.'[15] This was a rather minor affair compared to the murder in 1802 of Joshua David Llaingain by James David, a yeoman from Newchurch in Carmarthenshire. The deceased and his brother had brought a fiddler 'in a riotous and violent manner' to a marriage bidding. This had engendered 'general rioting and fighting', during the course of which Joshua had been shot. The accused was, however, acquitted by the Court of Great Sessions.[16]

Some weddings, of course, had to be arranged in a hurry. One woman born in north-west England in 1908 remembered the unforgiving crowd upon the occasion of such a wedding around the time of the First World War:

R: The bride and bridegroom used to walk to the church to get married. Now this here woman was pregnant, I think that was really cruel – she might not have been the willing party. It isn't always the girl's fault you know! A man's a man and he's blinking strong, isn't he, and they get really lust in them. They can overpower you, you know! But this here woman, she worked in the same mill as my mother and this here weaver has asked my mother if she was going to watch the wedding. She said that she couldn't as she had her washing to do, and she were working while Saturday dinner-time. Anyhow, when my mother went to work on the Monday they told her what the wedding was like. They stoned the woman because she was pregnant! That was at Emmanuel Church!
Interviewer: Who threw the stones?
R: Nasty-minded women you know.
Interviewer: What did the weavers think of that? Did your mother say?

---

15 *Once a Week Periodical*, 1 April 1879, p. 588.
16 Welsh National Archives Great Sessions Database 4/753/3, 19 January 1802.

R: My mother said that some agreed with stoning her. They thought it was a crime to have a child before you were married.[17]

If pre-marital sex offended conventional morality no doubt there were many hypocrites among the crowd. Why, though, should crowds object to marriages in which there was a significant age discrepancy or where one party had been married before? The origins of the objection may lie in the fact that in small communities there may have been only a limited number of young and eligible men and women. A person who took one of that number out of the pool might then expect to be the recipient of a certain amount of envy and, if he or she had already had one wife or husband or had been considered too old to marry, then active resentment might follow. One can also imagine that grudging tolerance might be the best that would be extended if the groom was from outside the village. Laura Knight observed of the village of Staithes in the first half of the twentieth century that, 'It was only a short while since no marriage outside the village was allowed; a few years earlier, any strange man coming to court a girl was stoned out of the place.'[18]

Conversely, stigma might be attached to anyone who could marry but refused to do so. Katharine Briggs reports the testimony in 1973 of an elderly woman from Painswick in the Cotswolds. She recalled that during her childhood she had witnessed a skimmington, 'directed against two ladies, the Misses Mason of Beacon House ... Their effigies were borne through the town and at last burned, presumably on Beacon Hill. The Misses Mason behaved with great courage and dignity. They walked quietly up and down the street looking at the procession, apparently quite unconcerned, and no one molested them.'[19] Briggs remarks that the only reason for the affair was to have been that neither of the Masons had ever married. The belief that it was appropriate for men and women to marry, but to marry within the ambit of community expectations, seems to have long endured. I am grateful for the information from a colleague that during her childhood in the 1960s in north-east England it was still customary for local children to cry out 'shammy wedding!' at weddings of apparently mismatched couples.[20]

Wrongful conduct after the wedding could also inspire rough music – and more often at the more serious end of the spectrum. George Roberts in his *History of Lyme Regis* gave what he thought were the three principle reasons for riding skimmington – and all involved married persons. The first cause was occasioned when 'a man and

---

17 The Centre for North-West Regional Studies, Lancaster. Elizabeth Roberts Oral History Archive: Neighbours. Transcript of interview with Mrs D.1.P (b.1908).
18 L. Knight, *Oil Paint and Grease Paint: The Autobiography of Laura Knight*, vol. I (1936 Harmondsworth), p. 95, cited in Snell, *Parish and Belonging*, p. 62.
19 Briggs, *The Folklore of the Cotswolds*, p. 117.
20 Thanks to Louise Falcini for this information.

his wife quarrel and he gives up to her'; second, 'When a woman is unfaithful to her husband, and he patiently submits without resenting her conduct'; and third, when there had been 'grossly licentious conduct on the part of married persons'.[21] Violet Alford listed husband-beating by wives as the second most common cause of rough music in France and, as we saw in Chapter 1, a desire to control overbearing wives or women in general featured strongly in the use of the branks, the ducking stool and indeed rough music in the medieval and early modern periods. The late-sixteenth-century frieze at Montecute House features just such a woman who belabours her husband for having helped himself to beer – in the next panel the subsequent skimmington is depicted. Jonathan Swift gives us a picture of the unenviable life of such a man:

> At home, he was pursu'd with Noise, –
> Abroad he was pester'd by boys,
> Within his wife would break his Bones, –
> Without, they pelted him with Stones,
> The Prentices procur'd a Riding
> To act his Patience and her chiding.[22]

During one such example from Northenden in Cheshire c.1790:

> A man dressed in female apparel was mounted on the back of an old donkey, holding a spinning-wheel on his lap and his back towards the donkey's head. Two men led the animal through the neighbourhood followed by scores of boys and idle men, tinkling kettles and frying pans, roaring with cows' horns and making a most hideous hulabuloo, stopping every now and then, whilst the exhibitioner made the following proclamation: 'Ran a dan, ran a dan, ran a dan, Mrs Alice Evans has beat her good man. It was neither with sword, spear, pistol or knife, But with a pair of tongs she vowed to take his life. If she'll be a good wife and do so no more. We will not ride stang from door to door.'[23]

Unruly wives remained an issue well into the nineteenth century. Charles Dickens remarked that in Surrey and Sussex, 'Rough music to a scold is among the customs of some villages. So recently as 1860, when a man was shut out of his house by a termagant wife, the boys and young men dressed up an effigy of the woman, imprisoned it in the pound for a time, and then burned it before her door.'[24] Margaret Burne notes one instance of the staging of a skimmington in the late nineteenth century

---

21 Roberts, *The History and Antiquities of the Borough of Lyme Regis and Charmouth*, p. 258.
22 Jonathan Swift, 'A Quiet Life and a Good Name', 1724, *Poems*, ed. H. Williams (Oxford: OUP, 1937), pp. 219–21, lines 49–54.
23 W. E. A. Axon, *Cheshire Gleanings* (London: Simpkin, Marshall and Co., 1884), p. 300.
24 Charles Dickens, *All The Year Round*, 3 October 1874, p. 581.

at Upton St Leonards in Gloucestershire to ridicule a man who had been beaten by his wife.[25] In Wales, as we shall see, a particular rough music form, the 'coolstrin' seems to have been performed entirely, or almost so, for the benefit of errant wives – although the practice may have disappeared altogether by about 1840. Theo (Theodora) Brown also reports that taming such creatures was one of the aims of the stag hunt in nineteenth-century Devon.[26]

Rather curiously the fiction of a wife having beaten her husband also seems to have been employed as an excuse for and prelude to prearranged festivities, as this notice from the Somerset County Archives describes:

> Notice is hereby given to all his Majesty's true and loyal subjects that on Monday the 24th Day of May next being Whitsun Monday in honour to an unhappy couple there will be a genteel Skimeton performed that day, in the Parish of Bradford, in the country of Somerset, to begin by 8 o'clock in the morning, at which the Public are Desired to Attend.
>
> Poor John received a severe drubbing every Day last Week; and Saturday last, by his lovely wife he was unmercifully beat because he would not [wait?] by for his wife whilst she fetched him some tobacco.
>
> Same day and place will be also Raceing, Running for young women, Jumping in the Bag, and the Evening to Conclude with other Amusements.
>
> Dated near the White Horse, Bradford, 24th April 1790.[27]

Similarly, the parade of effigies of women or of men dressed as women and accompanied by the traditional sign of a cuckold, a pair of horns, was thought in some localities to be a necessary prelude to the opening of a traditional fair and a mode of establishing its legal existence. It was claimed that by processing a rider dressed as a woman three times on three separate days, and fixing horns in three adjoining parishes, cattle fairs could be held at Bratton Fleming and Chittlehampton in Devon.[28] Alice B. Gomme noted that in Devonshire:

> The procession consists of two stuffed figures of a man and woman on horseback, back-to-back, preceded by a man carrying a pair of ram's horns on a pole or on his head, followed by noisy music of ladles, pots, frying pans, etc. and smacking of whips. After the procession the horns are nailed up sometimes to the church porch.[29]

---

25 Burne, 'Parish Gleanings from Upton St Leonard's, Glos', pp. 236–9.
26 T. Brown, 'The "Stag Hunt" in Devon', *Folklore* 63:2 (1952), pp. 104–109 at p. 108.
27 Somerset County Archives, DD/HP/23.e.
28 *The Transactions of the Devonshire Association*, 8 (1876), p. 640.
29 A. B. Gomme, 'Skimmington Riding', *Folklore Journal* 1 (1883), p. 365.

Similar rituals are said to have established fairs at Charlton and Lynton. The logic of the connection between the fair and the fictitious offence is rather difficult to determine. One could perhaps imagine that should a suitable target present itself then a fair would be a most suitable time for an episode of rough music, and that one might thereby become so associated with the other as to seem indispensable. The truth is, however, that this is mere speculation.

It seems fairly clear that there was a subsisting tradition in the first half of the nineteenth century of penalising rumbustious wives. For the second half, however, the evidence suggests that the practice was very much on the decline and had disappeared altogether in some areas. In the Cotswolds, Katharine M. Briggs expressed what seemed to be the general view that, 'If a woman was supposed to be a scold or husband-beater an effigy might be carried in procession but in more recent times the procession was mainly against the man.'[30] The stanging of unruly wives had ceased in Beverley, Yorkshire by the end of the century, and it was said of the village of Holderness in 1912: 'needless to say that wife-beating is the only misdemeanour punished by the stang'.[31]

By the end of the nineteenth century, in respect of marital relations, wife-beating is a much more common reason advanced for the performance of rough music than wifely insubordination. Most of the written records of the doggerel verses associated with rough music are from the second half of the nineteenth century and concern themselves with the punishment of such behaviour. I have already alluded to South Stoke, but at Beverley it was chanted, 'For Johnny has been beating his wife. He beat her, he bang'd her, he bang'd her indeed, he bang'd her, poor creature, before she stood need.'[32] At Hedon it was declared, 'If onny o' you husbans your gud wives do bang. Let 'em cum to uz, an, we'll ride 'em the stang.'[33] Efforts short of a full-blown stanging or skimmington were also made to encourage offenders to desist. Thus, in Gloucestershire straw would be scattered outside the house of a wife-beater to symbolise 'threshing done here'.[34] The same custom is also attested for Yorkshire.[35] In Monmouthshire, as a wedding ritual some straw was tied around the newly married couples' gate so that the husband could beat that instead of his wife.[36] Finally, during protests in Wales against agricultural conditions and extortionate road tolls, known as the 'Rebecca Riots', Rebecca's men also took it upon themselves to campaign for a moral reformation in the countryside and warned men of the unpleasant

---

30 Briggs, *The Folklore of the Cotswolds*, p 115.
31 Gutch, *County Folk-Lore vol VI*, p. 130.
32 Ibid.
33 J. Nicholson, *The Folk Speech of East Yorkshire* (London, Simpkin, Marshall and Co., 1889), pp 8–9.
34 Briggs, *The Folklore of the Cotswolds*, p. 115.
35 *Notes and Queries*, 9th series, vol. 1 (5 February 1898), p. 116.
36 *Byegones*, 24 May 1893.

consequences of beating their wives.[37] Thompson argued, cautiously, that there was an observable moral shift reflected in the redeployment of rough music from the punishing of gender-inappropriate behaviour by women towards the chastisement of men who assaulted women.

Again, chastisement and festivity were interposed. Around 1895 near Staines:

> An innkeeper was reported to have beaten his wife. This was a golden opportunity not to be neglected by his neighbours, so they 'tin-kittled' him right royally, until he offered the orchestra a plentiful supply of refreshment, whereupon they desisted for the time, but returned in less than a fortnight to serenade the landlady, who was said in the meantime to have walloped her lord. Since then, I believe, there have been several instances of this harmless though noisy amusement.[38]

The report begs the question of whether the affair is to be regarded as a justice event – that is to say, whether it was primarily designed to punish the wrongdoer and deter wrongful conduct, or whether it was intended primarily as a festivity, one in which the orchestra could be bought off by suitable liquid dole, which presumably the innkeeper had in plentiful supply.

Describing a skimmington on Midsummer's Day at Welburn in 1883 Hammerton concluded that, from the fact that it took place on 'a traditional date for community celebration and carousing', this suggested that 'the urge for a good time weighed at least as strongly as outrage against the offending husband'.[39] Nevertheless he agreed that: 'The evidence of growing intolerance in the nineteenth century to violence generally and violence to women in particular is undeniable.'[40] This is in line, of course, with the declining levels of violence and insult generally evidenced by Shoemaker, Stone, Cockburn and others.[41]

If the connection between punishment and a good time continued to be asserted it should not be thought that by the end of the nineteenth century the performers had ceased to act in earnest. In 1881, at Alderley in Cheshire, the sounds of violence caused a crowd to break down the door of a man called Bredbury. He was dragged out with a halter on his neck and taken to the village pond to be ducked. A constable

---

37 Williams, *The Rebecca Riots,* p. 241.
38 *Notes and Queries*, 9th series, vol. 1 (5 February 1898), p. 116.
39 James Hammerton, *Cruelty and Companionship: Conflict in Nineteenth-Century Married Life* (London: Routledge, 1992), p.16.
40 Ibid.
41 See, R. Shoemaker, 'Male Honour and the Decline of Public Violence in Eighteenth Century London', *Social History* 26:2 (2001), pp. 190–208. L. Stone, 'Interpersonal Violence in English Society 1300–1980', *Past and Present*, 101 (1983), pp. 22–33, and J. S. Cockburn, 'Patterns of Violence in English Society: Homicide in Kent 1560–1985', *Past and Present* 130 (1991), pp. 70–106.

intervened at this point and arrested the man who was holding the halter at the time. The local magistrate must have been somewhat sympathetic to the performance, since when the arrested man was brought before him he let him go with a mere caution.[42] Rough music was employed at Alderminster in 1922 against a man who habitually rowed with and beat his wife.[43] A local newspaper reporting the hussitting of a wife-beater in Woodley, Berkshire in 1930 describes a rather grim scene:

> Grey-haired women ... clasped hands and danced solemnly round a bonfire where the effigies of three people were in flames. No smile was on their face, and from their lips fell curses on a young husband ... All around them were a host of men, women and children, chanting monotonously and beating tin cans, old kettles and cracked bells in a melancholy rhythm.

If the reporter had perhaps been unduly influenced by Shakespeare's *Macbeth* when writing his copy, still the purpose of the hussitting was serious enough. The man had been summonsed by his wife at Wokingham Police Court for cruelty but the magistrates had refused to grant her a separation order. A villager informed the reporter that, 'We are judge and jury here and it will go hard with him if we get hold of him.' For three days the rough music continued with effigies of the man, his mother and his sister being paraded around the village and whipped before being consigned to the flames. The reporter observed that whilst children joined in for fun, for the older people 'it was a serious matter'. One of them told him that, 'We hope the man and his people will leave the village.'[44]

If marital relations were subject to close scrutiny, extra-marital relations were even more so. A stanging in 1837 at Northallerton in Yorkshire was occasioned by an ostler being unfaithful to his recent bride. An effigy was created, placed on a cart and paraded for three days, accompanied by the ringing of a bell, until burnt on the church below the green. Such an event may have been relatively common at the time, since the newspaper report states: 'It is between three and four years since a similar exhibition took place.'[45] In 1848 a Hertfordshire village was shaken by an incident: 'A gang of working men going about with rough music, intending to give a bad woman a ducking. She was a notoriously bad woman, and in the family way, and was saying she would swear the child to someone though she confessed she had been connected with many.'[46] At Oxton, Lancashire the inhabitants of the village, 'having

---

42 *Manchester Guardian*, 5 October 1881.
43 N. Teulon-Porter, 'Rough Music', *The Countryman* 52:2 (1955), p. 399.
44 See G. Seal, 'A "Hussitting" in Berkshire, 1930', *Folklore* 98:1 (1987), pp. 91–4.
45 A. Walker, *Yorkshire Miscellany* (Huddersfield: The King's England Press, 2000), p. 63.
46 The diary of John Izzard Pryor, cited in Gerald Curtis, ed., *A Chronicle of Small Beer: The Early Victorian Diaries of a Hertfordshire Brewer* (London: Phillimore, 1970), p. 107. Entry of 31 January 1848.

discovered that Robert Oswald, a gardener was living with his second wife, his first wife being still alive, dragged him out of his house, fastened him to the top of a high ladder, and in that manner paraded him round the village, accompanied by a large crowd of people, the proceedings being enlivened by rough music'.[47] One stanging at Gorton, Manchester in 1876 was inspired by the discovery that a painter was cohabiting with two women; a second was the consequence of a surgeon having had an affair with one of his patient's wives:

> Their effigies were paraded around the village on two long poles – called stangs in Lancashire – like that of Guy Fawkes is borne by schoolboys on Gunpowder-plot day. The rustics recited some doggerel verses composed by our local laureate describing the guilt of the offenders and then made a hideous noise, facing their dwellings, with sticks upon old pans and kettles. On the latter occasion Gorton Cotton Mills were closed half a day, in order that the eight hundred factory hands there employed might render us assistance and enjoy the fun.[48]

The affair is particularly interesting given the social status of certainly one of the victims – by no means all targets of such music were working men or ill-educated rustics. Furthermore, not only is there evidence of pre-planning but, if correct, the report might be taken to suggest the cooperation of the mill owners and managers in celebrating the proceedings. Another medical man, this time in Yorkshire, had already been treated to rough music around the year 1865 when his new bride had run back to her father's house because of her husband's attachment to his servant: 'Popular feeling was on her side. For several nights there was much excitement, and the stang was ridden consecutively with a great deal of noise and confusion. The end of it was that the servant was dismissed, the bride returned, and the young couple settled down amicably at last.'[49] At Redmire in North Yorkshire in 1901, an unfaithful husband was fashioned of straw, set on a cart and, 'the young bloods of the village, in all the glory of war paint, and with grim determination stamped on every feature proceeded to parade the streets'. After three nights of celebrations, hundreds of people had gathered from surrounding villages to see the burning of the straw man and the conclusion of a custom that, by that time, had not been held there for about twenty-five years.[50] Alice Mead of Leamington remembered being told a story of rough music just after the end of the First World War. A local woman had taken in a female lodger whilst her husband was away in the army. At the conclusion of the war the soldier had returned but had taken up with this lodger; pots and pans were

---

47 *Liverpool and Lancashire General Advertiser*, No 19087, vol. 37 (14 September 1847), p. 541, col. f.
48 Mr A. O. V. P., 'Riding the Stang', *Notes and Queries*, 5th Series, vol. 5 (25 March 1876), p. 253.
49 Henderson, *Notes on the Folk-Lore Of The Northern Counties of England And The Borders*, p. 30.
50 *The Craven Herald*, 31 May 1901.

resorted to and Alice remembered her grandmother saying, 'We lewbelled her out of the village.'[51]

Despite the differences of terminology, hussitting, lewbelling, skimmingtons and stangings all displayed similar features. However, a very particular form of rough music ritual seems to have evolved in the West Country in order to penalise sexual transgressions. Richard Kelly (Dartmoor Dick) remembered a 'stag hunt' in North Devon. A volunteer was selected: 'On his head were short deer antlers securely tied, his face was coloured brown and red, and he wore a loose sort of robe tied in at the waist.' Richard remembers being with his grandmother in Fore Street and seeing the 'hunt' in full cry:

> First came the 'stag' jumping in the air, turning and twirling and making a sort of shrill noise. Then came the red-coated mounted huntsman cracking his whip and urging on his hounds, who were also dressed up and making a sort of barking noise... The one and only constable tried to catch Steer and lock him up, but to no purpose; the policemen were always swept on one side; they were a small matter in the excitement of the chase. The hunt went on, up one street and down another, all over, all around the town, but not too near their goal. Any gates or barriers were an added attraction; Steer and the strong young 'hounds' could then show off their paces, etc. Crowds of people stood about or ran with the 'hunt'; especially the boys of the town; they would tell where the 'stag' had hidden in some back court to get his breath back and cause more shouting, etc. The fun of the chase lasted some time, to the laughter and jokes of the by-standers who knew where and what the end would be. That time it was a house off East Street, the top of Northfield Road, and at last there before the front door the 'stag' allowed the hounds to catch up and enact a very realistic 'kill'. The 'stag' carried a bladder full of ox blood, and as he fell down on the doorstep this blood was made to flow about and leave a decided mark there. Then members of the hunt told each other of a good job done, and everyone showed a marked delight and expressed the hope that the objects of the hunt would soon leave the town.[52]

The particular event described above took place in about 1875; Theo Brown has collected reports of such hunts from many Devon villages.[53] Accounts vary somewhat. A variety of sexual offences could be thus punished, for example one at Winkleigh was held in respect of a 'male pervert'. Almost invariably the part of the 'stag' seems to have been played by a youthful volunteer, but a local clergyman, A. H. Welldon Peek, believed that in Drewsteignton the offender was pursued in person. The 'hounds'

---

51 Palmer, *Folklore of Warwickshire*, pp. 59–60.
52 As reported in a letter of L. H. Wreford, 16 February 1950 to Theo Brown, cited in Brown, 'The "Stag Hunt" in Devon', pp. 104–9 at p. 104.
53 Bideford, Chagford, Chillaton, Drewsteignton, Exbourne, Gidleigh, North Lew, Okehampton and Winkleigh.

would gather around the offender's house, their leader sporting on his head a pair of ram's horns, and the men 'danced and howled round the house, making noises like a pack of hounds in full cry'.[54] The unfortunate was then brought out, 'given a fair start and hunted with howls and hunting cries. When caught he was generally thrown into the nearest pond or stream and then allowed to return home.' Welldon Peek asserts that the victim was never hurt, which makes one wonder about the accuracy of the account. We have enough instances of those species of rough music that involved dragging out the victim to know that this was rather unlikely. It may be that this account has simply confused an impersonator with the actual person that the hunt intended to shame.

The hunt, like other similar activities, was also associated with the opening of local fairs, such as the old 'Horn Fair' held in Winkleigh on 1 October each year. The form was much the same as described above: 'The Squire usually loaned the antlers from his hall, and they were returned to him after the "kill". The "stag" was made up to represent the animal as far as possible, and members of the hunt were dressed up for the part. They ran all day, calling at farmhouses for refreshments. It would be agreed beforehand where in the wood the "stag" should be found, but the "kill" always took place in the Square.'[55] Presumably, the hunt took place whether there were offenders to be symbolically pursued or not, but it is very probable that the name of some local reprobate was added to the proceedings each year in order to add some spice to the proceedings.

The hunt seems to have been suppressed quite early in most places in Devon. Robert Bevan reported to Theo Brown that there had been many stag hunts around Okehampton but by the end of the nineteenth century they had become 'very unpopular with the authorities'.[56] Richard Kelly remembered the last hunt taking place around 1875; Welldon Peek put the last one at Drewsteignton at 1878 with an attempt to stage one in 1894. Sabine Baring-Gould's novel *The Red Spider*, set in Bratton Clovelly, features just such a hunt and when it was published in 1887 such an affair was presumably still a genuine possibility. If the novel is correct, the stag hunt was a device particularly employed against sexual offenders, but there was in addition a somewhat milder version – the 'hare hunt' – designed to chastise scolding women.[57] However, Lawrence Molland believed that the hunt was in general abeyance in Devon by 1900, though North Lew is said to have held its last hunt just before the First World War.[58]

Of course one does not know the extent to which accusations of sexual impropriety had to be substantiated before rough music might be the consequence. Ursula Bloom

---

54 Brown, 'The "Stag Hunt" in Devon', pp. 104–9 at p. 106.
55 Ibid., p. 108.
56 Ibid., p. 105.
57 Sabine Baring-Gould, *The Red Spider* (London: Chatto & Windus, 1887).
58 L. Molland, *Transactions of the Devonshire Association* 98 (1966), pp. 29–30.

described an instance of rough music in Berkshire caused by the occupation of a cottage by an old man and his daughter: 'It was the usual case of incest, or suspected incest, for the village always suspected the worst (and generally got it), so, to show their righteous indignation, they had fallen back on the medieval custom of making effigies and burning them to the accompaniment of rough music.'[59] We do not know, and perhaps the crowd at the time did not, if there was any truth in the accusations against the victims.

The extent to which the fear of being thus exposed and ridiculed guided actual conduct is very difficult to assess. One is forced to ask an unanswerable question: how would people have behaved had this sanction not been available? Roberts, in his *History of Lyme Regis*, commented thus:

> Skimmington Riding is a great moral agent, not perhaps so much in restraining the vicious as causing them to shun public observation, thereby not holding out bad examples to the rising youth of both sexes; in a word it checks those instances of openly profligate and licentious conduct, which else might become too prevalent among the lower orders . . . it brands with infamy all gross instances of licentiousness, and exposes to lasting ridicule those who by their dissensions disturb the quiet and order of the neighbourhood . . . A Skimmington Riding makes many laugh; but the parties for whom they ride never lose the ridicule and disgrace which it attaches.[60]

These were not the only ones intended to amend their conduct in consequence of a skimmington. In cases of overbearing wives, further steps were taken to alert households to the fact that the community had their eyes upon them:

> When Young People ride the Skimmington
> There is a general trembling in the town;
> Not only her for whom the party rides
> Suffers, but they sweep other doors besides.
> Any by that hieroglyphic does appear
> That the good woman is master there.[61]

There were a number of signal behaviours available to warn those not the immediate target of a performance that they might conceivably be the next. I have already referred to the scattering of grain outside the gate or door of wife-beaters, which seems to have been a widely distributed phenomenon, but there were other practices.

---

59 Ursula Bloom, *Whitchurch, The Changed Village* (London: Chapman and Hall, 1945) cited in Palmer, *Folklore of Warwickshire*, p. 59.
60 Roberts, *The History and Antiquities of the Borough of Lyme Regis and Charmouth*, p. 258.
61 *Dr King's Miscellany*, cited in Roberts, *The History and Antiquities of the Borough of Lyme Regis and Charmouth*, p. 259.

For example, in Somerset at the turn of the twentieth century, the hanging of a sheep's fleece outside the door of a malefactor was a powerful sign of local disapprobation.[62] We can well believe that these practices together with actual rough music itself operated to some cautionary effect. The *Illustrated London News* commenting on a skimmington staged after a marital infidelity remarked: 'The fear of this public exposure is said to act as a great deterrent.'[63]

It is very much open to question, however, whether rough music rituals in English communities in the later period were systematic enough and regular enough to exert a great influence on day-to-day conduct over a sustained period of time. One can readily accept that the day after a skimmington wives might not be beaten, sweethearts visited, vices indulged – but what effect did they have in communities that experienced them only once in a dozen years or more? Accepting that many instances of rough music must escape us, still it seems fairly clear that in most communities rough music was a statistically very improbable response to the many vices that could in theory incite it.

Edward Shorter in his *The Making of the Modern Family*, seemed to envisage charivari in early modern Europe as a morally coherent and systematised practice, a key disciplinary tool such that: 'The traditional community was able to compel individual family members to follow collective rules through a disciplinary technique called the charivari.'[64] Maintenance of social hierarchy was, for Shorter, always at the forefront of the minds of the performers. Thus, he notices that adulterous wives were not put on donkeys and paraded through the community but rather their husbands, because their lack of supervision threatened male authority generally: 'What upset the community was not the actual sexual impropriety so much as the threat its consequences posed to community social order.'[65] Masters who slept with their female servants were left unpunished and this may be considered evidence that, 'traditional populations were not prudish, just circumspect'.[66] Furthermore, Shorter argues that although in France wife-beaters were sometimes punished, this occurred mainly during the month of May as a festive performance. There was no great incentive to penalise wife-beaters since charivari was an instrument to maintain the social hierarchy and, he says, 'since men were seen as the natural bearers of authority, their abuses met with considerably greater tolerance'.[67]

Leaving aside for the moment the fact that I believe such an interpretation may overplay the importance of charivari in the early modern context, there are certainly

---

62 Somerset County Record Office, Somerset Voices Archive, Ref no. A\CMQ/2/22.
63 Cited in Palmer, *Folklore of Warwickshire,* p. 159.
64 Edward Shorter, *The Making of the Modern Family* (London: Collins, 1976), p. 218.
65 Ibid., p. 220.
66 Shorter, *The Making of the Modern Family*, p. 220
67 Ibid., p. 223.

difficulties in applying such an analysis to the later English experience. Returning to wife-beating briefly: as we have seen, by the mid-nineteenth century such abuse was what most commonly inspired charivaric rituals in England. However, the danger with modelling rough music as a systematised strategy of social discipline is that it tends to be grounded in the assumption that neighbourhoods or communities were united in their social views and consciously instrumental in their application of the music. Rough music in my view is better modelled as an irregular eruption of moral outrage, an eruption that, whilst it was partially related to social ethics, was so closely connected to opportunity, festivity, chance and the vagaries of group dynamics as to resist being incorporated as part of a coherent communal ethical programme. In a somewhat similar fashion to the way that stock-market analysts are always able to tell us exactly why, after the event, a stock price has shot up, but never to reliably inform us before the event that they will do so, commentators (including myself) will readily offer the baldest explanations after the fact as to why a skimmington or stanging has been performed. However, in doing so we will often be relying on sources so impoverished and lacking in nuance that it is usually impossible to explain why it was that this particular cuckold was selected, or why that particular wife-beater was to be the target. Both stock pickers and historians are masterly predictors after the fact and are thus tempted to reduce very complex phenomena to simple economic principles or rules of social behaviour.

It is important to note that whilst rough music originated in group sanction of individual behaviour, such a group did not necessarily embody the community as a whole in either its actions or attitudes. Of course, it may have done so, but there is no reason to suppose that eighteenth- and nineteenth-century commentators were any more adept at divining the true state of opinion than their modern counterparts who so often confuse general opinion with the opinion of those who make the most noise. Insofar as differences within communities are acknowledged in the sources or subsequent commentary, this often takes the form of the simplistic assumption that those of higher station disapproved of the raucous unpredictability of rough music, whilst those of lower status and thereby unthinking disposition, delighted in it. If there came to be a certain rough truth to this, particularly in the later period, matters were nevertheless rather more complex. As we shall see, some educated commentators wrote approvingly of the moral lesson imparted. Some of the better-off seem to have financed such activities, or at least sanctioned them. Similarly, it is not safe to assume that everyone amongst the lower orders approved of such goings-on, either in general or in respect of a specific event. For the most part all one can say is that in a particular time and place a sufficient constituency of opinion had been mobilised in order to carry through the music. Most newspaper or journal reports were either unaware of, or had no interest in reporting, any dissenting voices amongst the lower orders opposing such performances, and we have few records of any constituency that might have remained disapprovingly aloof.

Common sense suggests that such constituencies did exist. For a start, many recipients of rough music must have had their own social allies, family and friends. Some others may have opposed the music out of conscience, some because, for them, participation was not socially safe. The aftermath of rough music was rarely remarked on – except where prosecutions resulted or where the target of the music subsequently did something dramatic such as flee the community or attempt suicide. How social relations were managed thereafter generally escapes us. The problem (as anyone brought up in a village knows) with offending the pub landlord is that that pub may be the only place in the village where one can go for a drink. Riding the stang for the local physician may be problematic if one becomes ill thereafter. The skimmingtons and stangings that are sometimes observable against persons of higher social status may on occasion have been sponsored by others of a somewhat similar or superior social position, for one can imagine that otherwise the actors would have been vulnerable to retaliation by the victim. The skimmington in *The Mayor of Casterbridge* is mounted against Farfrae's wife by the local rustics. However, by this point in the novel Farfrae had become the largest corn-dealer in the area, having pulled into his hands all the influence previously possessed by the former Mayor Henchard. If we try to transpose the novel into reality we can readily suppose that the farmers, small dealers, retailers, carters and farriers of Casterbridge would have felt it most unwise to offend such a man. The skimmington itself may have been performed by labouring men and women but still many of them must have got their employment from the men with whom Farfrae dealt. Hardy had no interest in pursuing the consequences of this useful plot device, but Farfrae would clearly have been in a position to do very real harm to the perpetrators.

There may then have been practical reasons why, when an incident of rough music occurred, certain sections of the community declined to participate. The most principled reason for abstinence, though, might be found where they quite simply did not agree that the intended target had actually done anything wrong. This conviction may have been based upon evidence – they may simply have disagreed that the circumstances indeed pointed to infidelity, abuse or so on. Or, they may not have agreed that the conduct complained of constituted an offence. A useful illustration of this latter point may be offered by the case of wife-sale. E. P. Thompson has shown that this was acknowledged in many rural communities as a legitimate mode of breaking the marital bond, but those who might be considered more respectable did not generally concur. In March 1790 *Aris's Birmingham Gazette* protested that: 'Instances of the sales of wives have of late frequently occurred among the lower classes of people who consider such sales lawful, we think it right to inform them that, by a determination of the courts of law in a former reign, they were declared illegal and void . . . a mere pretence to sanction the crime of adultery.'[68] The *Hampshire Courier* lamented that at Hailsham in 1814:

---

68 Palmer, *Folklore of Warwickshire*, p. 160.

A labouring man, of Westham, led his wife, a decently dressed woman, into the market in a halter, and there exhibited her for sale, in which situation, however, he had not long placed her, before a tradesman of a neighbouring parish stepped up and bargained for her at five shillings. She was accordingly delivered and her purchaser, after being offered seven shillings in advance for his bargain, took her off in triumph, amid the congratulations of a great number of spectators.[69]

Most of these partings appear to have been by mutual consent; thus when Richard Yates from Brockton in Shropshire brought his wife to Much Wenlock he began to have second thoughts, but his wife allegedly responded, 'Let be, yer rogue. I wull be sold; I wants a change.'[70]

Wife-sale seems still to have been a possibility as late as 1870 when a naval captain heard an altercation between two men in Dog Lane, Coventry caused by one having 'sold' his wife fraudulently to the other as child-bearing.[71] Respectable opinion, however, as *The Mayor of Casterbridge* indicates, was firmly against it. Slowly, the values of the 'respectable' classes imposed themselves upon the values of rural communities, such that by the end of the nineteenth century there was probably hardly anyone who could be found who regarded wife-sale as anything other than an outmoded, unseemly, relic of the past. Yet clearly, there was an intermediate period in which some within rural communities regarded wife-sale as a detestable act while others saw it as as a well-established and time-honoured practice. Rough music depended upon the development of a certain critical mass sufficiently animated and outraged by a practice so as to wish to act against it, but it did not necessarily signify the presence of an overwhelming feeling against the conduct complained of.

Thus when a Cotswold man from Burford openly sold his wife at Chipping Norton market for the handsome sum of £25 we cannot quite believe the report that the whole town was indeed 'scandalised'. The woman went to live with her purchaser but after three nights of rough music the man's effigy was burnt outside his door. The effect was salutary, since the purchaser is said to have thereafter paid the vendor £15 to take her back! Nevertheless, fifteen years later the idea that an undesirable partner could be sold by placing a halter around her neck was still a 'popular opinion' in Lancashire, and so in 1870 a man sold his wife for eight shillings in Bury market. However: 'The inhabitants of Bury have not taken the matter quietly, for they have burnt in effigy both the buyer and the person sold.'[72]

It is very likely that different opinions were held on many 'stanging matters' within communities and, in certain circumstances, interest groups mounted performances

---

69 *Hampshire Courier*, 31 October 1814.
70 R. Palmer, *The Folklore of Shropshire* (London: Logaston Press 2004), p. 155. Oral testimony of Mrs Swyney of Much Wenlock.
71 F. J. Odell, 'Wife Sales', *Notes and Queries*, vol. 151 (6 November 1926), p. 340.
72 Letter of T. T. W., *Notes and Queries*, vol. 4:6, issue 152 (26 November 1870), p. 455.

in support of their own particular agendas. Whilst knowing that rough music was often performed in the context of certain species of acts tells us something about the broad state of public mores, it does not necessarily tell us how a crowd would react in any particular set of circumstances. There are few circumstances that are not capable of bearing at least two different interpretations and there is no reason to suppose that the people in nineteenth-century communities were any less capable of logically incoherent and contradictory responses than their counterparts today. Context, in short, was almost everything.

Thus, when in 1823 a Mr Middleton from Weston in Somerset preferred an indictment against his servant for assaulting his three children, the people of Weston had no doubt whose side they were on – when Middleton returned home, 'the bells at Weston were set ringing, and he was burned in effigy by the populace ... part of his house has been unroofed; and within the last week stones have been thrown through the windows of his house'.[73] The welfare of Mr Middleton's children was not foremost in the crowds' mind. By contrast, in 1876 a mob in Folkestone broke into the house of a Mr Knight and Mrs Upton to rescue a three-year-old child 'half-starved and verminous'. The child was removed and the house besieged. Mrs Upton was burned in effigy and the house pelted.[74]

Such examples can be selectively employed to evidence a gradual moral evolution on the part of the crowd, but this is fraught with difficulty. For instance, in respect of gender relations, whilst a certain moral component in the popular acts against wife-beating is hard to deny, Anna Clark reminds us that these rough music rituals were, 'an outgrowth of masculine popular culture, and until the early nineteenth century revealed their hostility to women by punishing wives who dominated their husbands'.[75] This opens the possibility that in one place the brutality of a husband might be met with a resigned shrug, in another place and under slightly different circumstances similar conduct might lead to a man being stanged. Conversely, in one place the meekness of a husband might be ignored whilst in another, a similar man was judged unduly submissive and chastised. Men who attempted to seduce or assault women might be subjected to rough music but, at the same time, as Clark observes, women who complained of sexual assault might, on the rare occasions that their accusations were believed and their assailant's punished, invite popular retribution upon themselves. Thus, following an execution of a Bedfordshire man for rape, about two hundred people surrounded the complainant's house, 'exhibiting obscene effigies of herself and her parents.'[76]

---

73 *Morning Chronicle*, 30 August 1823.
74 *Illustrated Police News*, 15 July 1876.
75 Anna Clark, *Women's Silence, Men's Violence: Sexual Assault in England, 1770–1845* (London: Pandora, 1987), p. 50.
76 Clark, *Women's Silence Men's Violence*, pp. 49–50.

In the so-called 'Clitheroe case' of 1891, a Mrs Jackson, a woman of independent means, had become estranged from her husband, a man who had clearly married her only for her money. She had gone to live with her sisters but was then kidnapped outside a church and imprisoned in a relative's house. Given the apparent readiness of communities to penalise abusive spouses one might perhaps suppose that the husband's actions were such as to render him a suitable target for a spot of rough music. Far from it. Mrs Jackson secured her release via the law and *R v Jackson* 1891, but she did not secure the support of her home town. The newspapers had chosen not to represent the affair as a matter of spousal abuse but rather as a case in which the courts had officiously interfered and prevented the exercise of a husband's natural dominion over his wife. When Mrs Jackson returned to the town, her carriage was mobbed, demonstrations were held outside her sisters' home, effigies were made and the house was stoned.[77]

Those who participated in rough music were not principled reformers nor were they members of a plebeian equivalent of the Society for the Suppression of Vice campaigning to advance a well-thought-out social programme. Whilst there is sufficient consistency in the record to identify common causes in the performance of rough music, those causes rarely amount to sufficient explanation in themselves. During the hussitting of the wife-beater at Woodley in 1930 it was said that such an event had not occurred there for some thirty years. But is it likely that Woodley had been bereft of a wife-beater for all that time – or that such conduct had not come to the attention of the village? If, as Shorter seemed to imply, rough music was consistently deployed as an instrument of correction against scolding wives, adulterers, promiscuous youths, notorious gossips, aged grooms and the like, would anyone in the average English village have ever managed a sound night's sleep? Laurie Lee famously remembered that in Slad, Gloucestershire after the First World War, 'quiet incest flourished where the roads were bad' – the village did not approve, but nor did it overtly disapprove and no one ever complained to the magistrate, the vicar or the constabulary.[78] Accepting, then, that an overarching explanation or a legitimating cause might be necessary before rough music was performed, the intelligent question to ask is why it was that one particular instance of wife-beating occasioned a skimmington rather than another; why one case of infidelity was pounced upon whilst another was quietly ignored.

Much can probably be assigned to chance. Given that rough music was more prevalent at some times of the year than others, actions might be more likely to be

---

77 D. Rubinstein, *Before the Suffragettes: Women's Emancipation in the 1890s* (Brighton: Harvester Press, 1986), pp. 54–8.
78 Laurie Lee, see chapter 6, 'First Bite at the Apple', in *Cider with Rosie* (London: Vintage Books, 2002), p. 206.

sanctioned in certain seasons than at others. A period of leisure, a coming day of opportunity, and a certain turn in the public mood might play as much a role in the staging of an event as any immediate indignation or objective consideration of conduct. Thomas Hardy captures the sense of it:

> 'I say, what a good foundation for a skimmity-ride,' said Nance.
> 'True,' said Mrs. Cuxsom, reflecting. "Tis as good a ground for a skimmity-ride as ever I knowed; and it ought not to be wasted.'

The desire not to waste a good opportunity when it presented itself may be as good an explanation for many of the occurrences of rough music as any another.

The circumstances of the parties concerned no doubt also played a part in the calculation of who could offer good sport or whose penalisation would offer the most satisfaction. In the case of wife-beating, for example, it seems very likely that a particularly comely wife well-regarded by the village was more likely to attract sympathy than perhaps another. Such a woman might also have family in the village prepared to stir up trouble upon her behalf. On the other hand, the husband too was likely to have his allies and family who would depreciate such conduct – questions of likely retaliation might also be important.

Common sense suggests once more that it was someone who was an outsider who was most likely to be penalised – an outsider either in the sense of their origin or in the sense that their conduct distinguished them from the normative values of the community. John Harris, for example, notes that the reasons advanced for a man being forced to ride the ceffyl pren in the Rhydlewis area about 1880 was that he was an adulterer and a drunkard. That may have been so, but in truth the cause was the fact that as an auctioneer he had broken ranks with other auctioneers in the locality and agreed to conduct farm sales after the eviction of tenants.[79] It seems very likely that, at the time, even the participants did not fully articulate the reasons for their actions. A fascinating oral account survives in the Somerset County Archives of a skimmington that occurred around 1910 in the village of West Pennard.[80] An inhabitant, Bob Hiscox (b.1891) recalled the public demonstration and the 'skimmity dancing' that was held near the Apple Tree pub – and the reason he advanced for it was that a married man was 'carrying on with a woman'. Bob recalled the victim coming out into his garden and his wife standing shouting at the participants who were banging on milk churns. The girl allegedly involved wasn't present at the time but the village

---

79 J. Harris, 'The Early Career of Caradoc Evans' (University of Wales PhD thesis, 1986), pp. 3–7 cited in Jones, 'Popular Culture, Policing and the 'Disappearance' of the Ceffyl Pren in Cardigan, 1837–1850', pp. 19–39 at p. 26.
80 Somerset Record Office, Somerset Voices Archive, ref. no. A\CMQ/2/22, interview with Bob Hiscox (b.1891) and Edith Hiscox (b.1903).

did burn her paramour in effigy. However, when asked to describe the man in question it slowly emerged that the victim was already very unpopular for two reasons: first, he was a teetotaller, and second, he was a nonconformist – and the village liked neither. The unfortunate man was finally described as having a hunchback.

Bob Hiscox's description of the demeanour of the crowd upon that occasion probably aptly sums up the feelings demonstrated during the course of many rough music events, 'everyone enjoyed it' but at the same time the crowd was 'angry'. Here was no contradiction but a reflection of the intricate connections between celebration and chastisement, mirth and mockery – and a sobering reminder that oftentimes the community came together and became itself only through the identification, judgement and punishment of others.

5
Defending Economic Interests

In the previous chapter I considered those instances of rough music that were mainly said to have been inspired by inappropriate conduct in the fields of sexual or gender relations. Wife-beaters, wife-sellers, husband-beaters, adulterers, old men who snatched away young women – these were the people who offended the parish. However, the case of the Westonbirt 'groaning' has already suggested that manifestations of rough music might not always have been the result of disinterested moral outrage. In this chapter I intend to focus more on rough music or street justice employed not so much as an expression of general sentiment, but rather as a tool of particular constituencies of opinion or vested interest. The broad conflicts between the orders will be dealt with in Chapter 6. Here, I shall focus on individuals or smaller interest or occupational groups who often deployed the same symbolism and theatrical practice as we observed in the previous chapter but who, in protecting their own situations or advancing their own causes, turned the culture of public shaming and retribution against rather different targets. In order to do so, however, they had to seize control of public space and direct the behaviours of those within it. Some understanding of how they were able to do this may in part be gleaned by a brief consideration of the flammability of the crowd in the eighteenth and nineteenth centuries.

One Sunday in February 1822 a rabble of men and boys made 'a determined attack' on a paint factory in Clyde Street, Glasgow. The doors and windows were broken, the furniture thrown into the Clyde and 'such was the desperation of these ignorant people, that their dispersion was not effected till the successive arrival of two divisions of the military ... The work of destruction is the most complete that can well be conceived.'[1] The outraged mob had not been inspired by some bitter dispute over wages, conflict over a political cause, or even religious sectarianism. In fact the crowd had been roused to fury by the rumour that a large number of children had been murdered in the factory as the necessary ingredient in the factory's production

---

1 *Lancaster Gazette and General Advertiser*, 2 March 1822.

of red paint! According to the *Lancashire Gazette* the affair had begun when two children looking through the factory windows had seen bloody clothing (actually the paint-strewn garb of an employee) on the floor. From their vivid imaginations a riot sprang.

That such a large mob could be collected in such an unlikely cause tells us much about nineteenth-century popular culture. Life on the streets was volatile, passions were swiftly roused and violence often followed. Although many similar examples to the one cited above could be given, space prohibits mention of more than a couple of others. In 1828, an elderly woman was mobbed in Leicester by a crowd who tore off her bonnet, threw her down and then threatened to throw her into the river. The cause was an assertion made by a passer-by that the old woman was in fact a man in women's clothes. Immediate consternation was caused and there rapidly gathered 'a large concourse of people' who treated her very roughly. Things could have been very ugly indeed had not a woman from a nearby pub offered the woman shelter from the mob.[2] One would perhaps have supposed that the question of the gender of the victim could not have been in so much doubt; that the testimony of the woman's husband who arrived on the scene in the middle of the disturbance would have been determinative. However, once the rumour had taken flight, reason did the same and the crowd was not easily mollified.

The crowd was similarly unimpressed by the testimony of a police inspector who was assaulted outside a butcher's shop in Bethnal Green Road, East London, in 1834. The butcher, Mr Green, had unwittingly agreed to store some boxes for a surgeon, Mr Fuller. One of Mr Green's children had, however, opened one of the boxes and taken from it 'an anatomical preparation of a hand and arm' and carried it into the shop, with the result that:

> Some talkative female, observing the preparation in the hands of the child, soon circulated a report throughout the neighbourhood, and in a very short time a considerable crowd of persons, consisting of men, women and children assembled about the door. Some of the persons so assembled gave expression to their foolish and illiberal conjectures, such as that the arm was intended to be chopped up for sausage meat . . . the consequence was a disposition of the part of the mob to attack and injure the house and property of Mr Green.[3]

The arrival of Inspector Ebbs, who soon ascertained the facts of the case, did not quell the disturbance and two men incited an attack upon him. It was only the arrival of reinforcements that dispersed the crowd but 'with some difficulty'.

In the early nineteenth century we were still in a world where gentlemen could

---

2 *Leicester Chronicle: or, Commercial and Agricultural Advertiser*, 13 September 1828.
3 *The Examiner*, 17 August 1834.

shoot each other over who should read the newspaper,[4] where violent rioting could break out over the cost of the tickets at the New Theatre, and indeed, where a mob could be induced to believe that red paint is made out of the blood of the neighbourhood's children. Thus any consideration of popular justice needs to acknowledge the at times uncertain temper of 'public opinion', the partiality and excitability of the crowd and, perhaps above all, the ability of some to take leadership of the crowd and exploit it for their purposes. It is important as yet another salutary corrective to any model of popular justice as folksy, democratic and essentially benign. We have seen that skimmingtons and the like were often carefully planned to coincide with festivity but that they could nonetheless be very vindictive. In addition, spontaneous effusions of popular justice could occur that were rather likely to be squalid, unthinking and often regretted thereafter by the very participants themselves. There were always, though, those who had an interest in arousing a mob and I shall explore some of their activities here.

Dealing with Informers

One group who were often targeted for a dose of 'popular justice' were informers. Given the very limited resources available to the state, the authorities were often forced to make general use of paid informers in order to assist in the management of society. It was these men and women who identified those who had broken the trading laws and the weights and measures acts, they 'peached' on thieves, scouted out the hiding places of seamen who might be pressed, took rewards for convictions, gathered intelligence on the politically suspect and so on. They were as necessary and yet as repellent as leeches were once supposed to be and the magistrates themselves often professed to despise them. It was in the very nature of their occupation that these informers had to insinuate themselves into social and street culture. Thus they posed a threat not only to individuals but also to the community as a whole, by engendering a climate of distrust that imperilled normal social relations.

Informing was at best a precarious profession. Informers were very vulnerable to retaliation, partly because they were rarely well-paid and had to dwell largely unprotected amongst those upon whom they preyed. Once identified, there was often a strong impulse to drive them from the community and chastise them. Not infrequently, responses to the presence of informers were extremely physical, although this carried the risk of a firm response by the authorities. Shaming rituals and shaming punishments intermixed with this direct violence, but also played a non-violent part. They served to identify those who could not be trusted and thereby

---

4 See the duel between Mr Cahill and Captain Rutherford in September 1810 reported in *The Times*, 7 September 1810, p. 4, col. c.

rendered them less potent; they branded informers as dishonourable and thus had the potential to dissuade others from following in their footsteps. Sometimes they accompanied murder or grievous bodily harm, whereas sometimes they provided a useful alternative to it.

Informers were active in many spheres of life and amongst the most dangerous were those who reported serious criminal activity and those who, in time of war, worked for the press gangs. Beginning with the latter, in 1755 a group of quarrymen at Dennybowl Quarry in Cornwall swore to bury any of them that came near. Their mettle was apparently tested when three men of the press approached and the whole quarry fled – only to discover later that the three were in fact local girls who had dressed up in men's clothing and put cockades in their hats for a prank.[5] Those unfortunate enough to be taken by real press gangs did not forget those who had assisted their capturers. In 1783 at the end of the American War of Independence returning sailors arriving at Sunderland:

> Determined to avenge themselves on the informers ... Such of those fellows as had not left the town were accordingly hunted up, and were mounted, when found, upon a stang, and carried through the principal streets, exposed to the insults of the enraged populace, the women in particular, bedaubing them plentifully with dirt, rotten eggs, potatoes and turnips, and whatever missiles came ready to hand. The constables being powerless, and beaten off the field, the military had to be called in, when the mob dispersed, but not without threatening a renewal of the manhunt. Amongst the informers stanged at this time was Jonathon Coates ... who, after undergoing severe punishment, reached his home nearly dead. During the night, he heard a noise, which he supposed to be his tormentors coming for him again, when he crawled into a narrow dog-leap or slip of waste ground between Arras's and Baines's Lane where he died. The popular fury ran so high that his relatives durst not attempt to bury him in daylight, and his body lay in his house for a whole week until some soldiers were prevailed on to carry it by night [to the churchyard].[6]

In February 1793 with the outbreak of hostilities with France, seamen from North Shields, Newcastle, Sunderland, Blyth and the small ports along England's east coast made joint resolutions to resist the press gangs: 'On Tuesday the 19th they got hold of the press gang at North Shields, and, reversing their jackets, as a mark of contempt, conducted them, accompanied by a numerous crowd, to Chirton toll bar, where, dismissing them, they gave them three cheers, and told them never again to enter Shields, or they should be torn limb from limb.'[7]

---

5 *Oxford Journal*, 26 April 1755.
6 *Monthly Chronicle of North Country Lore and Legend*, 5:47, January 1891, p. 2.
7 Ibid.

Some of those intent upon resisting the press were likely seamen implicated in the smuggling trade. It is clear that there were coastal areas in which a significant proportion of the local population were complicit in the activity. That being so, resistance to the Customs and Excise authorities could readily take on the facets of a popular crusade as smugglers sought to cast informers and law officers as interlopers whose conduct placed them outside the bounds of normal human fraternity. In 1775, when five hundred gallons of smuggled wine were found on a punt off Queenhithe, the local watermen and porters set out to discover the identity of the man who had tipped off the authorities. When they found out they constructed an effigy of the man out of a barber's block and old clothes. They then paraded the figure around the neighbourhood before erecting a gibbet on the causeway. The figure was hanged and burned to repeated huzzas.[8]

Similar demonstrations were repeated in many places, but sometimes the mob went awry in the venting of their hatred. In *R v Worthington* 1822, William Worthington and others were indicted for assault upon two fishermen, John Smith and Edmund Paine, who had allegedly been informers for the Board of Excise. On 7 March 1821, Smith had been seized by a mob and dragged into the King's Arms in Deal. There he had been stripped, tarred and feathered, then tied to a cart and dragged around the town. During the progress the mob had encountered Edmund Paine who in turn was thrown into the cart and tarred and feathered: 'In this manner both the unhappy men, in broad day, were exhibited round the town, the cart being drawn by the mob, who cheered and shouted their progress, and heaped upon the men the most offensive execrations.'[9] During the proceedings Smith was blinded in one eye. It transpired, however, that the crowd had been entirely misinformed. Smith and Paine had never been in the pay of the Board of Excise. Rather they had been named on a list fabricated by a former excise officer, Mr Brown. Brown had been dismissed for having accepted bribes from smugglers and in revenge had compiled a list of his personal enemies and circulated it through the town.

The following year the preventative service had a significant success when it arrested a large gang of smugglers at Sandwich. An important witness in the prosecution at Maidstone Assizes was a Mrs Etridge. Nineteen of the defendants were capitally convicted but when the woman and her husband returned to Canterbury, 'they were treated very roughly by the populace, who stigmatised them as informers'.[10] She and her husband lodged with the prosecutor of the gang but a mob gathered outside his door, burned him and Mrs Etridge in effigy and smashed down his door. The mob was eventually dispersed but only two were subsequently convicted of riot. Qualitatively,

---

8 *Middlesex Journal and Evening Advertiser*, 7–9 September 1775.
9 *Morning Chronicle*, 23 March 1822.
10 *Morning Post*, 12 August 1822.

the degree of animosity exhibited in such cases was extreme and certainly more than that commonly expressed in the deployment of rough music as a punishment for sexual incontinence and the like. One gets a sense of a real struggle within communities: on the one side, to subdue them to the rule of law; on the other, to maintain collective solidarity in defence of important economic interests.

The trial of *R v Mead and Belt*, held at York Assizes, illustrates that struggle.[11] The bald facts were that late in the evening of 13 February 1823, Richard Law, a 'respectable farmer' had been returning home on horseback from Scarborough market with a friend called John Dodsworth. Accompanying them had been two servants, a Mr John Watson and a Mr Hineson. At Burniston the men had 'recognised' the home of a Mr William Mead. They had no high opinion of Mead and as they passed Watson had begun to sing a derogatory song about him. In response Mead had fired a pistol from his bedroom window, fatally wounding Mr Law. Subsequently, tried alongside Mead was Robert Belt who had been sleeping in the same room as Mead and who was alleged to have encouraged the firing of the shot. Most of the basic facts of the case were not in dispute. The question was whether the firing had constituted an utterly disproportionate response to 'an incivility' and was thereby murder, or whether at the time of firing the shot Mead had had good reason to feel endangered, in which case he might be acquitted upon the grounds of self-defence. Alternatively, it might be said that he had been reasonably provoked into firing and might be convicted of mere manslaughter.

There was much more to the affair than first met the eye. The pistol that had fired the fatal shot, 'had been lent to Mead by a Mr Coulson of Whitby, a customs collector, who had been intimately connected with those antecedent proceedings'. The antecedent proceedings included the fact that based on the evidence of Mead, the attorney general had previously laid an information against Law for smuggling. Law had been acquitted and had subsequently prosecuted Mead for perjury. At the time of the fatality Mead was actually on bail pending the trial. John Watson claimed at Mead's murder trial that, 'Mead has told a many tales about smuggling as people say.' That being so, the collector, Mr Coulson, had been correct in supposing that Mead's life was in some danger. Indeed, some days before the fatal shooting the shutters on Mead's house were staved in by persons unknown. According to one witness, 'It was the talk of the town the next day.'

On the day of the actual shooting there had been a violent encounter between Law and one of Mead's friends, a John Dobson. Dobson had been in the Globe Inn in Scarborough when he had been ambushed by Law and a mob. According to Dobson:

---

11 *York Herald and General Advertiser*, 26 July 1823.

James Law said, 'was my friend, William Mead along with me, we should neither of us go alive home.' I was an evidence against Law in London. They kicked me about and dragged me in all directions, both up and down . . . He said, 'it is of no use prosecuting the crown's evidence; we'll give them club law at home.' He cried out that to the whole mob . . . After they had done kicking me, I was taken to a pump and some of them threw water upon me, and all kinds of filth. They put me into the pump-trough, and some of them pumped upon me, whilst others beat me . . . I was then thrown into a state of insensibility. When I came to myself I found myself tied hand and foot to a ladder. They were carrying me about the streets. I can't recollect too much after that . . . [they] were going to have me down to the sea, to drown me; they said so. They had me to a place called Ayton, where I was rescued.

John Watson admitted at Mead's trial that he had seen Law kick Dobson in Scarborough that day, but denied seeing the more egregious acts or having been party to them himself. However, he admitted he was currently incarcerated in jail awaiting trial for his alleged part in the assault. He was also awaiting trial for an assault on one Dawson and conceded that he himself had been in that same jail before, charged with smuggling. It was a Dawson, Ann Dawson, who had that evening conveyed the news of the attack on Dobson to Mead. However, in consequence she attested, 'I durst not go back to Scarborough; I was afraid they would do with me as they did with Dobson: they said they would the same day as they abused Dobson . . . I am now afraid of returning to Scarborough after this trial.'

So on the night in question Mead had already heard of a brutal assault upon his friend. He must naturally have been fearful when that evening he saw Law and the three others outside his house. Watson's testimony could not obscure the fact that, far from passing the house by chance, the men had actually sought it out.

Watson contended, however, that throughout what transpired, the four of them had remained on their horses on the main road, which was some distance away from Mead's house. He said they had done no more, and had intended no more, than to sing the derogatory song, which he himself had composed. The question of whether Mead had actually felt himself under attack seemed to substantially rest upon the position of the men relative to the house. The house was separated from the road by a causeway that was raised some 3ft or so above it. A man on a horse on that causeway would have been right up against the house and looking in through its windows. The defence suggested that this was where the men had actually been when the shot had been fired. Mead's daughter, described as 'a little girl', was one of those who attested that this was so. Whomsoever paid for Mead's defence (and one presumes it was the Board of Excise) was thorough. A surgeon gave evidence as to the trajectory of the bullet, and a land surveyor was commissioned to produce a model of the scene and explain how the shooting had transpired. However, there was evidence of a palpable lack of cooperation with the defence: 'We applied for leave to go into the house, and it was refused ... I wanted the assistance of someone and applied to two or three persons in the village, but they refused to assist me.'[12]

The house had been placed under the charge of one of the local constables, William Haxby, whose partiality seems to have been somewhat suspect. Obviously, the authorities had wanted to know what had transpired inside the house, who had fired the shot and so on. Haxby had arrested Mead and his family but subsequently claimed that he 'had not said anything to him, either in the shape of a promise or a threat, to induce him to confess'. He had, however, to defend his conduct in respect of the girl, 'I did not take Mead's daughter by the nose, or whip her I'll swear.' Mead readily admitted firing the shot but he was subsequently visited, whilst incarcerated, by Haxby accompanied by a Mr Emmerson and a Mr Hornby, an attorney. Mead allegedly admitted, at that time, that Law was not at all involved in smuggling as he had previously alleged, and some attempt seems to have been made to get him to sign a paper to this effect. One wonders what pressure was exerted, because Mr Emmerson's sister happened to be married to John Watson and two of Emmerson's cousins had also been accused of smuggling by Mead. Haxby himself admitted that he had previously acted as a witness against Mead and on behalf of Law!

Others were called whose testimony was intriguing. William Wharton was a juryman at the assize but gave evidence that he had been called to Mead's house the day after the shooting and affirmed that the window of Mead's chamber had been broken from the inside. His evidence, under cross-examination, suggests that the defence believed that he himself was deeply implicated in the affair. 'I knew of a suit against Mead for perjury at the suit of Mr Law. I never subscribed towards the defraying of the expenses of that prosecution. I heard of an effigy being burnt of whom I knew not: I did not furnish a gown for it, nor do I believe my wife ever did. I have not subscribed or agreed to do so.' Wharton, though, admitted he had been subpoenaed to give evidence against Mead in London. In the event, Belt was acquitted and Mead was convicted of mere manslaughter. What interests most about the case is the portrait it presents of a divided community, each side with its own allies. One side, however, was able to rouse the crowd and to punish or intimidate the other, not merely through violence, but also through the appropriation of traditions of display and punishment.

A year earlier another criminal enterprise, this time a gang of burglars, had actually been able to lay hands upon a prosecution witness at Soham in Cambridgeshire. Between 1819 and 1821, there had been a series of burglaries at farms in the district and thefts of livestock. However, in April 1821 a gang of fourteen men were arrested in Soham and charged with these offences.[13] Others were implicated and in total

---

12 Ibid.
13 *Cambridge Chronicle*, 13 April 1821.

twenty-two men were put on trial. Sixteen of them were found guilty and the ringleaders were sentenced to transportation. On the evening of 9 April 1822, however, four men broke into the house of a John Horsley in Soham, dragged him outside and threw him in a ditch. Two more men joined them and Horsley was then 'hauled up town with nothing on but my shirt'. By this time a crowd had gathered and Horsley was periodically exposed to the mob before being taken to The Crown and then sat on an ass facing backwards. He was then taken and thrown into the local pond, after which he was paraded through the streets to the Red Lion where it was proposed to duck him once more. Three men then intervened, one of them being a surgeon and one, Mr Orman, the local clergyman. They were unable to recover Horsley from the mob but persuaded them that another ducking would amount to murder. Horsley was paraded again and then taken home to his bed. Horsley complained to Sir Henry Bate Dudley JP, who sent his deposition to the Home Office. Significantly, the *Cambridge Independent*, which reported the affair, described Horsley as a man who had been instrumental in bringing the Soham gang to justice. Horsley himself had no doubt of the reason for the affair; it was to damage his reputation and his testimony against one Thomas Tibbits, an associate of his assailants, who had been charged with a felony. Five of the primary assailants were subsequently jailed for two years, the other was acquitted.

Sometimes criminals could not lay hands on the witnesses against them but in those circumstances they often resorted to symbolic revenge. Mary Flinn, who identified three perpetrators of a £200 cash box robbery, was burned in effigy outside her house by a crowd of several hundred.[14] In *Ex Parte Leversedge*, an attorney instructed by the Burial Board to obtain a criminal information against a Mr Bennett, who had embezzled bread to be distributed to the poor under a bequest, complained that the man had responded by gathering persons, 'of the lowest class in a room in Winterton and distributed tea and tobacco to them according to their sex . . . The crowd afterwards went to the applicant's house where his wife was lying ill of gastric fever, and hissed and shouted and created a great noise. The applicant was burned in effigy . . .'[15]

In view of what was at stake, we can readily understand why the press was so fiercely resisted and why criminals went to such lengths to preserve themselves. The violence of shopkeepers is perhaps somewhat more surprising. Regulatory myths have led to the supposition that bureaucratisation and obsessive regulation are modern phenomena and ones that have but recently displaced a happy world of carefree and cheery social interaction. In reality, life in the eighteenth- or nineteenth-century towns was anything but unregulated, and breaches of the Sunday trading laws, violations of licensing hours, attempts to trade without the relevant permits, instances of furious

---

14 *Manchester Times*, 4 June 1870.
15 *Standard*, 1 February 1867.

driving, or cases of unlawful gaming were the very things upon which the majority of informers thrived. From respectable and even affluent occupational groups, down to beggars and petty hawkers, many were engaged in continual battles against the seemingly petty, sometimes nit-picking regulations that nonetheless inhibited and sometimes entirely jeopardised the earning of livelihoods.[16] Most of these regulatory breaches, then as now, were willingly colluded in by the general population or, at the least, their violation was regarded as hardly wrong.[17]

Although it was the traders who were most vulnerable to the activities of informers, they could often count upon the support not only of their fellows, but also their customers, neighbours and family groups, in raising a crowd and taking counter-measures. Jessica Warner and Frank Ivis explain that in the course of the opposition in London to the Gin Act 1736:

> There were at least nine instances in which informers were dragged along the streets or were forced to march in procession. This particular dimension to the demonstrations links them, if only loosely, to charivaris in which transgressors were placed on a cart or were paraded backwards on a horse or ass; in one incident, an informer was actually 'set upon an Ass . . . whilst others beat and pelted him, leading him up and down Bond Street.'[18] In the same incident another informer was 'dragged several times through the Horse Pond of the White Horse Inn.' This particular punishment, in turn can be linked to a subset of charivaris known as 'riding the stang.' At least eight informers were forced to 'ride the stang,' whether in a trough or a muddy ditch, or the Thames itself. In another incident, an informer was burnt in effigy, a practice typical of rough music.[19]

A man who had informed against a woman found himself humiliated and forced to march in a procession up Ludgate Hill,[20] a man who had pretended to be purchasing a medicinal dram for the sick was 'dragged to a dung-hill in Bishop's court . . . and there buried for some time with ashes and cynders',[21] and in Bristol a man who had similarly informed on an unlicensed liquor vendor was tarred and feathered.[22] Others were disposed of cunningly and more permanently. Informers might sometimes find

---

16 For example, *The Poor Man's Guardian*, 16 June 1832, protested about the imprisonment of a heavily pregnant woman who had been arrested in Hatton Garden for selling nuts from a basket.
17 I should say that there were other 'minor' offences that were viewed with profound hostility, such as selling short measures.
18 *London Daily Post and General Advertiser*, 5 August 1738.
19 Jessica Warner and Frank Ivis, '"Damn You, You Informing Bitch": Vox Populi and the Unmaking of the Gin Act of 1736', *Journal of Social History*, 33:2 (1999), pp. 299–330 at p. 310.
20 *Grub Street Journal*, 17 February 1737, p. 2, cited in Warner and Ivis, 'Damn You, You Informing Bitch', p. 312.
21 Ibid., p. 308.
22 *Read's Weekly Journal, or, British Gazetteer*, 17 December 1738.

themselves served up to the press, such as one taken up in 1743 and 'press'd by a Gang planted for that purpose'.[23] That same year another informer, John Markham, was 'taken out of a Gin shop' in St Katherine's and 'carry'd on board a Tender'.[24]

The Gin Act was repealed in 1743 but there were plenty of other lucrative opportunities later for informers. Some came from within the relevant occupations themselves and their fellows often closed ranks against them and expelled them. This happened to a journeyman shoemaker in London who had passed information to a magistrate. Interestingly, he tried to defend himself by saying that he had only gone to the magistrate in response to a personal injury that had been done to his wife and he promised he would not do it again.[25] Expulsion was not always possible, however, or did not always suffice, and then more direct street punishments were employed. Butchers feature prominently in accounts of these punitive street activities – large men, adept with heavy objects, they seem to have been highly regarded as 'hired muscle' and to have had a high degree of social cohesion. They could be quickly assembled in defence of colleagues and similarly to punish those who broke the butcher's fellowship. Thus in 1776:

> A number of butchers in Oxford market procured a cart, which they hung with black matting, and placed in it the effigy of a man with a halter around his neck, who they said was an informer against butchers, bakers, barbers, green-grocers, &c. for exercising their trades on Sunday. The cart was attended by three men, one of whom, in a black coat, a large curled wig, a calf's tail hanging down his back, with a book in his hand, represented the Ordinary; the others were intended to represent Jack Ketch and his Deputy. A man mounted on an ass preceded the cart, with a white wand in his hand, in imitation of the Sheriff, and was followed by near fifty butchers with large clubs, who acted as constables. In this manner they paraded round the principal markets in Westminster, after which they returned to the aforesaid place, where they hung the effigy on a high gallows erected for that purpose.[26]

A butcher who informed on several publicans in 1835 found that he had inconvenienced the drinking habits of his compatriots and a butcher's mob besieged him in his house.[27] Another in 1862, who had laid informations against tradesmen at Newgate Market for failing to give receipts, found that whenever he subsequently visited the market the porters and salesmen would cry out, 'Beware of the informer!' and no one would sell him meat at the proper price.[28]

---

23 *Read's Weekly Journal, or, British Gazeteer*, 7 July 1739.
24 *London Evening Post*, 21 June 1743.
25 *Read's Weekly Journal, or, British Gazeteer*, 17 December 1737.
26 *Gazeteer and New Daily Advertiser*, 14 June 1776.
27 *Essex Standard*, 30 October 1835.
28 *Bury and Norwich Post*, 4 November 1862.

A high degree of organisation is suggested by some of the elaborate humiliations heaped upon informers – a reflection of the ability of particular groups to organise, exert authority and exploit both resources and popular resentment. In 1822, for example, two thousand people gathered around the sessions house at Kingston to attack two informers who had filed informations under the Coach and Coal Acts. One of the terrified informers jumped from a bridge into the River Thames but was captured and beaten almost to death.[29] A little less dramatic was the case of Moses Pegg, an inspector of hawkers' licences who presumed in February 1832 to ask a man selling brooms from a cart at Great Wigston in Leicestershire to produce his licence. The vendor was unable to do so, but when Moses set off to inform on him to the local JP he was 'followed by upwards of a hundred men and boys who first knocked and then threw stones at him ... they threw him into a ditch and pelted him with sludge'. Five men were brought to trial for the assault on Moses, though it seems that his dignity was injured as much as his body. He denied he was a common informer and according to the *Leicester Chronicle* informed the court that he was 'a regularly authorised Inspector of Hawkers' Licences, which was an Irish sinecure, "all work and no pay" – although he confessed he received a share of all penalties, yet not more than paid his expenses, and compensated him for the anxiety of mind he suffered in the discharge of his duties'.[30] How sympathetic one should be to poor Moses Pegg I am uncertain – he seems to have had a talent for being assaulted. In October 1832 he gave evidence against a hawker trading without a licence. The result was that a crowd of 200–300 dragged him out of the Greyhound Inn in Leicester, pelted him with mud and punched him.[31]

In December 1832 an informer attempted to lay an information at the petty sessions at Linton in Cambridgeshire. The information alleged that the landlord of the Crown Inn kept his premises open on Sundays. The magistrates however, headed by Lord Godolphin, dismissed the information. But far from diffusing the affair, a large crowd gathered to do summary justice upon the informer. The magistrates attempted to escort the man safely back to his house but during the course of the journey they were stoned; one magistrate was cut severely. Ten men were subsequently convicted of the riot and nine received salutary jail sentences of one to two years.[32] One cannot but suppose that the vigour of the authorities in bringing the culprits to justice was very much stimulated by the status of the parties assailed. Generally speaking, very few of those taking part in such activities were ever prosecuted, especially if they had not played a prominent role and if there were numerous people involved.

---

29 *Morning Chronicle*, 22 August 1823.
30 *Leicester Chronicle*, 7 April 1832.
31 *Leicester Chronicle*, 5 January 1833.
32 *Morning Post*, 15 March 1833.

Estimates of crowd numbers at these affairs need to be treated with the greatest caution (nothing has changed in that respect today). However, some gatherings were clearly very large such as that at Saltcoats in 1855. The ostensible cause was that a tradesman had been informed upon and fined for having issued a receipt without the requisite receipt stamp:

> There could be no fewer than 5,000 persons present, who all seemed to be animated with the same spirit of detestation of the circumstances connected with this affair. The effigy was placed on a donkey, and surrounded by several parties carrying torches. At a respectable distance it was followed by a flute band, which at intervals, played 'the Rogue's March,' and other airs. After going various rounds, the vast assemblage congregated on the braes at Saltcoats Harbour, where, after suspending the effigy for some time, fire was set to it, and it was consumed . . . During the evening a brilliant display of fireworks was kept up throughout the town.[33]

Notwithstanding the assertion of the report, can we really accept that such a high proportion of the population of Saltcoats and nearby Ardrossan were so animated by the matter of a receipt – even given the detestation of the informing species? Clearly, there was a strong festive element here: music, a torchlit procession, a firework display! This begs the question as to what extent elements of the crowd actually knew anything of, or were personally animated by, the alleged cause.

The Saltcoats disturbance was unusual in respect of scale and, unlike many other cases, no actual violence appears to have been doled out to the informer or anyone else. Yet the readiness of familial groups, groups connected by occupation, or groups united by a strong geographic identity, to protect their interests by violence leads one to imagine that this must often have been a successful strategy that deterred the operation of many potential informers, prevented lawful arrests and precluded the suppression of popular justice activities once under way. Suffice it to say that by the very nature of things, one cannot know about those who were tempted to inform but on reflection decided against it. Similarly, one is more likely to learn of an arrest than the fact that no arrest was made because a constable had pondered the situation, turned around and quietly walked away. When the police tried to arrest two youths for breaking tree branches in Hyde Park in 1833 one of the youths warned the officer that he was a chimney sweep, 'Remember fellow, I belong to the black clergy and, if you touch me, I'll change your colour you blue devil!'[34] The mob of sweeps assembled to try to rescue the youths but on this occasion they failed.

Constables must have been all too well aware of the dangers of getting their heads staved in and could be discrete when it was called for. For example, on 22 June 1844

---

33 *Caledonian Mercury*, 21 December 1855.
34 *Morning Chronicle*, 29 July 1829.

a case of riot was heard against five defendants at the petty sessions at Newport, Hampshire.[35] The defendants had been part of a band that had 'tin-kettled' an informer's house at Ventnor for two nights running. The parish constable had heard the first night's disturbance but 'did not get up as he had no staff and thought he could do no good'. On the second night he went along and saw the burning of the informer's effigy but, 'did not take any particular notice as to who the parties were or who were the most active in the disturbance'. A member of the rural police was also there and did attempt to take down names, but he too 'considered that his interference would have been no use as there were between two and three hundred persons present'. True, five of the two hundred or so were eventually indicted but this was more due to the vigour of the undaunted informer than the activities of law enforcement.

Thus far I have been speaking of informers as though they were a professional group earning their living this way. The activities of such people were well attested. However, it was rather easy for an ordinary member of the community to become characterised as an informer if he or she had unwisely drawn attention to an offence. In 1845, a quarrier in Castletown, Monmouthshire mentioned to a gamekeeper, employed by Sir Charles Morgan, that he had seen a local farmer, Mr W. Rees, shooting at a hare. The result was that Rees was hauled into the court and fined £10. In consequence: 'The inhabitants of the neighbourhood are so exasperated against the informer, that, on the evening of Christmas Day, they assembled in large numbers, near Castletown, and first hanged him in effigy, then they shot the man of straw, and, as a last honour, they prepared a pyre.'[36] As so often, there are more questions about this affair than can be answered. Was it wrong to report any offence to authority or merely an offence of the type at which people generally connived? Did it matter that the accused was a local farmer and the complainant a somewhat absent magnate? Would so many people have gathered at all on Christmas Day had they not been offered some inducement – possibly hospitality provided by Mr Rees?

Even turning to law in order to remedy a wrong against oneself was not without its risks. *R v Crutcher* 1822 was brought by a Mr Clay, the proprietor of a coach plying between London and Blackheath, against a rival proprietor, Mr Brown, and his friend Mr Crutcher. Clay had previously laid a complaint against Brown because Brown had 'wilfully drove against him' – and Brown had been fined £5.[37] Clay had been entitled to a proportion of the fine but, as he was at pains to inform the court, he had offered to return that proportion to Brown. Furthermore, he

---

35 *Hampshire Advertiser & Salisbury Guardian*, 22 June 1844.
36 *Bristol Mercury*, 4 January 1845.
37 *Morning Post*, 12 August 1822.

stressed it had not been him who had desired the prosecution but his endangered passengers who had insisted upon it. Brown, however, had chosen to characterise the affair rather differently and had denounced Clay as a 'bloody informer, and he would take care he should not get his living upon that road'. One day, on returning from London, Clay had been met by a gathering of more than a hundred persons who had blockaded the road. Clay's coach had been forced to join in a 'tumultuous procession' and, encouraged by the two defendants, he had been grossly reviled. An effigy with his name inscribed on a clay tablet had been carried in front of his coach and at last burned at the coach stop. Continuing intimidation thereafter had induced his customers to abandon him and he had been forced to give up the business, until a group of sympathisers had subscribed to purchase a new coach for him. In his second action before the court, he sought relief from the harassment. He succeeded insofar as the two defendants before the court pleaded guilty to riot, but it is unknown whether their conviction prevented further harassment, or exacerbated it.

Perhaps the reason that Clay had been at such pains to stress that it had been others who had urged him to commence his original prosecution was that prosecutions for furious driving were very often advanced for personal profit. In 1831 a Mr Byers attempted to lay a complaint of furious driving at Lambeth Street, fortified by a paper from the Commissioners of Hackney Coaches authorising him to lay complaints against offending cab drivers.[38] The magistrates dismissed the paper and asked him brusquely if he had come forward as a common informer. When Byers admitted it was so, the magistrate replied: 'Then, we won't hear you; we will have nothing to do with you; we have long ago determined against listening to any complaints brought by a common informer ... The system of informers is decidedly bad. We shall resist it.' Byers, it has to be said, was nothing if not thick-skinned and persistent. In 1827 he had travelled to Winchester to meet with a Mr Rawlins who was to give evidence in some cases for him, but he and Rawlins had been besieged in the Five Bells Inn whilst an effigy was paraded through the High Street and burned on Giles Hill.[39]

Pursuit of informers has largely taken us away from village and rural parish and into the towns and cities. Often it has also taken us somewhat up the social scale from village craftsmen and labourers to independent tradesmen, some of whom were clearly men of some substance. Mr Law, the 'respectable farmer' had also been a man of some means, though exactly where we should place him I am unsure, given that we have sound reasons to suppose that much of it was not legitimately acquired.

---

38 *Hull Packet and Humber Mercury*, 21 June 1831.
39 *Hampshire Telegraph and Sussex Chronicle*, 27 August 1827.

The Directing Mind and the Defence of Interests

Evidence of the sponsorship of rough music and associated activities in order to advance personal causes may make us look more critically at those instances in which rough music was allegedly caused by the spontaneous eruption of popular outrage. Clearly, this did happen and, whomsoever first muted the idea of staging rough music, one can readily imagine that once the idea took flight the originator might be forgotten. Such instances, then, will have had no single directing mind. At the same time, however, the fact that simple mono-causal explanations of these phenomena were so often advanced by newspapers, diarists and antiquarians must in part be explained by the fact that they were reporting and not investigating. They had neither the resources nor the inclination to look beyond the immediate ostensible cause. The reports set out a kind of broad moral rubric and establish families of circumstances within which these practices could be legitimated. They tell us interesting things about general popular morality, but they rarely move beyond the general to the specific to tell us exactly why at this particular time and why this miscreant was selected as opposed to others.

Where cases went to law, however, like that of Mead and Belt, a more nuanced explanation of causes was sometimes proffered or can subsequently be recovered. We begin to see individuals exploiting the rubric and the elbow-room within popular morality, and using the crowd to impose on the community and upon public space their own interpretations of popular justice. In cases such as Clay we can observe a contest over the defining of acts, with his opponent placing him (seemingly successfully) in the category of mere informer and Clay representing himself as the agent of his aggrieved customers, and carrying with him a constituency who subsequently got up a subscription for him. There were, I suggest, many acts that bore more than one interpretation – and why one interpretation was preferred to another remains largely unfathomable. Thus, whilst as far as I know no one ever came out enthusiastically in favour of kidnapping wives, as the Clitheroe case demonstrates such an act could be portrayed as monstrous oppression of the weaker sex – or else the legitimate exercise of the authority conferred on the husband by marriage. The interpretations of events that seemed to arise holistically from the crowd were certainly, on occasion, interpretations given to them by others. Later evidence affirms the suggestion derived from Rollinson's study of seventeenth-century Westonbirt that 'popular justice' was on occasion a strategic tool employed by rather well-heeled backers.

As an example of someone from far outside the lower orders who sponsored an exhibition of public shaming in order to accomplish his own purpose, one could scarce do better than the case of William Martin, gentleman and wine merchant, who did battle in Tewkesbury in 1805 with the local tax inspectorate. In February of that year Martin had appealed against his income tax assessment. The revenue commissioners, however, did not favour his case. Shortly thereafter, two effigies of local tax inspectors, James Hawkins and Thomas Holland, appeared on a cart in the streets of Tewkesbury to be paraded and pelted with filth by the local townspeople.[40] Conducted around the streets to the sound of a funeral bell tolling from the church, the two figures were then taken to the river, ripped apart and thrown in, whereupon the church bell changed to a merry peal, which allegedly went on for six hours. A mock report was circulated of the final moments of the two figures, in which it was alleged that they had confessed their venality and despoiling of the good people of the town, 'I claim forgiveness of you though I have wronged you all alike with this my vile associate [meaning the said Thomas Holland], partner of my villainies, sharer of my gains. Words are wanting to convince you how my Conscience Goads me. Heaven hath now showered curses on my head!'

The townspeople, it seems, were not loathe to join in the fun at Tewkesbury, but nonetheless it seems rather surprising that Martin's sympathisers were able to monopolise the church bells uncontested for such a long period. At any rate, three people were eventually arrested at the scene and Martin, as the inaugurator of the whole affair, was detained shortly thereafter. Martin himself was acquitted before the other three, who were all labourers, were brought to trial. These three were charged with 'a conspiracy, combination and confederacy and agreement' to 'make and cause to be made a great noise riot (rout) tumult and disturbance at Tewkesbury aforesaid in the county aforesaid'. All three were convicted of 'endeavouring to bring the inspector and surveyor of taxes into ridicule and contempt'; one received twelve months' imprisonment, the others nine months each.[41] The acquittal of Martin under such circumstances suggests that, although the authorities clearly believed that he had inspired the procession, he had not actually participated in it and therefore it was difficult to convict him. Importantly, none of the other defendants were prepared to give evidence against Martin. It is indeed possible that none of them knew the true causes and had merely joined in the entertainment.

In 1819 a further assault was made upon the Inland Revenue, one that led to the conviction of nineteen men at the Somerset Assizes.[42] The cause was a dispute about the meaning of the Assessed Tax Act. The act exempted dairies from taxation, but the local collector had levied taxes on the ownership of milk carts. The locals, seemingly erroneously, had believed that the carts were also exempt and had blamed in particular the local tax assessor, Mr Barnstaple, and to a lesser extent the collector, Mr Howard. I say the locals, but of course the owners of these carts were not men at the lower end of their society and it was presumably they who had circulated bills

---

40 For the full account see S. Matthews, 'A Tax Riot in Tewkesbury in 1805', *British Tax Review* 337 (2002), pp. 437–4.
41 Public Records Office, King's Bench, KB 21/48.
42 *Morning Chronicle*, 24 November 1820.

amongst the adjoining parishes to the effect that effigies of the two men were to be exhibited at Middleroy on 1 and 6 December. A substantial crowd had gathered on the days in question and Barnstaple, who was resident there, had been 'burlesqued' and stoned. At the subsequent trial of the participants, the solicitor-general pressed for a deterrent sentence and was keen to point out that Barnstaple was indeed an official assessor, 'and not a common informer as he was described on the other side.' He went on to note that two of the men convicted were churchwardens of the parish and that one of them, Mr Andrews, was the 'High Constable of the Hundred', 'These were the principal persons in the district, for there were no Gentlemen resident there.' Not only is the comparatively high social standing of these defendants of interest but also the manner in which the convicted were subsequently dealt with. There were several trials concerning the affair and in total forty-three persons were convicted of riot. It seems that the labourers (the majority) and some boys also detained were not brought up for judgement. However, the key persons, described as yeomen, received heavy fines and were ordered to find sureties for their future behaviour. Of the leading three, the high constable and one of the churchwardens were convicted on a single indictment, fined £100 each and sentenced to two months in Coldbath Fields; the other churchwarden was convicted on two indictments, fined the same amount and imprisoned for three months.

To summarise, performance strategies could be employed as a means of protecting individual or group interests against the encroachment of the state by means of its instruments – be they informers, tax collectors or customs collectors. In the case of fishing or smuggling communities this could take on the appearance of whole communities setting themselves against the state – and I will revisit this issue in Chapter 6 when I come to examine the relationship of performance culture to political resistance. However, the tools of popular justice, such as processions and effigies, could also be employed in the competition between individuals. Why does one butcher inform against another? For the reward possibly, but also because if one sells on a Sunday and the other does not, then the law-breaker obtains an advantage. A subsequent heavy fine removes that advantage, but if in turn the convicted party can cast his accuser as a common informer then he may remove him from the business altogether. In the example cited earlier, the harassment that Mr Clay endured from Mr Brown seems quite clearly to have been the result of a concerted attempt to remove a competitor.

It was concerns about competition that led an angry mob of retailers to stage a charivari in the fashionable shopping promenade of Westbourne Grove in west London in 1876. The target of their wrath was William Whiteley, a linen draper who was rapidly expanding his shop into London's first department store.[43] Whitely

---

43 See Erika D. Rappaport, '"The Halls of Temptation": Gender, Politics, and the Construction of the Department Store in Late Victorian London', *Journal of British Studies* 35:1(1996), pp. 58–83.

had recently added a greengrocery and a meat department to his store and this made him 'exceedingly distasteful' to the other shopkeepers in the neighbourhood. They resolved upon collective action and at about midday on 5 November:

> A grotesque and noisy cortege entered the thoroughfare [Westbourne Grove]. At its head was a vehicle, in which a gigantic Guy was propped up ... vested in the conventional frock coat of a draper ... conspicuous on the figure was a label with the words 'Live and Let Live.' In one hand of the figure a piece of beef bore the label '5 1/2 d.' and in the other was a handkerchief, with the ticket '2 1/2 d. all-linen.'[44]

A procession of butchers followed the cortege, making their traditional hullabaloo by banging their cleavers on marrow bones as they escorted the effigy to a bonfire in Portobello Road.

Erika Rappaport notes that the events of 5 November were the termination of four years of antagonism that had resulted from Whiteley's expansion. During that time, 'Whiteley's enemies charged that, by selling an array of commodities, services, and pleasures to a mixed shopping crowd, Whiteley disorganised class, gender, moral, and economic categories.'[45] A rival tradesman wrote sarcastically to the local newspaper complimenting Whiteley on his 'startling succession of feats in the art of shutting up your neighbour's shop and driving him elsewhere, but this last daring and audacious feat – this vending of meat and greens as well as silk and satins – overtops them all'.[46] Others had already attacked Whiteley on a different front, alleging that his application for a liquor licence was fraught with moral danger. The very comfort of the store might induce women to overconsume and, furthermore, there was a veiled suggestion that the shop might become a place of prostitution. The women in the store, 'might be ladies or females dressed to represent them ... the place might be made a place of assignation'.[47] By 1876 it was no longer a possibility (in genteel Westbourne Grove at least) that Whiteley would be dragged from his store, ducked, set upon, tied to a ladder or any of the rest of it. However, it is noteworthy that the rhetoric employed against him referenced centuries-old ideas about fair dealing, just prices, sufficiency as opposed to unjust enrichment, and indeed, appropriate gender behaviour. Economically, Whiteley's opponents deployed terminology that harked back to regulated market activity in a market that had already largely surrendered to principles of entrepreneurialism and laissez faire. This tells us that, although Whiteley ultimately prevailed, there still remained a reservoir of sentiment predicated on the

---

44 'Guy Fawkes Day in Westbourne Grove', *Bayswater Chronicle*, 11 November 1876, cited in Rappaport, 'The Halls of Temptation', pp. 58–9.
45 Rappaport, 'The Halls of Temptation', p. 60.
46 Senex, 'Wholesale Butchery in Bayswater – The Victims', *Bayswater Chronicle*, 11 November 1876.
47 H. Walker, 'Whiteley's Liquor License', *Bayswater Chronicle*, 23 March 1872.

older notions of communal well-being and social obligation. It does not necessarily tell us, however, that the businessmen who opposed Whiteley were genuinely in sympathy with these sentiments. It might simply have been that they fell back upon them and paraded their own virtue simply because they had been less successful in modern competition.

What the case of Whiteley's department store and others that have gone before demonstrate is that the tools, techniques and performances associated with popular justice were not the unique property of plebeian culture. Granted it may have been the undifferentiated mass that participated with the most gusto in stangings, burnings and the like. However, the assumptions and associations, the affective states that such activities were intended to inspire, were the product of a shared cultural property in which the lower orders were indeed very often the participants but did not always provide the originating spark.

6

Political Resistance

The Ceffyl Pren in South Wales

The previous chapter has shown that it was not merely the disenfranchised that employed rough music rituals. All classes operated in the context of 'a society thoroughly drenched in ceremonial and celebration'[1] and acted out the issues of the day to the discomfort of their opponents. However, the enthusiasm of the better classes for using communal justice practices to penalise individual wrong-doing declined during the nineteenth century. It became apparent that rough music not only could provide the cognitive tools to mobilise crowds against morally deficient individuals but also against their betters and against what they believed was morally deficient authority. Thus rough music became a campaign tool employed during food crises, labour disputes, Chartist agitations and the like, a traditional and cohesive tool amongst groups not yet politically enfranchised and not yet endowed with a distinctive ideology. Small wonder then that authority, hitherto generally tolerant of rough music, began to depreciate it and to see within traditional ceremonial a challenge to their authority. Nowhere was this challenge more apparent than in south Wales.

Discontent in Wales sprang from many causes: overpopulation, the unemployment that followed the end of the Napoleonic War, low agricultural prices and so on. In Cardiganshire in particular, the problems were further exacerbated by the threatened enforcement of the 1812 and 1815 Enclosure Acts, which authorised the enclosure of 10,000 acres within Crown manors. I will not go into the full details of the subsequent campaign against the enclosures, but what is of interest here are the folk elements informing that resistance to the acts, as observed by David Jones.[2]

---

1 F. O'Gorman, 'The Paine Burnings of 1792–93', *Past & Present* 193 (November 2006), pp. 111–56 at p. 114.
2 See D. J. V. Jones, 'Distress and Discontent in Cardiganshire, 1814–1819', *Ceredigion* 5:3 (1966), pp. 280–9. H.O. 42/145 Depositions of John Hughes and W. Vaughan, 18 July 1815, cited in Jones, 'Distress and Discontent in Cardiganshire, 1814–1819', p. 283.

Horns were blown to summon the crowds, who duly assembled; women and even children played a prominent part in the disturbances. Gruesome but symbolic punishments were threatened, such as when a mob in 1815 threatened to bury alive the enclosure commissioners. Jones observes that the use of horns during the disturbances, 'together with the attempt to secure the people's "rights" through horrible threats, nightly meetings, and assaults upon officials, indicates the similarity of the Cardiganshire riots to the practice known as Ceffyl Pren (wooden horse)'.[3] There were other similarities. In 1815 a surveyor, John Hughes, was battered by women wielding frying pans who threatened to bury him in a pit that they claimed to have dug for that purpose.[4] In 1820 a house built on an enclosed plot was burned to the ground by a mob disguised as women and wearing handkerchiefs on their faces.[5]

Folkloric elements reappeared again amongst the 'Scotch Cattle' gangs who struck against blackleg miners and foundry men during the industrial disputes that were prevalent throughout south Wales between 1820 and 1835.[6] Overpopulation was again a cause of the general poverty and unrest in the 'black domain' but, more specifically, the disturbances were caused by the attempts of ironmasters and mine owners to reduce wages in response to a number of recessions.[7] What followed were a series of strikes from out of which emerged an increasingly sophisticated system of co-operation between labour in different collieries and factories, which was allegedly led by the Tarw Scotch (Scotch Bull). By 1830 there were committees in the works and mines throughout the area, holding weekly meetings and collecting subscriptions for the strike funds. Men bound themselves by oaths and withdrew from their employment to attend mass meetings on hillsides. The purpose of these mass meetings was primarily to intimidate their employers and those who continued to work during the disputes. 'Rough music' played an important part in summoning the men and in stimulating responses from those not yet loyal to the cause. Horns were blown and drums beaten and the mere sound of them from a nearby hillside was enough to cause the workers of Blaina Ironworks to abandon their work and go home.[8]

Mass meetings were also accompanied by the despatch of threatening letters, the posting of alarming notices (often featuring bloody bulls) and night visitations to

---

[3] Jones, 'Distress and Discontent in Cardiganshire, 1814–1819', p. 285.
[4] National Library of Wales, Nanteos MSS and Documents. Undated letter from J Lewis to W. E. Powell, cited in Jones, 'Distress and Discontent in Cardiganshire, 1814–1819', p. 285.
[5] D. J. V. Jones, *Before Rebecca: Popular Protest in Wales, 1793–1835* (London: Allen Lane, 1973), p. 49.
[6] Jones, 'The Scotch Cattle and their Black Domain', pp. 220–49.
[7] The 'black domain' is defined by Jones as the region extending from Rhymney to Abergavenny and Llangynidr to Caerphilly.
[8] PRO., H.O. 52/19, 31 March 1832, cited in Jones, 'The Scotch Cattle and their Black Domain', p. 234.

actual or potential strike-breakers and blacklegs. Such visitations adopted forms entirely familiar to plough bullocks and the like. Jones observes that they were:

> Usually carried out by small groups of from ten to twenty miners. The leaders of the party were disguised by masks, handkerchiefs and cattle skins; the remainder had blackened faces, and wore women's clothes, 'their best clothes', or simply reversed jackets. They announced their arrival by blowing a horn, rattling chains and making 'low noises'. At the home of their victim the 'Cattle' smashed the windows with stones or pick axes and broke down the door. Once inside it was a relatively easy matter to destroy the furniture and earthenware and to set fire to the clothes and curtaining.[9]

The origin of the term 'Scotch Cattle' is unclear but it is possible that there might be a relationship to plough bullocks. It might be thought, though, that the similarities between industrial unrest and popular justice/folkloric rituals are merely superficial – after all, there are only a limited number of ways that one can summon a large meeting, and the blowing of trumpets and the banging of drums is a fairly obvious one. The evidence, however, suggests deeper connection. Rough music and other forms of popular justice were a response to disappointed expectations, to failure to behave in ways that reinforced the assumptions upon which the community was formed. Similarly, doling customs, whilst not immediately punitive, reflected a created expectation and became punitive when that expectation was defeated. The industrial 'visitations' and those in other Welsh disputes, and similar disputes in England, were not randomised nor were they purely instrumental in the sense of trying to deter anyone who in any way assisted the particular employer's interest: they did not target the banker who lent him money, the teacher who taught his children, the gardener on his estate, his household servants and so on. Rather they targeted those who fell within, or should have fallen within, the community of the judgemental actors. Like other rough music practices they were intended to penalise those who had failed to conform to reasonable expectation, but this time by taking another man's job or failing to hold out whilst the strike was still on. In doing so, though there was some violence it was rarely indiscriminate – the behaviour of the Scotch Cattle, like that of the men of the later Rebecca Riots, was rule-based. The actors took upon themselves judgement of those they felt entitled to judge. The power to judge had to be invoked, however, and the community in action had to be constituted: festivity offered a rubric within which the magic could be performed and it offered a repository of symbols that could be employed to signal transgressive behaviour – notably by the adoption of women's clothing.

It is clear that the visitations owed much to rough music practice and, in particular, the ceffyl pren ('wooden horse') ritual. The ceffyl pren, like its English counterparts,

---

9 Jones, 'The Scotch Cattle and their Black Domain', p. 238.

had many variations – sometimes involving the parade of the victim himself, his effigy or a volunteer acting as his substitute. There were different degrees of elaboration. Sometimes the 'horse' consisted of no more than a ladder or a pole and therefore there was little or no outward difference between the 'horse' and the 'pole' employed in England. Jones observed, however, that in Cardigan an actual wooden replica of a horse was constructed and a substitute employed to mount the horse and harangue the assembled crowd. As previously seen, in cases of moral lapses a type of tribunal was often held to debate the case against the accused.[10] An announcement of an intent to carry the horse was often made well in advance of the actual performance and the ritual was traditionally repeated for the standard three nights.

As with the ceffyl pren's English counterparts, sexual and gender offences appear prominently in the reasons given for performances but it was similarly employed against other deviant behaviours. It may, however, have been applied with no more consistency than in England. Furthermore, the remembrance of the ritual does not necessarily mean that it was commonplace. Rosemary Jones cites an instance from Llechryd in 1837 where the ceffyl pren had seemingly been in abeyance for a generation before it was resurrected in order to punish an informer. [11]However, one important difference between England and Wales was that, given the particularly difficult circumstances of the population at that time and the perception of foreign domination, the ceffyl pren was able to inform an even deeper sense of cultural and national resistance. Discontent and distress amongst the Welsh population manifested itself both in a heightened desire to penalise immoral behaviour amongst its own and to renew moral standards, and also to protest against the impositions heaped upon it from outside – from rapacious industrialists, absentee landlords, grasping taxes, unjust tithes and so on. The ceffyl pren could be utilised for both, but it may have been rather uncommon before a sudden eruption of such activity in Cardigan around 1837.

In March of that year the magistrates of Cardigan wrote to the home secretary detailing the case of a house painter, Mr Gordon, who had given evidence against a man who had cut wood from a gentleman's plantation. The magistrates reported that he had been immediately threatened 'that the wooden horse should be carried against him'. They complained that such practices had become 'very prevalent', that the horse was being systematically employed in four parishes, and that attempts to suppress such practices had 'wholly failed to do so, and in cases of immorality or incontinence in any of their neighbours a right to visiting their delinquencies is

---

10 *Cambrian*, 6 April 1839.
11 *Carmarthen Journal*, 28 July 1837, cited in Jones,'Popular Culture, Policing, and the 'Disappearance' of the Ceffyl Pren in Cardigan, 1837–1850', pp. 19–39 at p. 27.

openly avowed and a determination not to be put down asserted'.[12] A petition signed by nineteen important persons in Pembrokeshire supported the claims of an increase in such activity:

> The practice to which we allude is that of carrying the 'wooden horse' to effect which a numerous party assembles at night, amounting in number sometimes to hundreds many having their faces blackened and their persons disguised, and proceeds with an effigy in the shape of a Horse along the public roads furnished with torches, and not infrequently with guns and in a noisy, tumultuous manner, and using most disgusting and obscene exhibitions, proceed to carry an effigy along the public road towards the house of the person against whom this procession is intended. Three times, once in each succeeding week, and on the last occasion it is burnt in some public place amidst the shouts and acclamations of the accompanying people. The object of this proceeding formerly was to check gross immorality and to visit against the offending party the crime of notorious incontinence, and while it was confined to those limits, and conducted without riot, the sense of the country connived at it, an indulgence, it is feared, that has given an impulse to the most dangerous practices and which is now too frequently resorted to as the vehicle of private malice and an obstruction to public justice.[13]

The Mayor of Cardigan himself fulminated that, 'the parishes concerned in these riots have violently resisted all attempts of the Civil power to put a stop to them, and at one of these assemblages last week no less than 15 persons were wounded with the Shot fired into the Mob. Public notice is given of these meetings and all the people assemble from miles around to give their Countenance and Support to them under the mistaken notion of asserting their legality.'[14]

The question to raise here is whether the behaviour of the crowd or the magistrates had changed, or indeed the behaviour of both. The petitioners had conceded that the practice had hitherto been tolerated: so was it that the practice had become more frequent or more violent, or that there were other reasons why that tolerance was no longer to be extended? One magistrate observed that, 'at the present moment when the Cardigan Union is about to be formed in the centre of the foregoing scenes of action, it is desirable that public feeling be in a wholesome and tranquil state'.[15] Rosemary Jones suggests that part of the reason for the attempt to suppress the ceffyl pren might be explained by a fear that it could be employed in resistance to Poor Law

---

12 HO 52/35/512. Letter of D. Saunders Davies and other magistrates to the home secretary, 11 May 1837.
13 HO 52/35/513–14.
14 HO 52/35/ 517–8. Letter of H. Lloyd Mayor of Cardigan dated 31 March 1837.
15 HO 52/35/513–4 D. Saunders Davies to HO, 11 May 1837, cited in Jones, 'Popular Culture, Policing, and the 'Disappearance' of the Ceffyl Pren in Cardigan, 1837–1850', p. 29.

reform.[16] It might also be the case that the magistrates – men with their ears to the ground – already had some inkling of what was coming in advance of the outbreak of the Rebecca Riots.

Whatever the reason, initial attempts to prevent such demonstrations did not go well. On 30 March 1837 the magistrates swore-in special constables and attempted to ambush a ceffyl pren procession in the town. Intelligence of this reached the procession, who marched up and confronted the magistrates. Two ringleaders were seized but the magistrates were in turn seized by the crowd who 'beat them severely', the special constables being either unable or unwilling to intervene. Interestingly, 'The ring-leaders were known, but neither the law nor its rigour was resorted to.'[17]

More success was had with the conviction of a John Williams at Cardiganshire assizes in July 1837 for his behaviour during the conduct of a ceffyl pren against the aforementioned painter Mr Gordon on 18 May 1837. The event had been led by a Thomas Haxby who had been 'running about with his coat turned, and his face disguised . . . making a noise like the neighing of a horse'.[18] Haxby had been arrested and lodged at a public house, but the crowd now led by Williams had broken in and released him. Haxby subsequently found himself acquitted but Williams was convicted of riot and assault – although he was sentenced to only one month of imprisonment.

Rosemary Jones believes that Williams's conviction 'reflected a hardening of attitudes among the ruling classes'.[19] This, I think, is not so certain, given the magistrates' responses to two ceffyl pren events at the end of the year. On 25 November 1837 a David Davies complained to the Mayor of Carmarthen that, 'your Police of the Town were allowed to form part of the procession which took place last night to carry me in effigy thus not only attempting an insult but committing a serious breach of the peace without an effort on their part or yours to prevent the one or preserve the other'.[20] Davies expressed his intention to complain to Lord John Russell. It was presumably in response to this threat that the magistrates requested a report from the chief police officer John Pugh, who was sanguine about the whole affair. Upon going upon his rounds at about 7.30p.m. he had heard the sound of music, 'there was a band consisting of three or four persons carrying torches who were followed by a crowd of persons and an effigy upon a pole'. Pugh followed 'at a distance' with fellow officers and, he says, 'when the people there came near the Town Hall burning the effigy I

---

16 Jones, 'Popular Culture, Policing, and the 'Disappearance' of the Ceffyl Pren in Cardigan, 1837–1850', p. 29.
17 Retrospectively reported in *Welshman*, 2 June 1843.
18 *Carmarthen Journal*, 28 July and 4 August 1837.
19 Jones, 'Popular Culture, Policing, and the 'Disappearance' of the Ceffyl Pren in Cardigan, 1837–1850', p. 31.
20 HO 52/35/450.

and the other police officers interfered and put it out. The people who were present almost immediately dispersed and in a quarter of an hour the Town was perfectly peaceable.'[21] No arrests were made at the time or subsequently.

However, the incident was repeated one month later and the mayor and justices found it prudent to compose a statement justifying their own actions and pre-empting what they clearly feared was another complaint from Mr Davies. In so doing they give us a rare insight into the operations of authority in these matters. First, they pointed out that in the first incident referred to above, 'the Crowd quietly dispersed and not a single assault occurred nor was any Complaint preferred before the Magistrates either on the following or any subsequent day connected with this affair'.[22] They pointed out that the entire police force at their disposal in the town consisted of only five or six constables. Nonetheless, on receiving Davies's complaint they called out special constables to guard his house but there was 'no disturbance and their being called out only excited surprise'. They explained in their statement that the affair had arisen because Davies had prosecuted an alderman, Mr Jones, who had libelled him in the *Welshman* newspaper. Jones had been sentenced to a month of imprisonment and this had inspired the first protest. A second protest had been anticipated upon Jones's release and in order to prevent this the magistrates had, 'sent for Mr Jones's son whose workmen / several in number / were reported to be the principals in the affair and he assured them that any workman of his Father's who appeared in the Crowd should be instantly discharged and that he was quite satisfied no such intentions existed upon their part'.

The likely date of disturbance was 23 December (the 24th being a Sunday, the Christmas Eve festivities were to be expected on the 23rd). A proclamation was cried through the town instructing people not to parade with torches on that day, and Mr Davies was told that 'any means he could point out for the purposes of preventing the annoyance which he anticipated should be readily afforded'. However, 'in the evening an Effigy with the words "Jim Crow" on its breast was again carried through the Town and publicly burnt as before'. The magistrates decided not to interfere, as John Pugh advised them that 'where the Effigy was burnt the Crowd as on the previous occasion would peaceably disperse which was the case and not a single assault again occurred'.

The Davies case serves as a useful illustration of the many factors that might condition responses to those lesser (and more common) skimmingtons, stangings and ceffyl prens in which the malefactor was physically unmolested. First, although the affair was obviously of great import to Mr Davies it does not seem to have animated

---

21 HO 52/35/454. Police Report dated 24 November 1837.
22 HO 52/35/153, fol. 450, December 1837. Statement of the Mayor and Justices of Carmarthen as to the Complaint of Mr David Davies.

the magistrates in the same way. No heinous act recognised by law was committed; possibly there was an obstruction of the highway, possibly a breach of the peace but there was no riot, no assault and no property was damaged. The affair had its origins in a personal and probably political conflict in which rough music was organised by one constituency against another.

Whatever the sympathies of the magistrates (and so far as one can read into the text one gets the sense that they thought Davies had brought these events upon himself) they had very few resources at their disposal in order to prevent such displays. John Pugh was aware that attempts to arrest the protagonists would likely turn very nasty indeed. He may also have simply not seen the harm in it, or been reluctant to take sides in a factional dispute. Whatever the cause, in the event he did little more than try to ensure that the crowd did not step beyond certain bounds, and this conversely must have suggested to the crowd that so long as they kept within those bounds their activity was lawful. Rosemary Jones remarked that the ceffyl pren was 'animated by a deep sense of ancient, prescriptive rights, based upon the widely-held belief that Hywel Dda had sanctioned its usage, a myth which had become so firmly cemented in popular consciousness that it was often reiterated by members of the gentry.'[23] Notwithstanding the alleged hardening of attitudes, nothing in respect of the burning of the effigy of Mr Davies could have disabused anyone of this notion.

Two cases were, however, brought in August 1839 against men who had actually attacked women during the course of a ceffyl pren. In one case the defendant was acquitted because he had been wearing a woman's bonnet and gown and the victim could not identify him for sure. In the second, an attack upon an unmarried mother, during which she was dragged out of her house, beaten and threatened with being thrown into a well, resulted in one man being sentenced to six months' imprisonment with hard labour. The two men who had actually broken down the door of her house and begun the assault were not brought to trial, however, because they too had been in disguise.

By 1839 the crowds had broader concerns. Merched Beca – the 'daughters' of the Rebecca Riots – had become active throughout south and mid-Wales, driven by the usual cocktail of misery and a campaign against unjust tax or tithe impositions upon the poor. David Williams observed that: 'It can, indeed, be said with complete certainty that the Rebecca riots were an extension of the ceffyl pren.'[24] In both distribution and form the identification is irresistible. One of the favourite targets of Rebecca were the toll houses – difficult to protect but levying what were, allegedly, usurious rates for passage. The assaults upon these houses were carried out swiftly

---

23 Jones, 'Popular Culture, Policing, and the 'Disappearance' of the Ceffyl Pren in Cardigan, 1837–1850', p. 27, citing HO 45/454.
24 Williams, *The Rebecca Riots*, p. 56.

in dead of night accompanied by a cacophony of horns and guns, but they were not indiscriminate:

> With soldier-like promptitude and decision, the work was commenced; no idle parleying, no irrelevant desire of plunder or revenge divided their attention . . . Meantime, all the movements of the assailants had been directed by a leader mounted and disguised like his bodyguard in female attire and having like them his face blackened and shaded by a bonnet or by flowing curls, or other headgear.[25]

In addition to attacking such targets, the two cases involving female victims (referred to above) illustrate the point that 'Rebecca's daughters', in addition to attempting to rid south Wales of unjust tolls and miserly employers, also had what we might now call a moral agenda. In at least a dozen cases they threatened to punish men who failed to marry the girls they had got pregnant.[26] They chastised wife-beaters, forced farmers to sell grain at a fair price,[27] and evicted bailiffs who had dispossessed tenants.[28]

Graham Seal asserts that although the threats issued by Rebecca were bloodcurdling: 'As with English agrarian disturbances conducted within a traditional ritual framework, violence of a serious kind was extremely rare in the Rebecca riots.' Rather, according to Seal: 'The few reported incidents of serious violence towards toll-keepers seem to be either the result of accidents, the result of some specific communal dislike of the keeper, or completely idiosyncratic.'[29] There is some difference of opinion here since David Williams had argued that the Rebeccaites did upon occasion carry through on their threats. It is perhaps not too pusillanimous to take a middle course. Seal was obviously keen to stress that 'riots' such as are observable in the cases of Rebecca, and in England in the protests against new threshing machines supposedly led by 'Captain Swing', were in fact workings-through of traditional ceremonials and dramas, which 'in the case of the Ceffyl Pren and the various English rituals of justice, utilised those existing ritual frameworks completely'.[30] I entirely agree, and if we think of a riot as an instance in which no rules of behaviour are acknowledged, then indeed 'riot' is the wrong term to apply to most of the observed rough music activities.[31] For Seal, I think that it is a desire to stress this that leads him to 'over-egg the pudding' when he asserts that there was a virtual absence of serious violence during such activities, and claims that in both the Rebecca and Swing riots, 'serious violence

---

25 *The Red Dragon*, vol. XI, cited in Evans, *Ask the Fellows Who Cut the Hay*, pp. 13–14.
26 Williams, *The Rebecca Riots*, p. 241.
27 Evans, *Ask the Fellows Who Cut the Hay*, p. 160.
28 Ibid., p. 172.
29 Seal, 'Tradition and Agrarian Protest in Nineteenth Century England and Wales', pp. 146–69 at p. 162.
30 Ibid., p. 164.
31 I say 'most' because I am not sure that some of the punishments meted out to informers, although wrapped up in the rubric of rough music, were not intended from the first to be fatal.

to persons as opposed to property, is almost non-existent across two countries and half a century of bitter antagonism'.[32]

I hope I have shown by now that violence was latent within traditional ritual and that traditional ritual did not always suffice to contain it. If the victim resisted or was aggressive then matters could slip rapidly beyond control. In our desire to rehabilitate the crowd and to tease out the nuances of ritual practice one can go too far in sanitising proceedings. After all, we are talking about crowds often composed of large numbers of highly charged, drunken young men endowed with a strong sense of grievance. The two assaults on women observed in Cardigan in 1839 were brutal and, as we shall see, similar assaults continued. Crowds did sometimes intend violence but also, as will be depressingly familiar to any criminal lawyer, once violence began it could readily escalate beyond anything that was initially intended. Indeed, it was the accidental killing of a woman during a demonstration at the home of a working miner that led to the hanging of Edward Morgan, one of the 'Scotch Cattle', at Monmouth jail in 1835 and turned the tide against the movement.

By 1843 the tide had also turned against Rebecca. One consequence of the Rebecca Riots and their suppression seems to have been the abandonment of that elaborate tribunal of morals, the coolstrin. In the first instance, if David Williams is right, it was the Rebeccaites who abandoned them, but it may also be that in the environment of the later 1840s, with increased policing and garrisoning, it was no longer possible or expedient to stage them. Evans describes a trial of an effigy in 1843, but thereafter the more formal 'courts' seem to have disappeared.[33] It is very likely, however, that less elaborate tribunals endured. It is also the case that, in respect to punishing moral offences, the ceffyl pren itself retained much of its vigour.

Rosemary Jones reports a number of occurrences during the period up until 1850 that were staged to punish sexual incontinence. In April 1847 a ceffyl pren was staged at Pencwm for a woman who had been unfaithful to her sailor husband during his absence.[34] Another took place between St Dogmaels and Cardigan on 26 May 1848, during the course of which a servant, James James, was carried upon the horse in female attire to act as 'spokesman' for the miscreant. James was arrested and the military had to be sent for to quell the resultant mob.[35] He subsequently received six months' imprisonment with hard labour at the quarter sessions. There was a further riding at Cilgerran in March 1849,[36] and three ridings in April 1850 near St Dogmaels to chastise a woman who had 'behaved herself improperly'. The woman concerned was threatened with being stabbed with a pitchfork, and with being tarred

---

32 Seal, 'Tradition and Agrarian Protest in Nineteenth-Century England and Wales', p.164.
33 Evans, *Ask the Fellows Who Cut the Hay*, pp. 41–2.
34 *Welshman*, 23 April 1847.
35 *Carmarthen Journal*, 2 and 30 June 1848.
36 *Carmarthen Journal*, 23 and 30 March 1849.

and set upon the wooden horse.[37] James Rees who had ridden one of the wooden horses in the 1850 ridings was sentenced to four months' imprisonment.

Several things are particularly noteworthy about these events. The numbers at these events were large, a 'vast concourse', and the degree of violence threatened towards their intended victims and actually employed against the police when they intervened was considerable. Bricks were routinely thrown and, in the case of James James, the gaol was besieged and, 'If had not been for the presence of the Military and the police, great outrages would have been committed.' It seems also to be the case that the police, supported by the military, were determined to intervene to prevent these activities in a way that they had not been in the case of Mr Davies in 1837.

In 1852 the commander of the troops in south Wales remarked that the police still required the support of the military, since 'the common people are more ignorant and excitable than in any other part of the country . . . are very prone to take the Law into their own hands, or perhaps more properly speaking have recourse to punishments of a wild and barbarous nature such as the 'Cyffil-pren' [sic]'. After 1850, however, when the ceffyl pren was finally displaced from the town of Cardigan, Jones observed that the practice was in marked decline. In part this was a product of a concerted campaign to tame popular culture, but Jones lists other causes, leading to 'a piecemeal fragmentation of the communal consensus which had been its mainstay'.[38] Amongst these were the decline of oral tradition, an increasing emphasis on individuality and privacy, and the new forms of socialisation that accompanied the rise of the sober and respectable classes. It was also the case that, as Jones writes, 'The chapel, with its harsh disciplinarianism, assumed responsibility for many of the moral policing functions previously ascribed to the ceffyl pren tribunal.'[39]

This last point is particularly interesting insofar as it causes us to reflect that the trajectories of rough music in Wales and in England need not have been one and the same. If one accepts that the upsurge in rough music in south Wales in the 1840s may have owed much to sensibilities of suppressed national identity, and its decline to the activities of the chapel, then neither factor was present in England. With the decline of the Church courts in England by the 1830s no institution equivalent to the chapel stepped in to take its place and, broadly speaking, whilst the form of rough music was changing, I do not see any convincing evidence of its actual decline in England until closer to the end of the century.

It is also the case that rough music was actually a long time dying in Wales.[40] In

---

37 *Carmarthen Journal*, 12 and 19 April 1850.
38 Jones, 'Popular Culture, Policing, and the 'Disappearance' of the Ceffyl Pren in Cardigan, 1837–1850', p. 35.
39 Ibid., p. 35.
40 All areas of Wales seem to have had their variants of ceffyl pren – in Glamorgan, for example, the practice was sometimes referred to as 'skymmetry'. See Redwood, *The Vale of Glamorgan*, p. 274.

the 1870s the police in Cenarth were still anticipating and trying to prevent ceffyl pren processions,[41] and examples of the practice – sometimes seemingly carried out with more vigour than their English counterparts – are attested as occurring sporadically throughout Wales until at least the end of the century. At Tenby in the 1850s, unfaithful men and women were still liable to be seized and paraded tied back-to-back on a wooden horse and pelted.[42] In Wrexham, the tradition of burning straw effigies of unfaithful parties continued into the 1870s at least.[43] In Conway, the parties themselves could expect to be strapped to a ladder and carried about the town;[44] and if E. A. Williams was right, the added refinement at Amlwch upon Angelsey of first stripping the parties naked continued into the 1890s.[45] It is true to say, however, that the ceffyl pren was never again to form such an important tool in a broad movement of social protest. To that extent, as an emblem of popular culture, the ceffyl pren was indeed declining in the second half of the nineteenth century. However, the values and symbolism that informed it were not extinguished. Rather, as in England, they remained entrenched within industrial culture and so re-emerged within the later labour movement.

English Music

In the last generation or so, the role that customary festive practices played in popular agitation in England has begun to be more fully appreciated with the work of Hobsbawm, Ingram, Rude, Thompson et al. At the heart of it is the simple observation that when people organise they tend to do so by either co-opting or imitating those institutions or symbolic forms with which they are familiar. Hobsbawm and Rude observed that the poor in English villages were generally familiar with only three forms of organised activity: first, organised labour; second, religious ritual; and third, customary collective rituals or celebrations such as 'beating the bounds'. Thus, 'the ambitious forms of organised protest and demand . . . modified the traditional collective practices of the village, which had once only served to organise the annual feasts, the processions and waits, the rural ritual . . . for the purposes of social agitation'.[46] Religious ritual could be subverted for the purposes of parody, as the Westonbirt 'groaning' and those cases of mock funerals demonstrate, but perhaps

---

41 N. L.W. MS. 21727B, Adpar Police Book 187–74, 2 and 20 December 1870, cited in Jones, 'Popular Culture, Policing, and the 'Disappearance' of the Ceffyl Pren in Cardigan, 1837–1850', p. 36 fn. 49.
42 K. Spalding, *Tales and Traditions of Tenby* (Tenby: R. Mason, 1858), pp. 95–6.
43 *Byegones*, 16 April 1879.
44 *Byegones*, 15 March 1882.
45 E. A. Williams, *Hanes Mon Yn y Bedwaredd Ganrif ar Bymtheg* (Llangefni: Cymdeithas Eisteddfod Gadeiriol Mon., 1927), p. 322.
46 E. J. Hobsbawm and G. R. Rude, *Captain Swing* (London: Lawrence and Wishart, 1970), p. 18.

post-Reformation it did not grant sufficient licence or was not sufficiently owned by the crowd in order for it to take the leading role in informing protest. Festive traditions, however, generated the community of misrule within which oppositional stances could be taken – especially if they were also supplemented by the occupational solidarity displayed by men in close-knit working groups. Since the cry of the crowd was so often the cry for justice it is no surprise that, in England as in Wales, justice rituals became co-opted as a means of expressing collective disapprobation of broader social circumstances. Thus, in the seventeenth century John Williams, leading the anti-enclosure protests in the west, adopted the transgressive behaviours of rough music and designated himself 'Lady Skimmington'.

In time 'justice' was to be linked to increased future expectation, but on many occasions and for much of our period justice was instead backward looking. It was generally associated with the re-establishment of sometimes rather idealised social relationships and the maintenance of traditional economic norms. Outside of the cash economy, the interests of the crowd were bound up in the continuing exercise of customary rights of gathering, gleaning, turbage and pasturing, which provided subsistence opportunities. Within the cash economy their primary concern was with the maintenance of food supplies at prices they could afford. Both these interests were increasingly threatened during our period. The former by continuing moves to enclose land, to bring it under sole proprietorship and single usage in order to 'improve' it for the interest of capital. The latter by the expansion of unregulated and wholly commercial inter-regional markets in foodstuffs.

E. P. Thompson's contributions to the study of the response of the crowd to these challenges and to their views of the 'moral economy' were, of course, many and profound. Not least amongst his insights was the appreciation that the 'mobs' and 'riots' of the eighteenth and nineteenth centuries raised in reaction to these challenges were, for the most part, no such things:

> What is remarkable about these 'insurrections' is, first, their discipline, and second, the fact that they exhibit a pattern of behaviour for whose origin we must look back several hundred years: which becomes more, rather than less sophisticated in the eighteenth century; which repeats itself, seemingly spontaneously, in different parts of the country and after the passage of many quiet years.[47]

The crowd often behaved civilly and did so in the firm belief that their actions were measured, fair and, above all, lawful. Looking at the cash economy to begin with, Thompson notes that in times of poor harvests and consequent shortages the central action of the crowd was not 'the sack of granaries and the pilfering of grain or flour' but

---

47 Thompson, *Customs in Common*, p. 224.

the action of 'setting the price'.[48] Broadly speaking, by the middle of the nineteenth century two contrasting views had emerged as to the proper operation of markets. One, the more traditional, believed in the tight regulation of price-fixed staples and regional self-sufficiency. The other, the more modern, believed in the development of capitalistic distribution networks in which the value of a commodity would become a floating market variable. The picture was of course very much more complicated than that and subject to the usual hypocrisies – for example, plenty of producers believed that they should be allowed to sell their goods wherever they liked at whatever price they could get for them, whilst at the same time holding that producers from other regions or even other countries should not sell into their markets if that threatened to undercut them.

An important point is the fact that these two opposing viewpoints did not simply reflect the contrasting interests as between rich and poor but also contradictory views within the elites themselves as to the role of authority and the nature of society. Put simply (and necessarily crudely) during our period, those in power moved from a regulatory to a more laissez-faire economic approach – they abandoned the position that their forefathers had but recently held. The process was uneven, contested, piecemeal, contradictory and, as Thompson and others have identified, took a very long time to accomplish. Whether, given urbanisation and economic change, the move to freer markets was inevitable is not my purpose here to consider. That move, though, sometimes left behind the poor, and offended those better-placed supporters who continued to have sympathy for their plight.

What one observes, then, in many of the tumults and riots of the eighteenth and nineteenth centuries is the crowd trying to assert a position that mayors, justices of the peace, sheriffs, court-leets and the like of a generation or so before would have regarded as really rather orthodox, but which the crowd now ran the risk of being penalised for. Communities clung to the notion of the fixed just price, such that bakers, for example, should sell bread at the same price whatever the cost of flour. They believed that goods locally produced should be exposed for sale in small amounts and at the local market. Intermediaries, certainly those operating on a larger scale, should be viewed with suspicion, and in times of dearth the export of goods (by which was meant sometimes no more than the transportation of goods beyond the nearest market town) should be prohibited.

It was not always clear, either to the leaders of society or to the participants themselves, whether collective action to fix prices was lawful. The law in this area was an irregular and contested territory and there was much within it to suggest that the traditional orthodox view of price regulation was the legitimate one. There were enough magistrates and sheriffs who thought so too, which give that view practical substance

---

48 Ibid.

right into the middle of the nineteenth century. The educated could refer to the Book of Orders from 1630. Throughout the eighteenth century all could observe that the assize of bread was still being held in London and many towns, and that regulations against forestallers and regraters were still being pretty widely enforced.[49] Court-leets were still exercising their customary powers to govern markets – for example, regrating remained an offence in common law until 1844, and Thompson notes that the number of courts-leets prosecuting for such offences may actually have been increasing at the end of the eighteenth century.[50] Other mechanisms to discipline the market continued to be upheld by the courts – the right of leet juries to confiscate or destroy any improper measures used by traders was upheld by the Court of King's Bench in 1852.[51] At the same time, however, at the centre opinion had shifted decisively in favour of free trade.

Pursuing the history of food price riots (or similarly of the anti-enclosure movements) is beyond the scope of this study so it must suffice to give just a few examples, noted by others, to illustrate the point that the crowd often acted in a rational rule-based manner. Furthermore, it was often emboldened and not dismayed by the responses of those in authority, notably the magistrates. Thus, when the Warwickshire magistrate Sir Roger Newdigate learned in 1766 that Bedworth colliers were marching on the houses of those who they believed had engrossed cheese, he met them at Nuneaton and led them into the houses of the suspects. The occupiers were persuaded to sell the cheese at a fair price; Newdigate and two others paid half a guinea each (as a kind of dole?) and the colliers went home satisfied.[52] When a London magistrate came upon a crowd demolishing a baker's shop in 1795, he seized the stock and found that the loaves were indeed, as had been alleged, under weight. He ordered them to be distributed for free to the crowd.[53] When, that same year, the people of Ely forced their butchers to sell meat at fourpence per pound, they asked Mr Gardner, their local magistrate, to supervise the sales – as the mayor had done in Cambridge the week before.[54] The scrupulousness of the crowd was notable, whilst at Portsea in Hampshire the butchers and bakers who refused to sell at the customary price had their premises ransacked; those who did adhere to that price 'were paid with exactness'.[55] To ensure fair dealing at Hanborough in Oxfordshire, when a

---

49 See J. Burnett, 'The Baking Industry in the Nineteenth Century', *Business History* 5 (1963), pp. 98–9.
50 Thompson, *Customs in Common,* pp. 209–10.
51 *Willock v Windsor*, 3 Barnewall & Adolphus 43, 1852.
52 H. C. Wood, 'The Diaries of Sir Roger Newdigate, 1751–1806', *Trans. Birmingham Arch. Soc.* 78 (1962), p. 43.
53 *Gentleman's Magazine*, 65 (1795) p. 697 cited in Thompson, *Customs in Common,* p. 223.
54 Lord Hardwicke, Wimpole, 27 July 1795, PRO, HO 42/35.
55 *Gentleman's Magazine*, 65 (1795), p. 343.

crowd intercepted a wagon of flour they sold fifteen bags and gave the money to the local constable to ensure it was passed on to the owner.[56]

The tolerance often extended to such activities may have owed much to an acute awareness on the part of magistrates and the like, of how vulnerable they were in the case of popular protest, and how scant were the resources at their disposal to quell disturbance. Thompson famously remarked that, 'A thundering good riot in the next parish was more likely to oil the wheels of charity than the sight of Jack Anvil on his knees in church.'[57] With the establishment of the Volunteers in 1794 as a militia corps raised to protect the country from invasion, and the fear of sedition, Thompson believed that after 1800 the nation was in 'different historical territory', with magistrates now being able and much more willing to repress price-setting actions.

However, it seems unduly churlish to suppose that any concessions to the needs of the poor were only extracted from the better classes by the threat of force. Evidence of genuine sympathy with 'the mob' is not difficult to uncover. In 1801, for example, during price-setting actions in south-west England, 'almost every corporate authority capitulated to the crowd's demands and accepted the maximum'.[58] In Totnes, a people's committee was elected that took control of the market there and negotiated a price agreement with local farmers and millers, assisted by aldermen and three army officers who took the part of the crowd. What interests most is what happened once the military had arrived and 'restored order' in the town. Many of the magistrates would not prosecute the offenders because, as Wells puts it, they 'were as convinced of the righteousness of the "moral economy" as the intended victims'.[59] Instead of prosecution, malefactors were obliged to circulate handbills thanking farmers for their leniency in not pursuing them; even the clerk to the 'People's Committee' in Totnes was not proceeded against, on the condition that he publicly burn the price agreement in the market place. The three officers were prosecuted but subsequently acquitted at the assizes.

It was said that many of the middling sort had sided with the price fixers at Totnes in 1801; even as late as 1867 when there were again food price disturbances in the south-west and at Oxford, 'it was scarcely credible how many respectable, well-intentioned persons moved about with the crowd, actually refusing to assist the special constables and paralysing their exertions'.[60] Robert Storch remarks that price-fixing was effective in restraining the price of foodstuffs at Oxford in 1867 and that food riots were still in the armoury of collective action:

---

56 PRO, Assizes 5/116, information of Robert Prior constable 6/08/1795.
57 Thompson, *Customs in Common*, p. 246.
58 R. Wells, 'The Revolt of the South-West, 1800–1801: A Study in English Popular Protest', *Social History* 2:6 (1977), pp. 713–44 at p. 724.
59 Ibid., p. 736.
60 *Torquay Directory and South Devon Journal*, 13 November 1867.

The old ways in which the populace traditionally had thought about and acted upon the questioning of provisioning were still alive and very well in 1867. Even among large sections of the provincial middle and lower-middle classes there had been few total conversions to the religion of free trade and little equation of the law of supply and demand with the dictates of Providence. The old notion of a popularly defined 'fair' price under current market conditions was a prominent feature of the incidents discussed in this article.[61]

In a rather different sense, the notion of just price and just trade was still being expressed in 1876 when the group of smaller traders burned the effigy of William Whiteley outside his department store in Bayswater (see Chapter 5).[62]

Storch sees the Oxford food 'riots' as 'vital survivals of the symbolic judicial functions the lower classes had traditionally arrogated to themselves'.[63] To an economic historian, food riots and price-fixing may be examples of the imperfect operation of, or the imperfect understanding of, markets. Political or social historians may find them of interest as strategies of resistance to new political philosophies, or exemplars of the diverging interests of the social orders. Such activities also have a place, however, within a history of rough music, because to the people of the time they were responses to very real personal wrongs. The baker who raised the price of his loaves had offended his community as much as if he had taken up with his neighbour's wife, or beaten his own, or obstructed a common right of way. The way of dealing with such behaviour was to dip into the tradition of festive and juridical practice. Where the baker returned to conformity with community expectations then the whole affair could take on a celebratory aspect, where he did not then it was appropriate to punish his recalcitrance.

Thus an attempt to set prices in Norwich in 1740 was constructed as a traditional perambulation:

> By sound of horns they met again; and after a short Confabulation, divided into Parties, and march'd out of Town at different Gates, with a long Streamer carried before them, purposing to visit the Gentlemen and Farmers in the neighbouring Villages, in order to extort Money, Strong Ale, &c, from them. At many places, where the Generosity of People answer'd not their Expectation, 'tis said they shew'd their Resentment by treading down the Corn in the Fields...[64]

Music, as ever, played an important role in the proceedings. In 1756, in an activity similar to the later Scotch Cattle, the Shropshire colliers from Broseley assembled

---

61 Storch, 'Popular Festivity and Consumer Protest', pp. 209–34 at p. 233.
62 Rappaport, 'The Halls of Temptation', pp. 58–83.
63 Storch, 'Popular Festivity and Consumer Protest', p. 234.
64 *Ipswich Journal*, 26 July 1740.

'with horns blowing' and marched to Wenlock Market.[65] In 1766 the blowing of horns raised a 'mob' in Gloucestershire. A 'mob', however, is a somewhat pejorative term for a group who listened politely when the deputy sheriff addressed them, cried out, 'God save the King' and then marched off to set prices.[66]

The correlation between acts of protest and traditional calendric customs and recreational activity is now well established. To give two examples, food rioters in East Anglia in 1816 timed their protests to coincide with the Ely Fair, and when in the same year protesters planned to attack the mills at Kettering in Northamptonshire, they proposed to gather the crowd under the guise of staging a football match.[67] The correlation between protest and festivity was not merely chronological or opportunistic it was also psychological; protest was embedded within the assumptions of the festive community – it was traditional practice, which created what Hindle calls the 'custom of disobedience'.[68] The labourers in these incidents were once more summoned by horns and other instruments: 'The festive attitudes of the rioters were emphasised by their frequent habit of bedecking themselves with garlands, scarves, handkerchiefs, and ribbons.'[69] They extracted dole for their performances by levying food, beer or money from households and entrusted it to an appointed treasurer. When an agreement on prices was reached the festivities commenced in earnest with the accumulated funds being spent at the local pubs.[70]

If the binding power of familiar performance provided a mechanism through which the crowd was gathered, still there was room for innovation. Many (though clearly not all) demonstrations, price protests and the like remained rather localised. The flags and symbols designed to rally the crowds to particular political programmes were not nearly as prominent as they were later to become. Instead the crowds dramatised their grievances. Thus in 1812 the women of Nottingham mounted a pole with a blood-soaked loaf surrounded by black crepe, which symbolised 'bleeding famine decked in Sackecloth'.[71] The blood-soaked loaf appeared again in 1831 as the symbol of revolt during the Merthyr Riots.[72]

The prominence of women is recurrent in price disturbances. A price riot in

---

65 T. Whitmore, 11 November 1756, PRO, SP 36/136.
66 Thompson, *Customs in Common*, p. 228.
67 PRO, SP 36/50.
68 S. Hindle, 'Custom, Festival and Protest in Early Modern England: The Little Budworth Wakes, St Peter's Day, 1596', *Rural History* 6 (1995), pp. 170–71.
69 Seal, 'Tradition and Agrarian Protest in Nineteenth-Century England and Wales', pp. 146–69 at p. 157.
70 *The Star*, 25 May 1816, *Cambridge Chronicle and Journal*, 22 May 1816.
71 J. F. Sutton, *The Date-book of Nottingham* (Nottingham, 1880) p. 286. See Thompson, *Customs in Common* p. 257.
72 G. A. Williams, 'The Insurrection at Merthyr Tydfil in 1831', *Trans. Hon. Soc. of Cymmrodorion*, 2 (1965), pp. 227–8.

Stockton in 1740 was invoked by a woman equipped with a stick and a horn.[73] Southey observed in 1814 that: 'Women are more disposed to be mutinous; they stand less in fear of law, partly from ignorance, partly because they presume upon the privilege of their sex, and therefore in all public tumults they are foremost in violence and in ferocity.'[74] Storch observed that during the 1867 food riots:

> In St. Thomas two women led the crowd,; women off-loaded flour from a wagon at Exmouth; women policed the prices in Exmouth's bakers' shops after the riots and held apron loads of stones for the men to throw at Torquay; Fanny Passmore and Mary Wotten led the crowds at Barnstaple and Newton Abbott respectively.[75]

In part, the role of the woman in the management of the household may account for their alarm and activism in response to price rises. Women, though, seem to play at least as prominent a role in rough music practice as men. It was often the women who gathered first outside of the house of the wife-beater, the morally incontinent man or woman and so on. Their role in broader protest owes much to their particular role as conjurors, signifiers and instruments of shaming. As we shall see shortly, and in the next chapter, to have something humiliating done to one in the sight of a group of women was (is) particularly disturbing to the male persona. Even worse, to have something actually done to one by a group of women signified a species of powerlessness that had very little to do with the presence of mere overpowering physical force. Conversely, to publicly do something vile to a woman was likely to invoke allegations of cowardice and the like, an imputation that was particularly damaging.[76] Women were in certain respects granted more licence within public space. The law was less likely to lay hold of them, and perceived gender differences – although marginalising women in many contexts – worked to make them very powerful operators on the field of shame. Wrongs, even whilst buried within the context of broader action, were personal wrongs and the woman who protested with a bloody loaf outside a baker's shop shamed the man inside for what he was doing to her – and shamed him by what she, in response, was publicly doing to him. She also, potentially, shamed those watching, if in taking action she dared to do what others did not. Action, though, was often symbolic and thus it was not merely in form but in substance that protests duplicated festive and rough music practice. Yes, protests could and did proceed to violence, but in the first instance they were extensions of ritual activity designed to express judgement, to chastise and hopefully

---

73 Edward Goddard, 24 May 1740, PRO, SP 36/50.
74 *Letters from England* (1814) ii. p. 47, cited in Thompson, *Customs in Common*, p. 234.
75 Storch, 'Popular Festivity and Consumer Protest', pp. 209–34 at p. 221.
76 Of course, this observation is not negated by the ready tolerance of domestic violence or the 'tough' attitudes to women in the penal policies of the time.

bring the subjects of their activities back into an appropriate relationship with their communities.

This was apparent during the Swing Riots that swept across south-east England in 1830. The aims of Captain Swing were chiefly the raising of agricultural wages, the reduction in tithes and the destruction of the threshing machines that threatened the employment of rural labour. This was to be accomplished by perambulations from farm to farm to destroy machinery and by agreements (accompanied by arm-twisting if necessary) with employers. There was indeed some wanton destruction and incendiarism, but amongst the more numerous elements the aim was demonstration followed by negotiation and, hopefully, celebration. For example, at Henfield in Sussex in November 1830 the labourers paraded, met the local farmers and agreed wages: 'Refreshments were given them in a field opposite the George Inn, and they afterwards paraded the town, headed by a band of music and dispersed without the occurrence of the least unpleasant circumstance.'[77] This was but one instance in which, as Bushaway puts it, 'The new form of proto-political was channelled through the medium of older ceremonial forms.'[78] Most of the disturbances occurred during November and December, traditional times for transgressive activity, and a good portion of the 'riotous' activity focused on obtaining doles from the farmers as well as getting their agreement to wage rises.

Even the machine-smashing that occurred during the Swing Riots had its analogue in traditional practice. Farmers were required to pay for the destruction of their property, thus at East Garston, near Lambourne, a participant boldly declared that he had come to 'break the machine all to pieces and have two sovereigns – the same as he had had in other places'.[79] There was more going on, however, than simply pecuniary acquisition. Describing stang riding in Yorkshire in the 1890s, Blakeborough observed that: 'To make the proceedings quite legal, it was considered a *sine qua non* that the stangmaster must knock at the door of the man or woman they were holding up to ridicule, and ask for a pocket-piece, i.e. four pence.'[80] Through payment the victim of the stanging accepted the justice that had been visited upon them and this acknowledgement paved the way for the restoration of social relations. For the most part, the crowd during the Swing Riots simply wanted their actions ratified, their cause compensated and appropriate social relations restored. The sum demanded as compensation note was not arbitrary, neither for a stanging nor a machine breaking. The crowd did not behave as a rapacious mob. When a farmer at Kintbury in Berkshire paid £3 following the breaking of his thresher the crowd offered to return

---

77 *Sussex Advertiser*, 29 November 1830.
78 Bushaway, *By Rite, Custom, Ceremony and Community in England, 1700–1880*, p. 130.
79 Hobsbawm and Rude, *Captain Swing*, p. 140.
80 R. Blakeborough, *Wit, Character, Folk-Lore and Customs of the North Riding of Yorkshire* (London: Henry Frowd, 1898), pp. 88–9.

£1 to him – as £2 was the sum that had been decided upon for such activity.[81] Whilst there were some broader political elements active within the 'rioters' it seems that for the majority restoring appropriate social relations was a question of dealing with people that the rioters knew – real people as opposed to abstract members of a certain class.[82] In general, labourers had no interest in travelling to distant places in pursuit of some sort of general campaign, rather they visited the places and farms that were known to them, without troubling to disguise their appearance.[83] Not that their appearance was unaltered by events; we hear that some of the crowds dressed in their best clothes to travel from farm to farm – they waved flags, blew horns and sported ribbons:[84] 'The followers of Captain Swing, the heroes of local mummers plays, and the participants in parish calendar rituals were the same people. In many cases their motives and their actions were much the same.'[85]

Their actions included doing festive justice – in much the same way that in the appropriate season rough music was visited upon village miscreants. The miscreants on one particular occasion in 1830, however, were the overseers of the poor. On 5 November some 150 women and children broke into the house of Thomas Abel, the assistant overseer and governor of the poor house at Brede in Sussex. Abel was dragged out and a noose placed around his neck. He was mounted on a cart and dragged six miles to Vinehall, outside the parish. It is probably significant that it was the women and the children who pulled the cart along whilst the men marched alongside wearing ribbons in their hats, carrying staves and marching in a mock military fashion.[86] Abel was 'ritually demoted and the normally powerless members of the community performed the main task, thereby confirming his total degradation and emphasizing their triumph . . . This ritual degradation was so potent that it was only after an absence of some time he was reinstated in his situation at the workhouse.'[87] Nine other parishes followed suit during the disturbances. At Ninfield, Samuel Skinner suffered the same fate, being taken to Battle in a cart similarly drawn by women and children.[88] These examples of revenge by the poor were not unique to these disturbances: in 1837 the overseer at Illogen in Cornwall was seized 'by a not very gentle sample of the female sex; held forcibly in his own cart, and carried off in

---

81 J. L. Hammond and Barbara Hammond, *The Village Labourer*, (London: Longman, 1978), p. 195.
82 Tricolours were occasionally flown in Kent during the disturbances.
83 Bushaway, *By Rite, Custom, Ceremony and Community in England, 1700–1880*, p. 131.
84 W. H. Parry Okeden, 'The Agricultural Riots in Dorset in 1830', *Dorset Natural History and Archaeological Society* 52 (1930), pp. 90–1.
85 Bushaway, *By Rite, Custom, Ceremony and Community in England, 1700–1880*, p. 136.
86 Thomas Abel's deposition, 6 November 1830 (PRO HO 52/10, ff. 402–3).
87 Bushaway, *By Rite, Custom, Ceremony and Community in England, 1700–1880*, pp. 134–5.
88 PRO HO 52/10 f. 501.

triumph to another part of the parish'.[89] When George Catch was dismissed from the Strand Union Workhouse, 'So intensely tyrannical and cruel had been the rule of this man, that the day he resigned the keys, the whole establishment rose up in open rebellion, and with old kettles, shovels, penny trumpets, celebrated their departure from the premises.'[90]

In the aftermath of the Swing Riots, when order had been restored, the authorities were inclined to concentrate on the arson, assaults, threats and so on that had accomplished the disturbances – though it must be allowed that by the standards of the time their vengeance was not unduly severe. Accepting that there were indeed a minority who resulted to extreme measures, one must doubt that the word 'riots' occasioned by people gathered into 'mobs' is appropriate at all. One could, if one chose, characterise what happened in many villages at the end of 1830 as merely blunt negotiations between employer and employee, set against a backdrop of deep agricultural distress. Such negotiations were far from novel – indeed in pattern they were not dissimilar to those that were conducted with harvesting or shearing companies each year. I do not want to underplay the size of the crowds or the degree of implied menace that might accompany their activities, but agreement having been reached one can readily understand that the actors did not necessarily understand why their activity should be later characterised as unlawful.

At Brede, for example, even the expulsion of Mr Abel had been accomplished after a careful agreement with the local farmers – who provided refreshment to keep up the enthusiasm of the crowd. For their part, the farmers wanted the labourers to join with them in demanding a reduction of tithes and this too was accomplished by negotiation. The labourers met the vicar cordially and at the conclusion, 'Mr Hele [the vicar] came out and we [the labourers] made our obedience to him and he to us and we gave him three cheers and went and set the bells ringing and were as pleased as could be at what we had done.'[91] The labourer from whose statement the quote came had little idea that he would later find himself on trial for his participation in such events. Graham Seal observes that the willingness of the local powers to treat with the labourers can only have reinforced the sense that their activities were legitimate – and points out that the first machine breaking at Hardres in Kent seems to have been inspired by criticisms levelled against threshing machines by a local magistrate – which were wrongly interpreted as authorising their destruction.[92]

It was not only the responses of the magistrates, farmers and clerics, however,

---

89 *Cornwall Royal Gazette*, 23 August 1837, cited in Bushaway, *By Rite, Custom, Ceremony and Community in England, 1700–1880*, p. 13.
90 R. Richardson and B. Hurwitz, 'Joseph Rogers and the Reform of Workhouse Medicine', *History Workshop Journal* 43 (1997), pp. 218–225 at p. 221.
91 Seal, *Tradition and Agrarian Protest in Nineteenth-Century England and Wales*, p. 160.
92 Ibid.

that gave succour to many of the activities observable during the Swing Riots, but also the fact that those activities fitted rather well into the repertoire of calendrical rituals or festive performances. The same can be said of at least some of the so called anti-enclosure riots of the nineteenth century that in fact had much in common with parish perambulations. The whole purpose of a perambulation was to establish the boundaries and strike down anything impermissible that had been erected in despite of the common interest. In that sense the perambulation itself was an example of ritual justice. Manorial courts might order the removal of fences but the right to take direct action against encroachments had been upheld on many occasions.[93]

One difficulty, however, was that laws and cases often operated to contradictory effect. So, for example, the Black Act was sometimes employed against those who broke down enclosures irrespective of whether it had been established that the enclosure itself was indeed lawful. One does not imagine that William Territ, rector of Bainton in Yorkshire who in 1748 organised his parishioners and broke down the enclosures erected, apparently unlawfully by the lord of the manor, anticipated ending up at York Assizes.[94] Bushaway lists a number of cases of men and women who found themselves in a similar predicament despite their conviction that it was the encloser who had offended.[95] Those desiring to accomplish particular economic ends did not hesitate to pick and choose according to their interests and to employ tautologies that described men as lawless for exercising their lawful rights. Thus the Select Committee on Commons Enclosure (1844) bemoaned the existence of Lammas lands in Nottinghamshire where:

> It occasions very great disrespect to the laws of the country generally... when the day upon which the land becomes commonable arrives [usually 12th August]... the population issue out, destroy the fences, tear down the gates, and commit many other lawless acts, *which they certainly have a right to do, in respect of the right of common to which they are entitled* [my italics]... the consequence is constant violence and abuse... (the men were) all voters which is a great misfortune, and they are misled with respect to their rights, and the value of them, by parties who have recourse at the periods of election to a course of agitation.[96]

---

93 See, *Arlett v Ellis* (1827), 7 B & C 47, ER 108. Earlier cases upheld this right, *Mason v Caesar* (Hilary 27/28 Car 2), 2 Mod, ER 86 and *R v Harding* (1769), 4 Burr. 2425, ER 98 (see Thompson, *Customs in Common*, p. 118).
94 W. E. Tate, *The English Village Community and the Enclosure Movements* (London: Gollancz, 1967), p. 152.
95 See Bushaway, *By Rite, Custom, Ceremony and Community in England, 1700–1880*, p. 83. In summer 1774 a shopkeeper, a carpenter, a yeoman and four labourers were charged and acquitted of throwing down hedges at Porlock, PRO Assi. 24. 42. Similarly, in 1789 a butcher, a husbandman, four yeomen and four needle makers were tried at Worcester for pulling down fences at Feckenham, PRO. Assi. 4.22 .
96 Thompson, *Customs in Common*, p. 124.

Pursuing the history of enclosure is beyond the scope of this book, other than to observe two points particularly relevant to this study. First, that although we know that the tide of history ran in favour of enclosure and the extinguishment of commoning and sundry-associated rights, direct action and resistance were not pointless. Aside from their physical acts, what was advanced in the cause of resistance was an alternative view of rights and privileges that sometimes, as the select committee above lamented, had real legal traction. Sometimes claims of right did indeed prevail – although it seems that legal claims accompanied by threats were more effectual than mere legal claims alone.[97] Second, in resisting enclosure those opposing the extinguishment of 'rights' often employed the types of justice rituals that are the subject of my broader study.

One example of successful resistance to enclosure offered by Thompson is that of the attack by the colliers of Coleorton upon the warrens and enclosures in Charnwood Forest, Leicestershire in 1749. Much violence followed and a number of arrests, but the right of commoning for 26 towns and villages was eventually recognised. An enclosure act was not passed until 1808 but resistance prevented its implementation until 1829.[98] Enclosure of the open fields outside Leicester was first attempted in 1708 but resistance was such that it took a hundred years to complete.[99] Of enclosures in Northamptonshire, J. M. Neeson observes that mobbing surveyors, destroying records and fence breaking sometimes delayed enclosures for decades and, 'If the landlords and farmers eventually won the battle for enclosure, rural artisans and agricultural labourers may have had some say in the terms of surrender.'[100]

Sometimes, of course, commons endured long enough to be of interest to 'better' society. Commoning as an economic resource was of no interest to them, but increasingly the preservation of open space for recreation was of interest. When the lord of the manor of Loughton enclosed Waltham Forest in the 1860s, one of those labourers who protested against it died in gaol. However, the affair became of interest to the Commons Preservation Society (founded in 1865) who brought influential figures such as John Stuart Mill into a campaign to restore commons rights. Those rights had allegedly been conferred by Elizabeth I on condition that they were secured by a perambulation through the forest at midnight on 10 November each year. This

---

97 Thompson, *Customs in Common*, p. 159, notes a rare case in which tenants were able to prove their entitlements. In 1880 during disputes over Wigley Common near the New Forest, tenants met to discuss the existence of an old paper that allegedly supported their claims. A copyholder remembered an old box in his possession that turned out to contain an exemplification under the Great Seal of a decree in Chancery from 1591.
98 Thompson, *Customs in Common*, p. 105
99 C. J. Billson, 'The Open Fields of Leicester', *Trans. Leics. Arch. Soc.* 14 (1925), pp. 25–7.
100 J. M. Neeson, *Commoners: Common Rights, Enclosure and Social Change in England, 1700–1820* (Cambridge: CUP, 1993), p. 280.

had never been forgotten, and when the Corporation of London took up the affair and won back some commons rights in 1879, five thousand to six thousand people allegedly took part in the revival of the custom.

The perambulation was a very real, relevant and powerful exposition of common right in the eyes of those who invaded Otmoor Common on 6 September 1830.[101] Until an act of Parliament extinguished common rights in 1815, ten townships had held rights there. In 1830 a minor case vindicated the actions of some small farmers who had flooded the moor in order to prevent their own lands being flooded. This was wrongly misinterpreted as making the previous enclosure invalid. What followed were ten days of assaults upon the enclosures and plantations, following now familiar patterns. According to a local parson, 'The depredators increased in number greatly and came in disguise with their faces blackened, and some with partly women's cloathes [sic]; they began cutting some trees ... Whenever a tree fell, a shout of exultation was raised with a blowing of horns.'[102] The day of the St Giles Fair was 6 September and it was this day that the townships chose to try to reclaim Otmoor by perambulation of the borders. Decorum, however, was maintained and an observer did not 'believe any individuals present entertained any feeling or wish beyond assertion of what they conceived (whether correctly or erroneously) to be their prescriptive and inalienable right'.[103]

The perambulation on Otmoor was, in the minds of the participants, only an extension of processing the bounds of the parish. This capacity of ritual practices to be enlarged or redeployed is perhaps nowhere better evidenced than in Poole's study of the march to Peterloo and the trial of Samuel Bamford.[104] Poole points out that the march took place in the middle of the summer wakes season, when: 'Almost every sizeable settlement in the manufacturing districts around Manchester had its wakes or rush bearing within a few weeks of the Manchester meeting.'[105] Far from being an invading horde determined to overthrow all authority, the whole affair was allegedly constructed as an extension of a traditional occasion equipped with rush carts, flowers, music and so on: 'We went in the greatest hilarity and good humour, preceded by our band of music playing several loyal and national airs; and ... our fathers and mothers, sweethearts and children were with us.'[106] Jeremiah Garnett

---

101 For full details of the disturbances see PRO HO 52 (9) Correspondence relating to Oxfordshire.
102 B. Reaney, *The Class Struggle in Nineteenth Century Oxfordshire: The Social and Communal Background to the Otmoor Disturbances of 1830–1835* (Oxford: History Workshop Pamphlet no. 3, 1970), p. 33.
103 *Oxford University and City Herald*, 11 September 1830.
104 R. Poole, 'The March to Peterloo: Politics and Festivity in Late Georgian England', *Past and Present* 192:1 (2006), pp. 109–53.
105 Ibid., p. 123.
106 S. Bamford, *Passages in the Life of a Radical* (London: A. M. Kelly, 1967 [1844]), ii, 81.

claimed that, 'A number of women, boys, and even children were in the procession, which had from this circumstance, more the appearance of a large village party going to a merry-making than that of a body of people advancing to overthrow the government of their country.'[107]

Whilst Poole presents a convincing case that the march had important festive elements, both sides in the recriminations that followed the 'massacre' set up simple binary versions of events. For the authorities, the marchers were in military array, keeping step and intent upon intimidating all those peaceable citizens in their way. Bamford, on trial with his fellows, attempted to portray the affair as little more than a popular excursion, a light-hearted festivity in which the good-natured and simple-minded participants were wrongly assailed. However, even if we reject the version offered by the prosecutor in the subsequent trials, still it would be unduly credulous to accept Bamford's representation entirely. Festivity and popular revolt have often been connected, and latent violence and celebration were never so far apart that we can for a moment accept 'festive' as a synonym for 'harmless'. At the level of group leadership all sides politicised festivity, thus for example, Dorothy Thompson remarked of the later Chartists that they were 'using traditional forms of processions, carnivals, theatrical performances, camp meetings, sermons and services to put across the message of the six points . . . Every aspect of the religious and cultural life of the communities was brought into service.'[108]

As a subset of traditional festive practice, rough music was primarily directed against individuals or pairs of individuals. A Sudbury farmer who would not permit gleaning on his land found himself dragged to the river and dunked.[109] A Huntingdonshire pindar who impounded animals grazing on what had once been common land found his effigy carried on a pole, whitewashed and then torn apart.[110] A man who enclosed the commons at Ilmington in Warwickshire was hanged in effigy in a churchyard and then burnt.[111] And so on. The participants may have been reacting to very personal wrongs but their actions necessarily acquired political facets if performed in the context of a broader movement or protest. So the ceffyl pren came to reflect not just a particular concern to maintain the moral community in Wales but also a general

---

107 *Peterloo Massacre: Containing a Faithful Narrative of the Events which Preceded, Accompanied and Followed the Fatal Sixteenth of August, 1819* (Manchester, 1819), 60–2, cited in Poole, 'The March to Peterloo', p. 118.
108 Dorothy Thompson, *The Chartists: Popular Politics in the Industrial Revolution* (London: Pantheon, 1984), pp. 118–19.
109 E. A. Goodwyn, *Selections from Norwich Newspapers, 1760–1790* (privately printed, Ipswich, n.d.), p. 20 citing *Norwich Mercury* 1772.
110 A. J. Peacock, 'Village Radicalism in East Anglia, 1800–1850', *Rural Discontent in Nineteenth Century Britain*, ed. J. P. D. Dunbabin (London: Faber, 1974), pp. 27–61 at pp. 46–8.
111 *Notes and Queries*, 12th series, vol. 9 (16 July 1921), p. 47.

determination to resist the operation of informers and to protest about general social conditions. The assaults upon the overseers of the poor at Brede and elsewhere no doubt reflected estimations of the individual character of the targets but nevertheless they were inextricably enmeshed in the broader context of Swing disturbances.

As previously alluded to, at the beginning of the nineteenth century the popular performative culture of which rough music was but a subset was broadly distributed and certainly not confined simply to the lowest classes. Nonetheless, it is fair to say that it was most deeply entrenched and exhibited with the most affective potential within those largely removed from formal education, economic security and political power. However, the more powerful classes were content to play a role in performance culture – so long as it served their ends. Certainly, in the nineteenth century they were much involved in trying to steer performance culture in particular directions and create new variations – such as royal or patriotic ceremonial – in order to fulfil their goals. As Hannah More recognised, however, performance culture would always retain its latent potential as a resistive tool overtly or covertly political. The role that popular performance might play in social opposition was but one reason why it began to be disowned in the nineteenth century by 'better' classes eager to redefine appropriate behaviour and to remodel acceptable collective practice. Those who continued in such activities became, over time, more clearly exposed as inhabiting the lower orders of society who still needed to be subdued by their betters. To civilise the nation it was necessary that rough music, as with other 'folk' customs and popular recreations, should be denigrated and suppressed, or at the very least remodelled in much the same way that the raucous Harvest Supper was to be reinvented as the insipid Harvest Festival. Independent traditions of policing and delivering justice were not easily suppressed, however, since there were groups and communities with sufficient cohesion to resist for a long time the pressure upon them. Having sketched then, albeit briefly, something of the role that rough music could play in mobilising oppositional forces, it is time to take a look at some of those types of resistive communities from which local justice traditions were most difficult to uproot.

7

Resistive Communities

If we are looking for a model of the type of community that policed itself, administered its own punishments, was capable of acting collectively to protects its interests and, to a degree, was able to resist the intrusion of outside authority, then we could do worse than start with the profile of the type of village disposed to riot offered by Hobsbawm and Rude:[1]

> It would tend to be above average in size, to contain a higher ratio of labourers to employing farmers than the average, and a distinctly higher number of local artisans; perhaps also of such members of rural society as were economically, socially and ideologically independent of the squire, parson and large farmer: small family cultivators, shopkeepers and the like. Certainly the potentially riotous village also contained groups with a greater than average disposition to religious independence. So far as landownership is concerned, it was more likely to be 'open' or mixed than the rest. Local centres of communication such as markets or fairs were more likely to riot than others.[2]

'Riot' was more likely to be fostered in communities with a certain cognitive independence, a less pronounced propensity to deference and a capacity to survive economic retaliation. A thriving performance culture was also an important element in the mix. Given the close connection between music and collective action, it is no coincidence that resistive communities had thriving traditions of traditional music and dancing. This has been noted by Ian McCalman, who observes that the radical underworld of eighteenth-century London drew upon 'the customary recreational culture practices of fairs, festivals, holidays, elections, taverns and charivaris'.[3] Far off in Lancashire, Richard Hendrix similarly observes that popular protests were

---

1 Bearing in mind all the previous caveats about what a 'riot' actually involved.
2 Hobsbawm and Rude, *Captain Swing*, pp. 188–9.
3 I. McCalman, *Radical Underworld: Prophets, Revolutionaries and Pornographers in London, 1795–1840* (Cambridge: CUP, 1988), p. 122.

much informed by 'the rural culture which survived in fairs and carnivals of the new towns'.[4]

Whilst the picture offered by Hobsbawm and Rude seems entirely convincing, one can also add other elements in an attempt to construct the idealised insubordinate community. The Swing Riots were peculiarly rural insofar as low agricultural wages and unemployment created by the new threshing machines were the primary grievances. However, it has become more and more apparent that many of the disturbances and protests of later eighteenth- and nineteenth-century England were not driven by agricultural workers but by the activities of artisan groups and skilled collective labour. Skilled collective labour does not, in this context, include factory labour, which was denied the independence granted to the colliers, quarrymen, shipbuilders and coal-whippers, that is, the occupations that appear prominently in accounts of collective action. Such men generally inhabited manufacturing or industrial villages where, by the standards of the time, they were often moderately well paid and able to support ancillary artisan and cultural activities. Groups of such men, rather like the butchers in London, exhibited comparatively high degrees of internal cohesion; they had internal social architectures that facilitated the development of strong bonds and enabled collective mobilisation. E. P. Thompson offers one particularly enlightening example of the activities of such men during a (successful) attempt to set fair prices at Haverford West in 1795. A local magistrate reported that he had been talking to a curate when suddenly a hullabaloo arose and the curate observed:

> Doctor, here are the colliers coming... I looked up & saw a great crowd of men, women and children with oaken bludgeons coming down the street bawling out, 'One & all – one & all' the colliers later explained they had come at the request of the poor townspeople who had not had the morale to set prices on their own.[5]

Similar examples are not hard to find throughout the eighteenth and nineteenth centuries. As mentioned in Chapter 6, it was the colliers of Broseley who descended on Much Wenlock to set prices,[6] and the Bedworth colliers who marched against engrossers.[7] Unsurprisingly, it was mining groups that were most active in food riots in the Forest of Dean,[8] and Wells points out that the disturbances throughout

---

4 R. Hendrix, 'Popular Humor in the "Black Dwarf"', *Journal of British Studies* 16 (1976), pp. 108–28 at p. 119.
5 PRO, HO 42/35.
6 T. Whitmore, 11 November 1756, PRO, Sp 36/136.
7 H.C. Wood, 'The Diaries of Sir Roger Newdigate, 1751–1806', *Trans. Birm. Arch. Soc.* (1962), p. 43.
8 See, John Turner, Mayor of Gloucester, 24 June, PRO, VO l.1087.

south-west England between 1800 and 1801 were led by mining communities and artisans in towns and organised by friendly societies.[9]

The contrast between rural and urban society is easy to overstate in the early nineteenth century. Dwellers in the town were, for the most part, but a short walk from the countryside. Although colliers were readily characterised as industrial workers even at the end of the nineteenth century, they might still cultivate plots and graze a couple of cows, whilst their wives and children might take in laundry or help in the harvest. It was the plurality of cash or subsistence resources that gave such groups dwelling in open industrial villages the opportunity for a degree of independent action and cultural separateness. We can observe this within radical politics and with Poole's observation that the crowd at Peterloo was substantially composed of the inhabitants of manufacturing settlements and small townships: 'class struggle in the industrial revolution turns out on closer inspection to be quite different; its most uncompromising radicals were Cobbettite smallholders and artisans not factory workers'.[10] In this respect, not so very much had changed by the time of the disturbances of 1867 of which Robert Storch observed that agricultural labourers were, by and large, absent from the subsequent prosecutions and those who were brought to court were: 'a cross section of the industrial and craft population of a southern agricultural county: precisely the same elements most prominent in any number of similar disturbances stretching back to the late eighteenth century'.[11] To get some sense of the types of community and types of people within them most able to protest, but also most able to govern themselves and maintain traditional cultural patterns, a brief visit to two such communities, one in Oxfordshire and one in Norfolk, and the research of Raphael Samuel and Neil MacMaster will be helpful.

Headington Quarry in Oxfordshire was an open village without any large proprietors or estate.[12] Headington was not a very old settlement, it had grown up as a squatter settlement upon the waste. The squatters simply occupied, built and then fenced off cottage gardens for themselves, and as the Charity Commissioners complained in 1869, they paid no rent.[13] They also exploited, gathered and grazed upon nearby commons and in due course the villagers, as one old time resident explained, 'took it for granted it was theirs'.[14] This was not so. Two of the commons, Open Magdalen and Open Brasenose, had once been part of the royal forest of Shotover, which was allegedly deforested in 1662. Any rights of neighbouring villages over the land had supposedly been extinguished at the same time and control of the commons was

---

9 Wells, 'The Revolt of the South-West, 1800–1801', pp. 713–44 at p. 740.
10 Poole, 'The March to Peterloo', pp. 109–54 at p. 125.
11 Storch, 'Popular Festivity and Consumer Protest', pp. 209–34 at p. 224.
12 See Samuel, 'Quarry Roughs', pp. 139–263.
13 Complaint of the Church Wardens 1869: Charity Commission archives, file no. 1585.
14 Headington Quarry Transcripts, Vallis fol. a. 1.

vested in the two relevant Oxford colleges. For the most part, however, the land was left open and neglected.

Attempts at the turn of the nineteenth century to enclose other areas of land in the locality under the 1802 Headington Enclosure Act were resisted. When an Oxford banker fenced off a path that had been the traditional route for funerals, the fences were broken and the villagers managed to get the vicar of Old Headington on their side: 'The inhabitants of Quarry say that as they are to be deprived of their funeral path they will not come to Church at all, but intend to have a Methodist preacher come to them.'[15]

What emerged in the Quarry was a feisty independent community that returned a census figure of 264 in 1841, which grew to 1,437 by 1901 – although given the independent tendencies of the inhabitants these figures may well be an underestimate.[16] It was a community well aware that its prosperity was in part predicated on the assertion of rights over the commons and it was active in defending them. The first half of the century brought few immediate threats, but from the turn of mid-century onwards the Quarry had to fight off a number of assaults upon its interests. Some battles were won, some lost. For example, in the 1850s a farmer, Richard Pether, did succeed in enclosing a stretch of open common and wood over which Headington Quarry claimed rights. However, this did not entirely prevent its exploitation by the village, who staged mass trespasses, continued to take wood and to illegally graze cows.[17]

The community came under further pressure when in the 1870s Brasenose College tried to exert its rights over Open Brasenose. Local resistance induced an agreement whereby it would leave one-third of the common unenclosed. In fact, though, the college soon abandoned any attempts to prevent the villagers exercising their traditional perquisites upon the rest of the common as well. The college bursar admitted in 1883 that the college had not enforced its rights over the rest either: 'There had been a tacit acquiescence by the College in regard to the exercise of certain limited privileges or indulgences on the part of certain persons.'[18] The Open Brasenose was thereafter leased to a John Chillingsworth, who at first tried to drive off the villagers but who was reluctant to invoke the law against them because he was uncertain as to his rights. Whatever the truth of it, this was one of those occasions upon which the claims of rights advanced from the villagers were sufficiently plausible and advanced with sufficient firmness as to allow them to profit from the legal indeterminacy that resulted.

---

15 Bodl Lib., MS. Oxford Diocesan papers, c. 657, fol, 21^r, 21^v, 22^r. Letter to the bishop. Cited in Samuel, 'Quarry Roughs', p. 153.
16 Samuel, 'Quarry Roughs', p. 141.
17 See, for example, *Oxford Times*, 2 September 1871 for a mass trespass; and *Oxford Chronicle*, 17 April 1880 for an incendiary fire.
18 Samuel, 'Quarry Roughs', p. 211.

By grazing animals on the common, collecting wood from the remains of Shotover Forest, cultivating their gardens, gleaning and employing their children in blackberrying, mushrooming and other such activities, the people of the village maintained their resilience in times of economic hardship. The village had also, of course, a place within the cash economy. The men quarried, hired themselves out as builders and specialised in particular in brick-making, the women for their part tended the gardens but also took in laundry. The brick pits:

> Provided the focal point around which village life arranged itself. The maypole was danced in an abandoned pit . . . the travelling showmen set up their roundabouts in the pits-old Mother Dolloway in one generation, the Bucklands in the next. The pit outside the Six Bells (the big pit) served Quarry in some sense as its village green. It was here that the morris men danced on Whit Tuesday, that the drum and fife band assembled on club days and Hospital Sunday; and that the annual sheep roast was held in November, the furnace being built up from the bottom end of the pit . . . In early Victorian times it had been an arena for village sports.

There was, then, a relevant and vital cultural life in the Quarry but it was a very traditional cultural life. Music, for example, seems to have been very important but Quarry did not adopt the later nineteenth-century fashion for brass bands. An authentic and vibrant Morris tradition endured well into the twentieth century, long after it had begun to decay elsewhere. Likewise, the community endured. Samuel notes that it did not suffer the destitution seen in much of the late Victorian countryside, and that amongst the census for the Headington workhouse, 'there is a remarkable paucity of Quarry names'. As for the oral testimony of the older villagers, 'in all the hardships of which they speak, no mention is made of those two great standbys of the out-of-work elsewhere: the workhouse and parish relief'.[19]

Samuel observes: 'Whereas in many working-class communities there was a gravitational pull towards respectability in the later nineteenth century, in Quarry the "roughs" were able to hold their own.'[20] Holding one's own and taking care of one's own were not simply a matter of taking action to confront would-be expropriators from the landowning classes, it also meant protecting one's interests from encroachment by one's 'neighbours'. Territorial imperialism rather than class consciousness was in evidence when in the 1870s the whole parish of Headington was given a piece of land known as the 'Rec' in compensation for the loss of rights over part of the Open Magdalen. The men of Headington Quarry promptly drove the men of Old Headington off the land.

These vigorous communities were best placed to resist the encroachment of the

---

19 Samuel, 'Quarry Roughs', p. 227.
20 Samuel, 'Quarry Roughs', p. 162.

police and others, and naturally enough it was in them that retribution was most likely to be delivered without reference to official avenues of complaint. In Headington Quarry, the suspicion of outsiders was seemingly general: 'If you'd been a stranger walking through there they'd have suspected you of nosing about; when they knew you they was alright – they was the best of blokes – but you didn't have to interfere with them . . . you had to mind your own business.'[21] Strangers who didn't mind their own business were at some hazard:

> We used to get some saucy buggers come out of different places . . . when they throwed their old swank about they bloody got 'comidated – 'cos there was some handy blokes in this village at one time – there was an old horse trough up there . . . the old pub at the top here . . . this . . . bloke (he was a saucy bugger), well they got hold of him one Saturday . . . and dragged him down – do you know they bloody near drowned him – they got him and put him in that bloody horse trough and he got away, got through the village, and he soon got away back towards Oxford bloody wet through.[22]

Such occurrences were probably not uncommon in villages throughout the land. Laurie Lee, remembering his childhood in Gloucestershire, recalled a far more savage retribution visited upon a returnee from New Zealand. The man had made his fortune overseas and was foolish enough to brag of it to an audience in the village pub. Bragging turned to belittling the villagers – and who actually murdered the man as he made his way home was never discovered, for the police were unable to penetrate the villagers' wall of silence.[23]

Well into the twentieth century, 'there was no fetching the police, no messing about – they'd have you in the pit . . . or outside the Chequers'.[24] It is of course true that after the Police Act 1856 the slow spread of the county constabulary brought something of a pacification of rural areas – relative, that is, to what had gone before, but the advance of authority was not uncontested: 'They hated a copper to come through this village. They wouldn't interfere with 'im, but if he come in there trying to cause a barney, 'ee never went home right.'[25] To the list of those who didn't go home right we can certainly add some of those who visited the village at election time to campaign for the Conservative Party. Upon one occasion a Tory squire was set upon and dragged from his horse, and in 1909 the electioneering

---

21 Heading Quarry Transcripts Edney, fol. a. 1. cited in Samuel, 'Quarry Roughs', p. 148.
22 Samuel, 'Quarry Roughs', p. 148.
23 Laurie Lee, chapter 6, 'Public Death, Private Murder' in *Cider with Rosie* (London: Hogarth Press, 1959).
24 Heading Quarry Transcripts, conversation at the Mason's Arms, 21 December 1969, see Samuel, 'Quarry Roughs', p. 163.
25 Headington Quarry Transcripts, P. Philips fol. 9, see Samuel, 'Quarry Roughs', p.151

wagon was overturned in the village.[26] It seems that any form of authority could likely be challenged. Compulsory schooling was a source of resentment in many communities. In part this was because it made no allowance for the seasonal employment of children, and in part because it also failed to acknowledge local festive calendars. The application of discipline by strangers was also problematic, and when a firm disciplinarian was appointed as head at the Quarry school in 1894, his activities soon inspired the smashing of the school windows and two assaults on the headmaster himself.[27]

A not dissimilar community to Quarry was that of the village of Pockthorpe just outside Norwich, described by MacMaster as a deviant and independent working-class community that shared 'many of the features of the "open" village and the associated deviant subcultures which flourished in the interstitial and marginal zones that significantly escaped the web of normal authority and power structures'.[28] Pockthorpe was also engaged in brick making and was dependent upon the neighbouring Mousehold Heath for its raw materials. The people of Pockthorpe also grazed their animals there, trapped rabbits, picked berries and gathered turfs and wood for fuel. As with Quarry, the plurality of the resources offered by the heath, allied to the nature of the trades employed there, allowed a measure of independence:

> The occupational structure of the hamlet leant itself to a considerable degree of freedom from employer control: in stark contrast to the hundreds of deferential workers in the Colman food factory, was a reservoir of carters, drovers and general labourers employed in seasonal, occasional or one-off jobs, who owed no one allegiance. If deference was shown at all it was to the small employers, the publicans, cart-owners and brick masters, who were internal to the community and its values.[29]

The origins of the community lie in the general decline of the manors and in the neglect of the manorial lords of the dean and the chapter of Norwich Cathedral under whose jurisdiction the heath lay. Since no significant revenues were forthcoming from the heath they had little inclination to manage it. The heath was also outside the imaginative space of the Norwich magistrates, who were fully engaged in policing the city. They continued to shut the gates at dusk until the end of the eighteenth century. Under no effective authority, Pockthorpe was settled by handloom weavers in the early eighteenth century, who were unopposed. Brick making came later with

---

26 'Memories of Old Quarry', *Oxford Times*, 19 December 1909, p. 14, col. 6.
27 Samuel, 'Quarry Roughs', p. 149, citing Bodl Lib., MS. Oxford Diocesan papers, c. 657, fol, 21^r, 21^v, 22^r.
28 N. MacMaster, 'The Battle for Mousehold Heath, 1857–1884: "Popular Politics" and the Victorian Public Park', *Past and Present* 127:1 (1990), pp. 117–54 at p.124.
29 Ibid., p. 134.

the decline of the weaving industry and soon the hamlet was also serving as a conduit into Norwich for smuggled goods and poached meat.

Perhaps what is most interesting about the community is the way that, as it grew, it came to invent its own traditions. It created its own self, as it were, so successfully that it was able to secure loyalty and mobilise itself in the face of threats from outside. The inhabitants, in arrogating to themselves the authority to govern, turned to the adoption of carnivalesque cultural forms:

> One clue to Pockthorpe's long-established sense of identity can be found in the annual custom dating from the mid-eighteenth century of electing a mock mayor. In a classic inversion ritual and parody of official Norwich mayoral proceedings, the inhabitants would elect their own mayor, parade the streets in an elaborate and ludicrous retinue with its own version of the city snapdragon, and listen to bombastic speeches promising, for example, to abolish all duties on tea and sugar. Through such symbolic means the hamlet asserted its sense of apartness and independence from the city authorities: as one contemporary observed, Pockthorpe was like a 'nation apart.'[30]

In Norwich, the snapdragon is first referred to in the city records in 1408, appearing on St George's Day (23 April) to be combated by the saint. A procession, subsidised dining and other festivities were maintained by first the Guild (1385–1548) and then the Company (1548–1731) of St George. After 1731, what continued to be known as 'Guild Day' fell to be organised by the mayor, but after the passage of the Municipal Corporations Act 1835 the celebrations were much reduced and finally abandoned in 1850.

In founding the Pockthorpe Guild and adopting its own dragon and mayor in 1772, then, the community was connecting itself to a very old traditional form that had hitherto been the property of others. It was expressing a collective identity and corporate independence. The very act itself was assertive but it was perhaps not until the demise of the celebrations in Norwich itself that it became resistive. In the city, concern for order, decorum and public security had led to the event becoming prohibited (there is evidence that it was still popular), but the people of Pockthorpe were not to be subdued and carried on the tradition of processing the snapdragon, which they did right up until the First World War. Opportunism, as ever, allied itself to ritual practice, with the spectators having to pay a penny in order to avoid being snapped in the dragon's jaws. Interestingly, Pockthorpe was not alone in having its own dragon: another brick-making village, Costessey, on the outskirts of Norwich, also had its mock mayor, and its dragon or 'gyle'.

In 1844, in a kind of coup d'état, Pockthorpe established a committee that took over the heath. This was not contested by the manor, but it was contested by men

---

30 MacMaster, 'The Battle for Mousehold Heath, 1857–1884', pp. 130–1.

from neighbouring villages. The men of the rival villages were displaced and the Pockthorpe Committee established a differential regime on the heath that was favourable to its own community. A list of charges was established for taking materials but outsiders had to pay more than those from Pockthorpe. Similarly, although outsiders could take materials, they were obliged to employ Pockthorpe men to dig them out and cart them away. The result was a remarkably well-organised system of taxation, or extortion, depending upon one's viewpoint. A ranger was appointed over the heath and the poor of Pockthorpe benefited from the receipt of tickets financed by the heath revenues, which they could exchange for goods and food in local shops. A boon, then, for the inhabitants – on the other hand, however, a brick maker who was not from Pockthorpe later recalled that around 1860 he had been stopped on the heath and told to pay dues or else his cart would be destroyed.[31] In 1863 the deputy bailiff of the manor confessed that he did not interfere with affairs on the heath because he was 'too afraid of the persons'.[32]

MacMaster's portrait of Pockthorpe is of a self-governing community, capable of sophisticated approaches to the control and disposition of resources whilst at the same time territorial, aggrandising and more than willing to enforce its 'rights'. The physicality of the men involved in brick making may do much to explain how Pockthorpe was able to intimidate city and manorial officials and subdue (for a time) its neighbours.[33] But this was not an indiscriminately violent and plebeian community: it had some men of education, small-scale employers, shopkeepers and others familiar with the necessary organising principles of civic life. Pockthorpe invented its history and then, usefully, forgot the invention. The adoption of ritual traditional activity was an important tool in this process. The result was that within a generation the inhabitants were, with seeming sincerity, asserting that they had always held rights over Mousehold Heath. As MacMaster comments: 'The case provides a well-documented example of the relatively short time required to invent a tradition.'[34] Pockthorpe was probably more self-governing by the middle of the century than it had been at the beginning – and this, as MacMaster observed, was not a unique phenomenon:

> The decay of manorial courts on estates close to large towns was widespread during the nineteenth century: the repeal of the corn laws, increasing imports of cheap foodstuffs and the marginal quality of soils on commons combined to make them unprofitable.

---

31 *Eastern Weekly Press*, 18 June 1881, cited in MacMaster, 'The Battle for Mousehold Heath, 1857–1884', p. 133.
32 Norfolk and Norwich Record Office, T. C., 50., 7.
33 See, for example, R. N. Price, 'The Other Face of Respectability: Violence in the Manchester Brickmaking Trade, 1859–1870', *Past and Present* 66:1 (1975), pp. 110–32.
34 MacMaster, 'The Battle for Mousehold Heath, 1857–1884', p. 136.

The collapse of ancient manorial structures close to large centres of population led to all kinds of invasion.[35]

This begs the question as to whether the opportunity for and the inclination to resort to species of informal justice may not actually have been growing in rural areas during this time.

Pockthorpe, however, had a relatively short time to enjoy the benefits of the heath. As early as 1857 the Norwich town council discussed transforming a part of it into a people's park. This was in response to the very limited space available for supervised leisure within the city walls. The local Tories opposed the scheme and in consequence received vigorous support from Pockthorpe. The plan was long delayed but in July 1880 the Ecclesiastical Commissioners transferred ownership of the heath to the city. The council cleverly wooed the brick makers on the heath by allowing them to become legal tenants of the city upon payment of a levy of 6d per 1,000 bricks instead of the 9d that the Pockthorpe committee levied.

The plan to fence and landscape part of the heath advanced, and the economic interests of Pockthorpe were engaged. Resistance took on forms akin to traditional folk protest. There were a number of mass trespasses and trenches were dug to stop corporation-authorised brick makers from pursuing their activities. In May, eleven of the ringleaders were sent to Norwich Castle prison for a week's hard labour. On their release they were met by a huge crowd and subsumed into a well-orchestrated procession led by a brass band, flags and banners acclaiming the 'Defenders of the People's Right to Mousehold Heath'.[36] Music played an important role in binding the protest and on 6 June 1881 the people gathered to ring bells and sing into the night.[37]

MacMaster notes that supporters of Pockthorpe lost no time in wrapping themselves in the rich imaginative texture of English liberty – references in the press spoke of Kett's rebellion in 1549 and the like. A legal challenge was mounted and was defeated in Chancery in 1883. A statutory enquiry was completed by the Enclosure Commissioners and a local act in 1884 established twelve conservators to manage the transformation of the heath into a leisure space equipped with sports pitches and gardens . This was not accomplished easily, and for a long time thereafter the people of Pockthorpe continued to poach on the remaining heath: they camped, staged prizefights, gambled and tore down the signs setting out the new by-laws.[38]

In essence, though, the interests of Pockthorpe were defeated. Their case illustrates the vitality and flexibility but also the duplicity of folk traditions. To substantiate themselves the people of Pockthorpe borrowed traditional forms from others and

---

35 MacMaster, 'The Battle for Mousehold Heath, 1857–1884', p. 126.
36 *Easter Weekly Press*, 4 June 1881.
37 Norfolk and Norwich Record Office, T. C., 50., 9.
38 Norfolk and Norwich Record Office, T. C., 50., 5.

then adopted the rubric and rhetoric of traditional protest to defend rights that had become theirs only by force majeure. The weakness of Pockthorpe's position, which became apparent once the city took interest in the heath, was in no small degree a consequence of its exclusionary parochialism. Pockthorpe had no prospect of support from the other communities around the heath whom they themselves had expelled or disadvantaged, nor could they expect much sympathy from the working classes within the city who were eager for recreation:

> The hamlet's auto-defence had much in common with the kinds of traditional crowd action – enclosure and food riots – which were endemic in the eighteenth century. In this sense the dispute pointed more towards the past than the future: there is little evidence that the defensive radicalism of Pockthorpe prepared the ground for, or linked up with, the strong labour movement that emerged in Norwich at the turn of the century.[39]

For a very long time communities such as Pockthorpe exhibited not much in the way of class solidarity and often pursued local and particularist agendas at the expense of what one might call the 'fellow workers' from elsewhere. Perhaps one factor inhibiting the development of such class consciousness was the economic pluralism that sustained households. The economic interests of a brick maker in Headington or Pockthorpe might be as much secured by maintaining rights of grazing, gleaning and commoning against the claims of brick makers from nearby villages as it might be by trying to act collectively with them to demand higher wages or, in the case of the self-employed, higher prices for the bricks themselves.

For a long time the situation was much the same in respect to the workers employed within the manufacturing sectors of towns and cities. There was often little sense of solidarity with those pursuing similar occupations in other regions. Even within the cities and towns themselves, structural graduations within local labour markets inhibited the development of common labour strategies. Thus in Birmingham, for example, artisans' societies 'were strongly sectional and as such they reinforced both the separation between the skilled and the unskilled within the workforce and the divisions between the different occupational groups within the skilled sector itself'.[40] Until at least 1840 the primary site of production in Birmingham remained the small workshop. In all such enterprises disputes with masters:

> resembled rather family differences than conflicts between social classes. They exhibit more tendency to 'stand in' with their masters against the community or to back them

---

39 MacMaster, 'The Battle for Mousehold Heath, 1857–1884', p.154.
40 Clive Behagg, 'Custom, Class and Change: The Trade Societies of Birmingham', *Social History* 4:3 (1979), pp. 455–80 at p. 455.

against rivals or interlopers than to join their fellow workers in an attack upon the capitalist class. In short we have industrial society still divided vertically trade by trade, instead of horizontally between employers and wage earners.[41]

During the first half of the nineteenth century, workers who were members of trade societies were disciplined and controlled by methods that owed more than a little to the practices of the medieval guilds. The case of James Tuckfield and the Bristol shipwright dispute in 1826 serves as a useful illustration. At that time, the Bristol Shipwrights' Club was involved in a wage dispute with Scott's shipyard in the city and the men had withdrawn their labour. One of their number, however, James Tuckfield, left the club and returned to work. The club met and determined to punish him with rough music, 'he deserved to have a ride for it, whether or no'.[42] What followed was a very traditional skimmington or stanging with Tuckfield mounted on a pole and carried through the city centre and around the shipyards for between three and four hours. It was said that three or four hundred were present, cheering and abusing their victim.[43] Notably absent were the local constables, who refused to turn out; and, among the hundreds of onlookers, allegedly none could be prevailed upon to identify the ringleaders of the affair.

Aside from having soot rubbed into his face and being somewhat bruised by the pole, Tuckfield was uninjured and it is clear that the crowd did not intend it. It is notable that the route taken allowed refreshment at a number of dockyard pubs, and Gorsky remarks that the role of beer in the progression 'points to the ambivalent relationship between the shipwrights and their victim, for while the theatre of the ride was a drama of violence and hostility, the shared conviviality of the ale offered friendship and reintegration into the community'.[44]

What was staged in Bristol was not one of those most extreme forms of rough music designed to chastise someone quite beyond the pale, but one of those charivaris in which due submission and appropriate repentance could yet restore social relations. Tuckfield duly submitted, agreed to rejoin the club and supped with his 'hosts' before being abandoned, presumably the worse for wear in all senses, in a local pub. Perhaps what was most unusual about the affair was that Tuckfield subsequently broke his promise and filed an information against the ringleaders.

In addition to the cases that I have noted in previous chapters, Gorsky can add several instances in which 'blacklegs' were stanged and in some cases dunked – at

---

41 S. and B. Webb, *The History of Trade Unionism* (London: Chiswick, 1920), p. 46.
42 *Bristol Journal*, 4 November 1826 evidence of John Davis. Cited in Gorsky, 'James Tuckfield's "Ride"', pp. 319–38 at p. 324.
43 Gorsky, 'James Tuckfield's "Ride"', p. 326.
44 Ibid., pp. 327–8.

Taunton in 1725 and 1726, Tiverton in 1749[45] and Stroud in 1825.[46] Gorsky remarks of the Bristol case: 'The theatrical form, and the reference which the riding made to folk-custom contrasts sharply with the familiar images of organised labour, be they the mass platform of Radical/Chartist politics or the more violent responses to blacklegs.'[47] He is surely right about the contrast, but it is not so much that the Bristol affair was unusual as that our portrait of organised radical politics is incomplete and prone to underestimate the importance of traditional culture.

Clive Behagg's study of Birmingham's workshops reveals a world in which traditional and ritualistic elements intermixed with many forms of coercion.[48] It was a world governed by careful rules and procedure and accompanied by graduated sanctions for disregarding them. Thus the rules of the Operative Carpenters specified that men who worked at below the society rate should be 'sent to Coventry'.[49] In 1838 the Loyal Albion Society called Joseph Corbet before them for having disobeyed the society's resolutions on apprenticeship. He was unable to answer the charges against him and was expelled for 'his overbearing, unmanly conduct in setting at defiance our long established laws and practices and thereby rendering himself unworthy of the name of Albion'.[50] Amongst the file smiths, if any man worked with a man who employed a boy to do what 'is considered a man's work he is in a manner outlawed, no man will work in the same shop with him'.[51] The tinplate workers were similarly robust: 'If a workman proves unruly and not willing to be bound by the union it is very easy to make the place too hot for him; he finds his tools missing, his coat stolen, his hats mashed, remarks of a personal nature chalked on his bench.' Rough music was commonly employed, with 'tin-kettling' of individuals being common in the first half of the century,[52] and so was the now familiar burning of effigies.[53]

Much was done to defend the small employer, the small workshop and the notion of the just wage to accompany the just price. As the nineteenth century wore on, however, local vertical loyalties predicated upon customary relationships between employer and employee began to give way to broader horizontal affiliations that

---

45 W. E. Minchinton, 'The Beginnings of Trade Unionism in the Gloucestershire Woollen Industry', *Trans. Bristol and Glos. Archaeological Soc.* 70 (1951), pp. 134–5.
46 Place MSS, 27802, 53.
47 Gorsky, 'James Tuckfield's "Ride"', p. 320.
48 Behagg, 'Custom, Class and Change', pp. 455–480.
49 *Bye Laws for the Government of the Operative Carpenters and Joiners Society of Birmingham. Established 31 May 1833.*
50 *Bristol Journal*, 10, 17 and 24 March, 7 April 1838.
51 Behagg, 'Custom, Class and Change', p. 478.
52 *Birmingham Mercury*, 4 January 1851.
53 For instance, during a picket of a bone button manufactory in 1837 that was trying to drive down piece rates an effigy of the wife of the owner was burnt and thrown into his yard.

transcended limitations of place and even identified communalities of interest amongst different sections of the labour markets. This was happening even in the places that were the most insular. Fisher observes that in the first half of the nineteenth century the free miners of the Forest of Dean were 'aggressively parochial in their attitudes. The Forest was "the country" and other places in England, especially the counties beyond Gloucestershire, were "other countries". People born outside of the Forest were "foreigners".'[54] However, there was a rapid change after the mid-century and by 1871 miners in Dean were affiliating themselves to the Amalgamated Association of Miners. *The Forester* observed that:

> A very natural dislocation has taken place, and the old order of things is breaking up. Any man with eyes to see can perceive it. Not only has the 'foreign' element permeated the ranks of the employers; it has entered in amongst the workmen as well ... It is patent now that the events which are happening in our day are exciting the minds of our colliers; that direct pressure is being brought to bear upon them by workmen of other districts, who will not suffer this or any other hitherto quiet corner of the labour market to fail in contributing its quota to the general movement ... the result is that the clannish relationship in which employers and employees have been bound together is perishing – dying, in fact – before our eyes.[55]

Much was swept away in consequence, so for example, in Dean by the end of the nineteenth century, 'The master was tyrant and oppressor, not a brother free miner. In all the exchanges and quarrels of union and coalmasters there was not a single reference to the heritage and traditions of the free miners.'[56]

As a system of communication and practice, however, rough music endured and transmitted itself into a new unionised, politicised and increasingly distinct lower order. Reputation continued to be a powerful determinant of working-class behaviour and consequently shame and gender mockery remained favoured instruments by which to notice, correct or punish social deviance. This seems to have been particularly the case within collier and quarrying communities. During the Tyneside miners' strike in 1879 the Usworth women were particularly prominent in harassing blacklegs with their rough music.[57] A series of strikes until the end of the century saw similar activity.

Merfyn Jones's study of the north Wales quarrymen also reveals a very close-knit labouring community:

---

54 Fisher, *Custom, Work and Market Capitalism*, p. 104.
55 *The Forester*, 6 October 1871.
56 Fisher, *Custom, Work and Market Capitalism*, p. 104.
57 D. Douglas, 'The Durham Pitman', *Miners, Quarrymen and Saltworkers*, ed. R. Samuel (London: Routledge & Kegan Paul, 1977), pp. 207–95 at p. 276.

Central to the quarryman's cultural pursuits was the caban, the lunchtime canteen which was also the union office, debating chamber and scene of a permanent test of literary skill. The caban had strict rules of behaviour and often had a very formal structure of chairman, secretary etc. It was a unique creation of the quarryman: eisteddfod and friendly society and trade union all rolled into one ... But the caban was much more than a mere canteen, for it was also organised for educational, cultural and, at times, agitational activity.[58]

It was also a place of judgement or mediation, grievances being aired and adjudicated under the chairmanship of the presiding 'sergeant'. The conditions under which the quarrymen worked were arduous, wages were low and there was a very active tradition of trade union activity. However, Jones shows that it was not simply material advancement that the quarrymen sought but recognition of their dignity. Disputes could be engendered by slights and cultural insensitivities, behaviour was highly nuanced and driven perhaps as much by reputational considerations as economic circumstances. In 1882 a newspaper reported with outrage the case of a quarryman who had told his manager that he could not face his creditors because of his low wages, and who was told scornfully that he should 'walk towards them backwards'.[59]

The causes of some of the disputes in the quarries remind us that these were still very traditional communities. Men took holidays on days such as Ascension Thursday whether the management would allow it or not. They were still integrated into the agricultural calendar. For example, a lockout at Dinorwic in 1885 was sparked by new management rules that attempted to prevent the men absenting themselves to assist during the hay harvest. This was particularly problematic as many of the men were still farming their own lands.[60] Music continued to play an important part in communal activity – though by this time the musical tradition in Wales was in the hands of brass bands. On 15 December 1885 the management tried to reopen Dinorwic but the approach was peacefully picketed by quarrymen and their wives. This was the same day, however, that the managers of the quarry had chosen to recall the instruments of the quarry band. The band dutifully arrived to return them but as they passed the picketers they struck up a tune and, 'emboldened by the music, the crowd fell in behind and a great body of men, women and children marched into the quarry' – the consequence was that the managers were expelled.[61]

In the quarry disturbances of north Wales we can observe the full panoply of sanctions that a labouring community can apply against those who break ranks,

---

58 R. Merfyn Jones, *The North Wales Quarrymen, 1874–1922* (Cardiff: University of Wales Press 1982), p. 57.
59 *Y Genedl Gymreig*, 5 April 1882, cited in Merfyn Jones, *The North Wales Quarrymen*, p. 79.
60 Ibid., p. 151.
61 Merfyn Jones, *The North Wales Quarrymen*, p. 153.

sanctions in this case augmented and enlivened by a sense of resistance to outside domination. A case in point is that of the lockout at Penrhyn, which lasted from November 1900 to November 1903 and which was particularly embittered by the reopening of the quarry with blackleg labour in June 1901. During that time, blacklegs found themselves excluded from local pubs, shopkeepers wouldn't serve them, barbers wouldn't shave them and those who had cows couldn't find anyone who would buy their milk.[62] Cards were issued to put in house windows declaring '*Nidoesbradwryn y tŷhwn*' [there is no traitor in this house]. Blacklegs were called *cynffonnau* [flatterers] or 'tails', described as beasts and had their names and addresses published in radical newspapers.[63] Some blacklegs were expelled from their Welsh Methodist chapels and turned instead to the English-dominated Anglican churches; their children could only be taught safely in separate classes. If the strikers campaign utilised a number of modern elements there were nevertheless plenty of traditional motifs, notably in the employment of music. In general, the campaign against the strike-breakers was as much audible as physical: they were hooted, serenaded with the blowing of seashells and castigated in song.[64] The timing of these collective activities coincided, as we might by now expect, with traditional festivity and the spontaneous gathering of crowds – as illustrated by the demonstrations in Bethesda on New Year's Eve 1901.[65]

The bitterness of the dispute endured for several generations. Jones reported that some seventy years later in Bethesda there remained a place where strike-breakers had lived that was still known as 'Tell-tale Street' and the memories of whose families had been on which side were still preserved.[66] Given what was at stake, it is perhaps surprising that there was not more violence engendered by the dispute than there actually was. In fact for the most part there was a very careful discrimination between property damage and actual personal violence. Jones has an explanation:

> The reason why the commotion was always contained was because it was meant to be so. The violence of the community was a judiciously used instrument, only one of range of pressures and controls available. Hooting and shouting and making threatening noises in the night are not, in this context, examples of 'violence' but rather expressions of a traditional, extra-legal, non-violent means of internal social control. Very often violence flared when those carrying out these practices were interfered with or provoked by blacklegs or police.[67]

---

62 *Yr Eco Cymraeg*, 22 June 1901.
63 *Y Werin*, 13 June 1901.
64 *Yr Herald Cymraeg*, 4 June 1901.
65 Merfyn Jones, *The North Wales Quarrymen*, p. 240.
66 Ibid., p. 266.
67 Merfyn Jones, *The North Wales Quarrymen*, pp. 243–4.

The term extra-legal is an appropriate one, when employed in respect of some of the shaming practices observable during the course of such disputes, since the participants were aware that such activities were not formally lawful but nonetheless believed that they were not unlawful per se and that custom and long practice entitled the community to carry them out. For their part, the strikers were adamant that, as a sympathetic newspaper put it: 'The men that had returned to work had broken a law.'[68] Here, as elsewhere, opposing rhetorics employed all the cognates of 'The Law' with equal conviction as to the correctness of their interpretation of its contents.

It was said in remarks to the Standing Joint Police Committee of the time that if the strikers in Penrhyn had actually wanted to harm blacklegs they had the power to 'blow them to atoms'. John Williams remarked of the demonstrations outside their houses: 'If there were a hundred policemen the windows would have been broke just the same ... It is something else and not the police that induces people to keep the peace.'[69] To a degree, the authorities seemed to accept this; it is notable that Caernarvonshire County Council and Bethesda District Council both opposed the deployment of extra troops and police as unduly provocative, and the chief constable of Caernarfon was adamant that his police would only act against actual breaches of the law not sweep hooting crowds from the streets merely because their behaviour was annoying.[70]

It was notable, once again, that women played an important role in the strikers' campaign. They featured prominently in the processions to the houses of strike-breakers, holding aloof banners.[71] Groups of women picketed the quarry in January 1901, with stones in their aprons ready for any blackleg to appear.[72] Jaclyn J. Gier-Viskovatoff and Abigail Porter remark: 'The history of female popular protest in British mining regions points to an older tradition of protests by women that suggests a continuity of form, if not content, in women's activism.'[73] Women continued to deploy attacks on masculinity as punitive and corrective performances long into the twentieth century. At Maesteg in 1906 a miner who refused to join the union was splashed with pig slop by miner's wives, his shirt was torn off and he was painted with black lead.[74] The practice of 'white-shirting' was quite common by the 1920s:

---

68 *Yr Herald Cymraeg*, 25 June 1901.
69 Standing Joint Police Committee report, p. 37, cited in Merfyn Jones, *The North Wales Quarrymen*, p. 244.
70 Merfyn Jones, *The North Wales Quarrymen*, p. 253.
71 For example, that of 30 June 1901 reported in the *Daily News*, 2 July 1901.
72 *Yr Herald Cymraeg*, 22 January 1901, cited in Merfyn Jones, *The North Wales Quarrymen*, p. 233.
73 Gier-Viskovatoff and Porter, 'Women of the British Coalfields on Strike in 1926 and 1984', pp. 199–230 at p. 200.
74 Rosemary Jones, 'Women, the Community and Collective Action: The Ceffyl Pren Tradition', *Our Mother's Land: Chapters in Welsh Women's History, 1830–1939*, ed. Angela V. John (Cardiff: University of Wales Press, 1991), pp. 17–42 at p. 27.

> There was a man that was lodging in the village here and he went to work. And so we women got together, we decided to go to the pit to meet him coming out. And we had sticks and brooms, you know, like you had and one of our members pinned a white nightdress on a broom and we marched right to the pit and waited for him to come out. And when he came out we marched behind him bleating and whatyoucall until he came up to a house here in the avenue where he was lodging and we chanted outside and then went away to our homes, like. We heard next morning that he had gone away in the night.[75]

He might have felt that he got off more lightly than some of those actually seized by women in 1926: 'We got hold of them, and we used to give them a rough time, and I said, "Take their trousers off, they won't go to work without any trousers." So that's what we did, we used to take their trousers off, take their food off them and throw it away.'[76]

What one observes at Penrhyn and elsewhere in the early twentieth century are industrial disputes that appear, at first sight, to be very modern but on closer inspection can be seen to be fully informed by traditional justice ritual. It should not be thought, however, that such ritual survived in the context of heavy industry or mining alone. Rather, it remained embedded in what we can speak of by the end of the nineteenth century as working-class culture, and offered tools of resistance in many contexts in which the new class found itself confronting unwanted authority. A case in point is that of education. Whilst the benefits of compulsory education may be apparent today, at the time it threatened the livelihoods of working families – this was particularly so since school calendars were often set without any regard to the necessary seasonal employment of child labour, for instance at harvest time. Similarly, school authorities had little regard for celebratory customs and traditional leisure activities. As such, education imposed upon customary family rights and practices and it also, in its relentless pursuit of order and uniformity, clashed with the independent culture observable in many working-class households.

Imposing education took a great effort of will – one often characterised by the liberal use of corporal punishments within school and the fining of parents. Resistance took many forms, sometimes expressed in the behaviour of individual pupils themselves:

---

75 Angela John, 'A Miner Struggle? Women's Protests in Welsh Mining History', *Llafur* 4:1 (1984): 78, cited in Gier-Viskovatoff and Porter, 'Women of the British Coalfields on Strike in 1926 and 1984', p. 200.
76 Interview with Mrs. L. P., recorded 25 October 1974, now in the University of Wales, Swansea, Oral History Archive, South Wales Miners' Library, cited in Gier-Viskovatoff and Porter, 'Women of the British Coalfields on Strike in 1926 and 1984', pp. 212–3.

larking about was an important part of an informal, irreverent and independent street culture, which profoundly influenced the identity of children and their attitude to authority during their growth to maturity. Also the evidence from interviews suggests that during the period 1889–1939 there was a significant increase in larking about, produced by the clash between the independent traditions of working class youth and the attempts to control and discipline it made by the complex web of educational, welfare and penal institutions that developed from the late nineteenth century onwards.[77]

Sometimes resistance expressed itself in collective action; obviously confrontational were the series of school strikes, two of them nationally coordinated, which flared up intermittently in British schools from the 1880s until the Second World War. Humphries remarks: 'The characteristic features of both these major strikes – notably their nationwide scale, the widespread use of pupil pickets, street marches and demonstrations – were all derived from the practices of the emerging labour movement.'[78] This is no doubt right, but one might also add that with the corpus of customary practice there was also a tradition of pupil activism manifested, for example, by their stanging of their fellow pupils in cases of transgression of schoolboy codes and by their barring of teachers in their classrooms in order to secure a day's holiday.[79] Protest was not futile and although school strikes invariably collapsed, nevertheless, where they were based on very specific grievances that did not necessarily challenge the principle of authority itself, then at least some of their objectives might be attained. Brutal teachers, for example, were sometimes dismissed or transferred to other schools.[80]

It is doubtful that any of these strikes could have been sustained were it not for the support of parents and certainly there were many instances in which parents clashed with teachers, sometimes violently: 'Explosions of resistance were often celebrated as moral victories and assailants proclaimed as heroes by the local working class community. Street collections would be made to pay the fines and rosettes were worn by sympathizers in court or on the day of release from prison.'[81] Around 1900, when a habitually violent Bristol teacher hit a small boy his mother promptly came to the school and assaulted her. She was subsequently fined £20 for the assault but: 'All the women made a collection, and then went and fetched her out of prison with rosettes

---

77 S. Humphries, *Hooligans or Rebels? An Oral History of Working Class Childhood and Youth 1889–1939* (Oxford: Blackwell, 1981), p. 122.
78 Ibid., p. 97.
79 For the exploration of the custom of 'Barring-Out' see Christina Hole, *British Folk Customs* (London: Hutchinson, 1976), pp. 25–6. For more on the employment of rough music against tyrannical teachers see, L. F. Newman, 'Some Notes on Life in East Anglian Villages in the Early Part of the Nineteenth Century', *Folklore* 56:2 (1945), pp. 285–354.
80 For instance, after a successful strike at Fishponds. See Humphries, *Hooligans or Rebels*, p. 113.
81 Ibid., p. 87

and white hats on.' Eventually the teacher was attacked by her own pupils and put into a bin.[82]

Aside from the evidence of collective solidarity, what is of interest are the attitudes on display. Arthur Burley remembered being savagely caned by a master at Perranwell School in Cornwall c.1918 for having rescued another child from a beating:

> So we went up to the master's house. Father knocked on the door, and the master's wife come to the door, and she said, 'Hello, Mr Burley, how are you?' Well, father said, 'I haven't come to inquire about health. I've come here to see your husband.' So she went in and told him he's wanted at the door. So when he came out he said, 'Good evening, Mr Burley.' Father said, 'While I've been waiting for you to come out, I've noticed in your passage you've got a hall stand with walking sticks and umbrellas in there.' Now father said, 'I could break all thy walking sticks and umbrellas around your back, but I aren't going to. But outside your gate is the king's highway, and when you go out there – it may not be tomorrow mornin', it might not be the mornin' after, it might yet not even be this week, but one mornin' when you go out – and you get down to the village, I shall be waitin' for you with a stick.' And he said, 'I'm going to beat you with a stick right up through the village and *the women in the village'll all see me doing it.* [my italics][83]

The solitary visit of Mr Burley might seem to be far removed from the hubbub of rough music, yet on closer inspection there are interesting related elements. There is a visit to the house and the possibility of latent violence that is yet constrained. The threatened violence was not indiscriminate; Mr Burley did not threaten to punch or pound the miscreant teacher but to visit upon him the very act that he had visited upon his son, a beating with a stick. Revenge was both practical and symbolic. It was not the beating, however, that was primarily to be feared – else Mr Burley might have performed it then and there. What was most important was the fact that it was to be inflicted in public on the king's highway, the teacher was to be put on display and beaten 'right up through the village'. The consequences of this were emphasised and made particularly egregious by the fact that 'the women in the village'll all see me doing it'. In the event, the corrective therapy was never applied – the teacher fully saw the error of his ways.

As the nation advanced into the twentieth century, reputation endured as being the touchstone of working-class respectability and character, and therefore its converse – shame – still wielded a powerful sting. What we might call traditional, orthodox forms of rough music continue to survive in rural communities. However, there had been many changes in popular culture over the course of the nineteenth century.

---

82 Ibid., p. 87.
83 Interview with Arthur Burley (b.1906, Perranwell) cited in Humphries, *Hooligans or Rebels*, pp. 84–5.

Respectable elements having largely abandoned rough music, its practices had been exposed as potent and undesirable manifestations of resistance to authority. This was all the more so since some of its assumptions and practices had helped to construct – and thereafter had embedded themselves in – the politically and ideologically constructed 'working class'. As such, along with violent popular recreations and raucous, anti-hierarchical and economically deleterious festivities, rough music was better discouraged, marginalised or if possible suppressed.

There was nothing very original about that sentiment. However, as we shall see in the next chapter, many others had seen the sponsorship of popular performance culture as a method by which the mob might be directed and contained – indeed they had very few other instruments by which to accomplish that purpose. As the nineteenth century wore on, however, other instruments became available – notably in the form of the professional police. The result was a sporadic, piecemeal but nonetheless steadily advancing campaign against undesirable facets of popular culture – and it is to the implications of that campaign that I shall turn next.

8

Performance and Proscription

Patriotic Performance

Thus far I have employed several broad categorisations in my exploration of punitive performance. I have observed it as one facet of the life of rural or semi-rural communities wherein it was applied to the punishment of general moral offences and I have suggested that there were particular types of 'resistive' community in which it was most strongly entrenched. I have noted it as a tool employed to advance the very particular interests of social subgroups such as smugglers and I have also considered it as a feature of particular occupational groups, usually semi-skilled or skilled, semi-autonomous, who were endowed with a long tradition of disciplining their own. It is time, then, to take a brief look at the way that elite groups used punitive performances to advance their own interests. Those interests were often political, but a detailed political study would take me a long way from my purpose here. That purpose is simply to allude to, and to illustrate, the kinds of popular performance that elites were prepared to continue to endorse through the long nineteenth century, whilst contrasting them with the types of activity discussed in other chapters that they were increasingly willing and able to proscribe.

As mentioned in previous chapters, at the beginning of our period elite groups were themselves intimate with popular culture on many levels. The reformation of public space had not yet operated to keep the orders physically apart and, socially, gentlemen were still prepared to speak 'flash' and consort with the lower orders (to a degree) whilst patronising bull running, gambling, boxing, cock fighting and other such activities. Popular street culture was, in short, very familiar to the elites. They did not simply observe it, they also participated in it. They also knew how to employ its more punitive attributes when competing amongst themselves. William Hogarth's series of paintings and engraving *Chairing the Member* (1755) reminds us that political life at this time retained its riotous, carnivalesque character and the chairing itself obviously connects to a whole range of traditional celebratory practices.

During the course of the riotous politics of the time, heads were sometimes cracked but much of the street activity, as with rough music per se, was aimed at the symbolic excoriation and vilification of opponents. The list of political and military figures who suffered such a fate was long indeed, including Cromwell, Marlborough, Walpole, the Pretender, Admiral Byng and many others thereafter.[1] On a somewhat less illustrious level when an electoral contest was threatened for the county of Lincolnshire in 1779, the Tory Sir William Manners dined the freemen of Grantham and burnt the incumbent Whig, Lord Brownlow Bertie. The Whigs won the contest, however, and Sir William was bound over to appear at Lincolnshire assizes.[2] In 1788 Arthur Young opposed a Wool Bill that would have banned the export of wool. The bill would have harmed the producers (whom he favoured) but would have driven down the price of wool and so favoured the cloth manufacturers. The cloth manufacturers were therefore rather angry with Young and those in Bury chastised him by burning his effigy. However, an admirer of Young responded with a proposal for a counter-contest, the construction of another effigy, this time 'to be worshipped by the real patriots' in order to 'make up to you in some measure the disgrace you have undergone (as is creditably reported about town) of being burnt in effigy by the wool manufacturers'.[3] The vigorous street politics of local vested interest continued well into the nineteenth century. For example, when in 1849 the Tories in Wakefield wished to resist municipal incorporation they organised a huge Guy Fawkes bonfire, provided a band and vittles and cheered from their balconies as the crowd below fought with the police who were trying valiantly, and unsuccessfully, to suppress the festivities.[4]

In the eighteenth century, two figures stand out in respect of the sheer number and the distribution of the immolations that were staged against them. The first was Lord Bute, whose effigies were consumed throughout the kingdom in the 1760s. Bute was excoriated as far away as the American colonies, and at Exeter his image hung on the city gates for two weeks. John Brewer's portrait of Bute at this time is that of a man under siege; he reminds us that prior to the development of professional policing, and in the chaotic conditions of the Georgian city, it was difficult for even the highest to escape the attentions of a well-roused crowd.[5] The crowd, though, was not simply a reservoir of unthinking bellicosity it was also a reservoir of performative possibility. In the case of the opposition to Bute this took the form of the adoption of the symbol of the Jack Boot and the Petticoat, 'the mob's Hiero-glyphics' for Lord Bute and the

---

1 O'Gorman, 'The Paine Burnings of 1792–93', pp. 115–53 at pp. 148–9.
2 Lincolnshire Archives 2 SIB/4/37 2 SIB/4/38, Unsigned letter 28 April 1797.
3 Arthur Young, *The Autobiography of Arthur Young with Selections from His Correspondence*, ed. M. Betham-Edwards (London: Smith, Elder, & Co., 1898), p. 173, cited in Rachel Crawford, 'English Georgic and British Nationhood', *English Literary History* 65:1 (1998), pp. 123–58 at p. 123.
4 *Leeds Times*, 10 November 1849.
5 See, J. Brewer, 'The Misfortunes of Lord Bute: A Case-Study in Eighteenth-Century Political Argument and Public Opinion', *The Historical Journal* 16:1 (1973), pp. 3–43.

Princess Dowager.[6] In response to the burning of Wilkes's *North Briton no. 45* and the pillorying of Williams who had printed it, the boot and the petticoat went up in flames or hung from the gibbet.[7] As Brewer observes, there were further elaborations or inventions. In some counties they 'dressed up a figure in Scotch plaid, with a blue ribbon, to represent the favourite, and this figure seemed to lead by the nose an ass royally crowned.[8] A crowd even occupied Tower Hill in 1771 and paraded the effigies of Bute and the Princess Dowager before they were decapitated and burnt by a chimney sweep dressed up as a cleric.[9]

The second figure, who inspired perhaps even greater detestation, was Thomas Paine. In the winter of 1792 a wave of burnings swept across the country in response to his works. During that winter and the following spring some 1,000–1,200 loyalist associations were formed to counter the perceived radical threat and almost all of them contemplated burning an effigy of Paine. There was, in a sense, nothing very new about this, loyalist associations had acted in similar fashion in immolating their enemies during the Seven Years' War and the American War of Independence and had acted again in opposition to the Catholic Relief Act 1780. The scale of activity was, however, unparalleled. O'Gorman has identified at least 412 actual immolations of Paine's effigy during that winter.[10] The performative rhetoric employed was very much informed by the way in which communities themselves penalised social deviation. The burning of Paine's effigy at Dover on 17 December 1792 serves as a case in point:

> He was drawn through the town in a cart; in his hands were *The Rights of Man* and a pair of old stays. Preceding the procession were transparencies in abundance, adapted to the occasion; the clergymen who attended repeatedly directed him to reflect on the misery he was likely to bring on the inhabitants of this happy isle, had not Providence, which generally checks the projects of malicious minds, interfered; and about seven o'clock in the evening, he arrived at the place of execution, amidst the hisses of persons innumerable, when the sentence which had been passed on him was at the request of the populace read by the executioner ... It is remarkable, the first object that caught the flames was *The Rights of Man*, and the last visible remains, the Stays. The whole time the bands were playing and the populace singing 'God Save the King'. The torches, flambeaux and fireworks were more than could be expressed. The multitude then adjourned

---

6 Horace Walpole, *Memoirs of the Reign of King George the Third*, ed. Sir Denis Le Marchant, 4 vols. (London, 1845), I. 330, cited in Brewer, 'The Misfortunes of Lord Bute', p. 7.
7 Walpole, ibid., ii, 80; Walpole, Letters, V, 407–8; ibid., VI, 191; *Gentleman's Magazine* (1765), p. 96; *Parliamentary History of England from the Norman Conquest to the year 1803*, ed. William Cobbett, 36 vols, (London, 1806–20), vol. 15, cols. 1380–4.
8 Walpole, *Memoirs of the Reign of King George the Third*, I, 280.
9 Walpole, *Memoirs of the Reign of King George the Third*, IV, 307.
10 O'Gorman, 'The Paine Burnings of 1792–93', p. 144.

in procession to King Street where the malefactor's confession was read to between two and three thousand persons.[11]

By turns all the facets of judicial riding, public execution and rough music ritual were on display during these affairs: 'Tom was almost always paraded in some sort of cart, notably a rushcart (a contemporary symbol of loyalism), bedecked in symbols of royalty, particularly ribbons and garlands, oak branches and even royal arms.'[12] He was also placarded, forced to bear the instruments of his crime and carried through the streets to the sound of bells.[13] The confessional speeches that were drawn up for him recalled the last moments on the scaffold but also employed the same device adopted by the wine merchant at Tewkesbury (as discussed in Chapter 5) who wished to chastise the tax inspectorate. A notable feature of the Dover performance was the device of a lady's stays. As we have observed with skimmingtons and other forms of popular justice, the employment of female attire was one way of ridiculing those whose conduct had threatened to upend the natural social order. There were other features particularly reminiscent of rough music: in Leeds Paine was stanged on a pole; on another occasion the practice observed during the 'stag hunt' in south-west England (as discussed in Chapter 4) was reported, in which a bladder of blood was affixed to Paine's effigy so that it could be stabbed at the appropriate moment.[14]

It has to be said that elite groups were also implicated in actual violence, as opposed to symbolic, anti-radical violence at this time. This was well illustrated by the anti-Painite riots in Manchester: 'The best-documented disturbances reveal more than a faint trace of upper-class influence.'[15] For three days crowds patrolled the streets holding placards and banners bearing the words 'Church and King'. They attacked the property of known reformers whilst the magistrates simply stood by. A constable was observed to be encouraging the rioters with cries of 'Good lads, good lads', and 'persons of respectable appearance . . . went among them whenever they seemed to droop, and applauded and cheered them, sometimes with whispers, sometimes with "Church and King for ever, lads, down with the Rump".' O'Gorman acknowledges the degree of premeditation observable in many of the events of 1792:

---

11 *Kentish Gazette*, 28 December 1792, cited in O'Gorman, 'The Paine Burnings of 1792–93', p. 124.
12 Ibid., p. 125.
13 At Castle Donnington, 'A solemn bell was rung during the procession and a peal of bells after the execution', *Leicester Journal*, 9 November 1792. At Minchin Hampton 'the bells rang all day', *Berrow's Worcester Journal*, 31 January 1793, see O'Gorman, 'The Paine Burnings of 1792–93', p. 129.
14 *True Briton*, 22 January 1793.
15 Alan Booth, 'Popular Loyalism and Public Violence in the North-West of England, 1790–1800', *Social History* 8:3 (1983), pp. 295–313.

The manufacture of the effigy in all his elaborate finery, the deployment of the parades and processions, the organisation of the music, the supply of food and drink, the construction of the bonfire and the manufacture of the gibbets and gallows demanded considerable preparation . . . Although loyalist reports try to give the impression that the people were acting on their own initiative, it is difficult to take them seriously.[16]

Here, I believe, O'Gorman's interpretation is open to some challenge, as all of the above activities are well-documented in the case of non-political stangings and skimmingtons. However we wish to define them, the crowd had more resources at their disposal than O'Gorman would seem to allow.

For E. P. Thompson, of course, the notion that these activities might have been genuinely popular is unthinkable: 'These carefully fostered demonstrations of loyalty, however popular the momentary bribery and license may have made them, have an increasingly artificial air.'[17] The events of winter 1792 were intended to 'revive and inflame the technique of mob violence', violence led by the 'numerous societies of magistrates and gentry already formed in response to the popular societies'.[18] Such a strategy was bound to fail and: 'Each bonfire of the effigy to Paine served to light up, in an unintended way, the difference between the Constitution of the gentry and the Rights of the people.'[19]

Thompson's account is brief but there is much to object to in what is essentially a portrait of brutish louts dragged out of the tavern to practice thuggery at their masters' bidding. Perhaps the first point to make is that whilst loyalist associations numbered amongst their ranks – mayors, aldermen, JPs and sheriffs – there were also constables, shearers, glaziers, shoemakers and many other artisanal trades.[20] As to bribery, although food and drink were handed out at Church and King burnings, and more rarely some small sums of money, this does not in any way distinguish them from other manifestations of popular culture. Doles, as we have seen, were not unusual and 'common consumption of food and drink was a time-honoured means of defining membership of a community and, to an extent, of shared subscription to its values'.[21] In the village of Swingfield, in Kent, 'Every labourer and his wife, and every other poor woman in the parish, had a pint of beer to drink the King's health, besides a shilling piece to put in their pockets to carry home to the children.'[22] This did not suffice, however, to raise a rampaging mob.

---

16 O'Gorman, 'The Paine Burnings of 1792–93', p. 137
17 E. P. Thompson, *The Making of the English Working Class* (Harmondsworth: Penguin, 1986), p. 123.
18 Ibid., p. 122.
19 Thompson, *The Making of the English Working Class*, p. 123.
20 O'Gorman, 'The Paine Burnings of 1792–93', p. 139.
21 Ibid., p. 144.
22 O'Gorman, 'The Paine Burnings of 1792–93', pp. 140–1.

Thompson describes the 'Church and King' burnings as 'a skirmish in a political civil war',[23] during which: 'It is as if the authorities sensed some sea-change in the opinion of the masses, some subterranean alteration in mood.'[24] I prefer to see these performances as events that can be firmly located in the context of a broad and performative culture that utilised very traditional mechanisms for expressing community disapprobation. If anything is remarkable about these burnings it is how successful they were in invoking collective hostility to revolutionary sentiments whilst at the same time constraining the violence that might otherwise have erupted. Booth, for example, notes that no one was killed during the course of more than thirty such 'riots' in north-west England.[25]

Thompson was motivated by his desire to identify and define an emerging class equipped with its own rather benign but unique and resistive cultural forms. It seems to me that in doing so he underestimated the degree to which patterns of social performance were shared with the middling and even the higher orders. Perhaps he wanted to clearly set the moral economy of the crowd against the political economy of the state without weakening the argument by fully acknowledging the consensual dealing in ideas, performance and practice that passed between the two. If elite groups consciously manipulated popular performance, so did non-elite groups. Similarly, those at the top of society might be as much captured by the affective power of performance culture as were those below (as discussed in Chapter 3, Dr Porter certainly was, for example).

If few of the conflagrations that swept across England and Wales after the Paine burnings were of the same scale, opinion formers regularly added new characters to the stock of national bogeymen. Some were national enemies. Napoleon, of course, made frequent appearance, as at the Bury Festival of 1814 that was 'to conclude with a bonfire and burning of Bonaparte's effigy'.[26] In time there were others, such as Nana Sahib after the events at Cawnpore and Kruger during the Boer War. Religious opponents also continued to be vilified. In 1850, for example, Nicholas Wiseman was elevated to the new Catholic Archbishopric of Westminster and geographic diocese were organised throughout England and Wales. This scarcely signified a new papal assault upon the Protestant majority but, after a slow start, the newspapers realised the rabble-rousing opportunities that these events presented. *The Times* launched an assault upon 'The wanton interference of a band of foreign priests' and assured its readers that Englishmen would resist the return to 'Romish Bondage'.[27] A letter from Wiseman read out in churches on 28 October 1850 unwittingly stoked the flames

---

23 Thompson, *The Making of the English Working Class*, p. 123.
24 Ibid., p. 127.
25 Booth, 'Popular Loyalism and Public Violence in the North-West of England, 1790–1800', p. 296.
26 Suffolk County Archive (Bury St Edmonds Branch) EE 500/27/1, 17 June 1814.
27 D. G. Paz, 'Popular Anti-Catholicism in England, 1850–1851', *Albion* 11:4 (1979), pp. 331–59.

when it spoke of the Catholic Church 'governing' English counties. The consequence was that on bonfire night a solemn procession was held through London in which the effigy of Wiseman, accompanied by men dressed as monks, was destroyed.[28] Similar acts were repeated in many English parishes.[29] The authorities, of course, obligingly stood aside on such occasions, as they were still doing when the Kaiser took his place in the hall of villainy.[30] It might be thought that these events did little actual harm but such can hardly have been the point of view of those who found themselves, often on the basis of simple ignorance, lumped into the proceedings as supposed supporters of the offender. At Shapwick in Somerset, for example, 'The whole village was so excited – they were all out burning the Kaiser's effigy – together with that of the local conchie.'[31]

Impudent Immolations: Containing the Flames

There were, then, many patriotic performances designed to stigmatise authorised targets, which continued to be encouraged throughout the nineteenth century. However, from the first there were those who had doubts. The problem with such acts lay partly in the perceived difficulty of keeping them within proper bounds; the revelry of such occasions could easily spill over into riot. Even during the bonfire mania of 1792 there was disquiet. A Captain Crawford, for example, confessed to his superiors that he had erred in allowing his regiment, the 2nd Dragoon Guards, to burn Paine's effigy in Dorchester, Bridport, Trowbridge and Bradford on Avon. He accepted the need for 'moderation and tranquillity' but pleaded that he had been attempting to raise the morale of a regiment that had suffered much from ill-discipline.[32] Some newspaper editors of the time complained that there were too many bonfires, that decent people did not express their loyalty in such a fashion and that all the bonfires were doing was actually drawing more attention to Paine's works.[33]

The danger, of course, was that whilst sponsoring tumultuous festive activity against external enemies and exploiting its possibilities in the contest with political rivals, elite groups were continuing to nourish a system of popular protest that could slip beyond their control. The secretary of the London Corresponding Society, reacting to the Birmingham food riots of 1795, put it succinctly: 'You did not shoot us when we were rioting for Church and King... but gave us plenty of good ale and

---

28 *The Times*, 28 October 1850, 6 November 1850 and 9 November 1850.
29 *Illustrated London News*, 9 November 1850.
30 See Christina Hole, 'Winter Bonfires', *Folklore* 71:4(1960), pp. 217–27.
31 The Women's Library, ref 396/4b. Bristol Women's Party paper.
32 HO42/23 folios 231B–231C.
33 *Stamford Mercury*, 21 December 1792, *Newcastle Advertiser*, 5 January 1793, *Newcastle Chronicle*, 26 January 1793. See O'Gorman, 'The Paine Burnings of 1792–93', p. 136.

spirits to urge us on. Now we are rioting for a big Loaf we must be shot at and cut up like bacon pigs.'[34]

The Queen Caroline affair in 1820, however, affirmed that there were still elite groups willing to exploit street disorder to further their interests. The accusations of adultery levied at the Queen (for an offence of which her husband George IV was assuredly guilty) split the country. There was an upsurge of popular sympathy for the Queen, perhaps not so much because of her own virtues, as the hypocrisy of the proceedings taken in Parliament against her. Anti-Caroline magistrates and clergymen, judges, ministers and the monarch himself all suffered the crowd's retribution. The Mayor of Canterbury had his windows put out for refusing to allow a public burning of the Queen's enemies and the effigy of the magistrate at Lincoln was torched.[35] At Chatteris in Cambridgeshire, the crowd 'broke open the belfry after the vicar had refused to give them the keys, but then proceeded in charivari fashion with drums and horns to his house where they played music, groaned, and hissed until four in the morning'.[36] Anti-Caroline newspaper proprietors were targeted and many of their newspapers torched.[37] Both time and resources were applied to the sanction of the Queen's enemies, for instance to the construction of a 30ft effigy of an archbishop to be dangled from a ship's mast on the River Thames.

Much property was damaged and many were abused, attacked or stoned, but what strikes one once more is how much of the activity was constrained within the traditions of festivity and, again, how often both damage and violence were occasioned by the refusal of 'victims' to acquiesce in festive performances. This is illustrated by what Laqueur describes as the 'typical' fate of Revd Charles Jarvis at Cheltenham.[38] Jarvis refused to allow a crowd to ring his church bells to celebrate the arrival in the town of the Queen's solicitor, Thomas Denman. A crowd broke into the belfry nonetheless and punished him in response by breaking his windows. Denman himself, meanwhile, found his horses unhitched and his coach pulled through the town by a welcoming throng, who he only at length succeeded in persuading to go home. Many other clergymen who refused to participate in public displays of affection or loyalty for the Queen suffered similar reprisals and so too did magistrates who refused to

---

34 British Library Place MSS., Add. MSS. 27, 813. Letter of June 1795.
35 *Stamford News*, 24 November 1820, p. 2 cited in Thomas Laqueur, 'The Queen Caroline Affair: Politics as Art in the Reign of George IV', *The Journal of Modern History*, 54:3 (1982), pp. 417–66 at p. 425.
36 Ibid., p. 426.
37 The editor of the *Chester Courier* was burnt in effigy with 'the lying edition pinned to his chest'. After hanging for a while, the effigy was lowered into the flames as boys and girls danced around a nearby maypole, *Liverpool Mercury*, 1 December 1820.
38 Laqueur, 'The Queen Caroline Affair', p. 426.

allow illuminations upon her acquittal.[39] Punishments were visited upon the images of those who had given evidence against her, burnings of course but also further elaborations. For example, an effigy of Theodore Majocci, a principal witness against the Queen, was ground up by mill stones at Warrington,[40] at Oldham he was beheaded by a man dubbed 'John Bull'. All the traditions of festivity were employed during the course of the affair. Laqueur reports, for example, that at East Barnett a group of men turned the Queen's acquittal into a doling opportunity and extracted beer from the wealthy in the town to support a celebration – taking modest revenge upon the lord of the manor who refused to supply refreshment.

No doubt this was all very satisfactory to the political opponents of the monarch, but by the end of it all matters had become dangerously muddled. It had ceased to become clear that the mob was still being led in the cause of high political rivalry (dressed up as principle) as opposed to having been hijacked by disaffected radical groups protesting against the very institutions of the state itself.

The bonfire was the natural means of expression for a crowd who were not simply supporting Caroline but saying what could not safely be said individually and were reaching out to castigate those beyond the reach of any other form of retribution. Many places had long-established traditions of immolating local hate figures. To give but one example, Castle Cary annually burned such a miscreant. In 1768 it was Mr Justice Creed who was so honoured after having been overzealous in prosecuting the churchwardens of Carey before the Episcopal Consistorial Court at Wells – in consequence of which it was said that, 'the whole parish are against the Justice'.[41] As the authorities well recognised, then, whilst the bonfire could be a tool of patriotic celebration, it could also be a device for galvanising resistance and expressing disdain. The questions they had to ask themselves as the nineteenth century advanced were, could they continue to contain it and exploit it? And, furthermore, did they want to?

The answer in part is there in the first section of this chapter – the bonfire was contained and exploited. However, this was not achieved without a struggle – and a struggle that was probably all the more fierce in consequence of what was happening elsewhere. I shall shortly visit other aspects of popular culture but it suffices for the moment to say that many calendar customs, popular sports and traditional gatherings were under attack and disappeared during the course of the nineteenth century. It is very likely that as more and more customary activities disappeared, resistance hardened around those activities that were particularly valued. In addition, the activities that were most likely

---

39 For example, magistrates in Norwich received anonymous threats for this reason. HO 40/15, 21 November 1820, pp. 179–280.
40 *Stamford News*, 8 December 1820, pp. 2–3.
41 James Woodforde, *The Diary of a Country Parson 1758–1802 passages selected and edited by John Beresford*. Entry of 5 November 1768 and 2 January 1769, cited in Bushaway, *By Rite, Custom, Ceremony and Community in England, 1700–1880*, pp. 53–4.

to survive were those that could be defended by reference to the very values of those who might oppose them. The 5 November celebrations were a case in point, since their avowed loyal and patriotic purpose was difficult to condemn. Aside from the obvious entertainment value of the celebrations, from the point of view of mischief-makers they were particularly to be welcomed as taking place under cover of darkness. Also, the bonfire was a very flexible popular form. In fits of moral outrage it was used to vilify alleged homosexuals acquitted by the courts in Exeter in the 1780s,[42] to attack a church minister in Manchester in 1852,[43] and in 1876 to chastise police inspectors who had been overzealous in enforcing the Sunday Observance Acts.[44]

If there was a continuity of form throughout this long period there was, however, a slow draining away of upper-class patronage of such activities. The temper of public life softened from, shall we say, the 1830s onwards. Increasingly alarmed by the vigour of popular culture, elites became much more circumspect in their use of the 'mob'. If politicians continued to hate each other, steadily they had the decency to stop burning each other's effigies, and ceased challenging their opponents to duels or attempting to rouse crowd violence against them. The constituency that had always abhorred performance justice with its rites of desecration, riotous assemblies, copious drinking and associated ribaldry grew substantially throughout the second half of the nineteenth century. Steadily the engines of state power passed into 'respectable' hands. Street patriotism had been revealed as difficult to manage, and whilst its utility was to a degree still acknowledged, the licence accorded it was ever more closely circumscribed. Where no wholesome purposes (as defined by those managing society) could be discerned, then the bonfire – like the the uncharted fair, the plough bullock and the street musician – was likely to be threatened.

In defending the bonfire, however, popular culture had at its disposal not just physical but also ideological and rhetorical resources. Sustaining Guy Fawkes was its association with constitutional liberty and its connection to a series of folk-law beliefs that privileged hard-pressed classes who were grateful for their day of misrule. So, for example, it was widely supposed that on that day normal laws were in abeyance. Thus in Yorkshire and Lincolnshire laws of trespass were suspended and anyone could shoot on another's land. In Oxfordshire, boys knew that they could gather firewood from anywhere provided they could recite a 'bonfire oath'.[45] Since property owners who refused to acquiesce might be targeted for retribution, one supposes that many gave way on that day with a good or ill-feigned grace that can only have sustained the claim advanced. As mentioned, since older church festivities and customs such as

---

42 Robert Holloway, *The Phoenix of Sodom, or the Vere Street coterie* (London: J. Cook, 1813), p. 27.
43 Manchester Archives, L105/7/1.
44 *Annual Register* 1876.
45 Charlotte S. Burne, 'Guy Fawkes Day', *Folklore* 22:4 (1912), p. 417 and p. 422.

mumming, pace egging and plough bullocking were in decline during this period, so it may well be that the importance of 5 November as a day of liberty, riot and score settling may actually have increased through the nineteenth century. At any rate it was around the festivities associated with 5 November that the conflict between popular culture and Victorian respectability crystallised.

Participants in the bonfire societies, best attested in the south of England, saw themselves as the heirs to an authentic patriotic tradition that targeted such established villains as the Pope but which also upheld common rights, and the 'vast majority were of course, artisans and labourers and represented a clear cross-section of the trades of the southern market and county towns'.[46] As we shall see, such men associated the right to meet, to celebrate and to castigate with a species of constitutional liberty that those in authority were wrongly inclined to subvert. They were robust in claiming their entitlements:

> Guildford was notorious for its riots. Men known as 'guys' assembled outside the town in early morning and entered the High Street marching in military fashion and carrying bludgeons and disguised in grotesque costumes. They would build a bonfire outside Trinity Church of palings, railings and palisades, that had been broken down by the victorious rioters and taken from the houses of all to whom they owed a grudge. Sometimes even doors, carts and household appliances were seized and burnt.[47]

Such men saw no contradiction between their unlawful appropriation of the combustibles of their opponents and their enthusiastic appearance in 1863 to celebrate the Prince of Wales's wedding.

The proprietorial influence that such groups, predominantly composed of young men, exercised over their communities is well attested in Hare's study of Worthing, West Sussex and its 'Skeleton Army' and 'Bonfire Boys'. The Skeleton Army came into being in 1883 in order to oppose the activities of the Salvation Army, which had recently arrived in the town. Hare has shown that the army was substantially formed out of the local Excelsior Bonfire Club and adopted its banners, regalia and so on. As with George a Greene two centuries or more before, the Skeleton Army swore oaths to each other in local taverns, established rules and organised themselves into a military hierarchy of 'captains' and 'generals'. Their officers carried skull-headed sticks and sported large sunflowers about the town, recalling 'the taste for gaudy and grotesque adornment sometimes shown by mummers or Morris dancers'.[48]

---

46 Robert D. Storch, 'Please to Remember the Fifth of November: Conflict, Solidarity and Public Order in Southern England, 1815–1900', *Popular Culture and Custom in Nineteenth Century England*, ed. R. D. Storch (London: Croom Helm, 1982), pp. 71–96 at p. 75.
47 Burne, 'Guy Fawkes Day', pp. 415–16.
48 C. Hare, 'The Skeleton Army and the Bonfire Boys, Worthing, 1884', *Folklore* 99:2 (1988), pp. 221–31 at p. 227.

Their targets, the Salvation Army, were depreciated for their parades, and their loud denunciations of the drinking and the sometimes saucy seaside atmosphere that drew visitors to the town. They seemed, then, to pose a threat both to profitable enterprise and general plebeian culture. Initially, the Salvationists adopted a rather low profile but from 1884 they commenced a full suite of missionary and proselytising activities. This resulted in an informal oppositional alliance between middle-class entrepreneurs (notably hoteliers and other beneficiaries of the holiday trade) and working-class youths. Violence followed but the police were initially reluctant to intervene because of the support that the Skeletons enjoyed amongst some of the leading men in the district.[49] Matters came to a climax between 18 and 21 August 1884 when Salvationists were attacked and Dragoon Guards had to be summoned from Brighton to quell the disturbances. Their colonel read the Riot Act but the crowd were unimpressed:

> The concluding portion of the Colonel's speech was met with howls of derision which lasted a considerable time and terminated in the people singing 'Rule Britannia' with special emphasis on the chorus, 'Britons never, never will be slaves'. 'I don't want you to be slaves,' shouted the Colonel. 'Then speak as a gentleman ought to speak, and apologize; roared a man in the crowd, and 'apologize' was angrily exclaimed in all directions. 'Now will you go home quietly?' asked the Colonel, and from a hundred throats the response was an emphatic 'NO!'[50]

However, notwithstanding the strength of local feeling, the disturbances led to the jailing of a number of the Skeleton's ringleaders in October 1884.

The festivities on 5 November that year were rather muted owing to the absence of the Skeleton's leaders but the campaign against the Salvationists continued. Music, as ever, played an important part. Ballads mocking the Salvation Army and threatening consequences if they did not quit the town were openly sold and printed in local newspapers, and a raucous procession passed the house of the magistrate responsible for calling in the dragoons, 'an attenuated version of the behaviour associated with rough music'.[51] Skeleton activities naturally enough became focused to take place on 5 November. Bonfire night in 1885 was a lively affair:

> A large assemblage of sportive youths and men, attired in fantastic garb, took place early in the evening and, after a preliminary exhibition of fireworks, tar barrels were obtained and rolled through the streets. The police at first attempted to stop the blazing tubs,

---

49 Ibid., p. 225.
50 *The Worthing Intelligencer*, 23 August 1884, cited in Hare, 'The Skeleton Army and the Bonfire Boys, Worthing, 1884' p. 227.
51 Hare, 'The Skeleton Army and the Bonfire Boys, Worthing, 1884', p. 229.

but their action was resented, stones were freely thrown ... No further resistance was offered by the police.[52]

Yet the tide had already turned against the Bonfire Boys and the Skeleton Army. In a spirit of protest the crowd had begun to attack those who had trespassed upon other traditional privileges. Notably, the Skeleton Army had torn down fences that had been erected across a supposed right of way by a newcomer, a Mr Duke, and burned an effigy outside his front door.[53] They had also smashed up the toll house on the Norfolk Toll Bridge and, in the cause of local particularism, had descended upon Shoreham. Attacks on property were already alienating the middling supporters of the Skeleton Army. Those supporters were drawn predominantly from those who benefited from the money brought into the town by the holidaymakers intent on having a good time. The sober activities of the Salvationists had seemed to threaten that trade but now those supporters began to calculate that more damage was being done to the reputation and business of the town by the Skeletons than by the Salvationists. By 1887 local tradesmen were enrolling as special constables in order to protect the Salvationists and the magistrates had decisively set themselves against the Skeleton Army. On 5 November that year, police were brought in from other towns and were able to arrest key members of the Bonfire Boys and prevent the custom of rolling tar barrels through the streets. By 1888 the celebrations were firmly under the control of the authorities and conducted with decorum.[54]

The events in Worthing both followed on and foreshadowed what had already happened or was to happen elsewhere. In Guildford middle- and upper-class groups had repudiated the activities of their bonfire 'Guys' as early as 1864, when they had elected a mayor who was committed to ending the practice. The attempt to do so had resulted in a riot and the death of a constable. The following year, though, lancers had been brought in who had cleared the streets and some of the ringleaders had been arrested. The last attempt to hold a 'proper' bonfire at Guildford had been in 1868. In Folkestone the rowdy tradition survived that of Worthing, but only just. The practice of rolling flaming barrels down the steep and windy Tontine Street to the harbour ended in 1890. Prohibition in Folkestone was accomplished with the carrot as well as the stick. The respectable classes formed themselves into a Carnival Society, which sold tickets to an annual dinner and funded a procession and modest hospitality. Collections en route continued as before – but this time the proceeds were converted into a donation to the local hospital rather than a subsidy for the local pubs. All sections of the community derived some benefit, but after 1890 there was

---

52 *Worthing Gazette*, 13 November 1885.
53 *Worthing Gazette*, 1 November 1840.
54 Hare, 'The Skeleton Army and the Bonfire Boys, Worthing, 1884', p. 226.

no bonfire and no more effigies were paraded through the town.[55] At Exeter the more exuberant facets of the bonfire were also suppressed by the end of the nineteenth century – in part because of the danger that the tar barrels posed to the fabric of the cathedral. Still, it took the military to accomplish the deed.[56]

At Lewes, the bonfire famously continues to this day – but not in its original form. Etherington's comprehensive study essentially divides the history of the celebrations into two.[57] The period up to 1847 was one of 'anarchy' and 'disorder' that inspired fairly consistent attempts by magistrates to suppress the celebrations. Arrests of 116 men took place between 1806 and 1847. Only six were subsequently discharged by the magistrates, the rest were fined or sent on to the quarter sessions, where they received sentences of up to six months' imprisonment. However, the attempts to suppress the celebrations were undermined by two things. First, the police presence was wholly inadequate. The East Sussex Constabulary was not formed until 1840. Even then it had only fifteen constables, and only a sergeant and three constables were actually stationed in the town. Second, the festivities continued to be supported by persons of some importance. Some subscribed to pay the fines levied on the Bonfire Boys at court and to pay for the festivities themselves. Etherington identifies one of the supporters as the town's high constable, Benjamin Flint, a local grocer and Tory who refused to call the police into the town in 1846. Others refused to serve as special constables when called upon to do so. In 1847 some 170 inhabitants were summonsed to serve, but 108 were reluctant and sent a memorial, delivered by two merchants, a chemist and a butcher to the Earl of Chichester opposing the magistrates' actions, 'as it would materially affect feelings and private interests'.[58]

Nevertheless, the assistance of eighty men from London ensured that a concerted attempt was made in 1847 to suppress the festivities. Eight men subsequently appeared before Lord Denman in March 1848, two being awarded six months of hard labour and the rest one month. Surveying the ages of 114 Bonfire Boys arrested up until 1847 Etherington found that over 80 per cent of those arrested were under thirty-one and only one of them was not resident in Lewes or the immediate neighbourhood. There were some exotic occupations listed – one was an attorney – but most of the defendants were either agricultural labourers or skilled workers such as tailors, butchers, bakers or shoemakers. A young close-knit group, then, not so different from the allies of George a Greene.

After 1847 respectable elements in the town proposed an alternative diversion – a

---

55 Burne, 'Guy Fawkes Day', pp. 412–13.
56 Burne, 'Guy Fawkes Day', p. 416.
57 J. E. Etherington, 'The Sociology of a Recurrent Ceremonial Drama: Lewes Guy Fawkes Night 1800–1913', unpublished PhD thesis, The Open University, 1988.
58 Ibid., p. 171.

band with free food and beer was provided in Wallands Park by the generosity of local dignitaries keen to keep festivities out of the town itself. By 1850, however, the celebrations had returned to the streets. However, this was not a victory per se for the Bonfire Boys but a victory for both bigotry and conciliation. It was the anti-Catholic demonstrations of 1850 (referred to earlier in this chapter) that encouraged the town's authorities to allow a mock representative of Cardinal Wiseman to deliver an oration in the town square as a precursor to a papal burning. The anti-Catholic element (for which the event is now notorious) was actually something of an innovation, it had not been nearly so prominent before, and the three years after 1850 led to the development of what Etherington calls 'an emerging traditional form'. There was in effect a tacit agreement that the police and magistrates would not interfere with proceedings so long as the Bonfire Boys kept both the subject of their celebrations and the manner of them within newly defined limits:

> The bonfire boys evolved an increasingly formalised celebration. Adapting to changed circumstances, symbolic embellishments were added while activities previously included were abbreviated or omitted. Street fires and squibbing continued, but rioting and confrontation ceased. Tar barrels and disguise were retained, but they became an integral part of the processions and instead of physically assaulting their opponents they burnt their representations in effigy. Anti-Catholicism, previously hinted at, now became a central object of the celebrations.[59]

This period also saw the emergence of permanent voluntary associations of Bonfire Boys, the Lewis Borough and Cliffe societies being formed in 1853 in place of the informal alliances previously observed. What one sees after 1850, then, is an independent popular tradition made subservient to the national patriotic programme. This meant burning effigies of Fawkes and the Pope but the tradition of also burning effigies of other national enemies such as the emperors of Austria and Russia who were destroyed in 1855. It also meant from 1863 (when celebrations were organised by the bonfire societies for the marriage of the Prince of Wales) regular affirmations of loyalty. So Queen Victoria's Silver and Diamond Jubilees were celebrated, the coronation of Edward VII and so on. Similarly, the speeches made by the 'bishop' on 5 November took on a conservative hue – for example denouncing socialists during the miners' strike of 1893 to 1894. Above all, topics of popular local controversy were avoided. The secretary of the bonfire society declared in 1893 that, 'the committee desired it to be known that they would not countenance anything that had a local bearing'.[60] Much had by then been forgotten. The case of Lewes stands not as an example of the power and longevity of customary practice but of the way that

---

59 Etherington, 'The Sociology of a Recurrent Ceremonial Drama', pp. 241–2.
60 Etherington, 'The Sociology of a Recurrent Ceremonial Drama', p. 311.

ownership of form might be allowed to remain vested in the populace so long as it could be divested of subversive content.

Reforming Popular Culture

The interest of the authorities in controlling large groups of young men equipped with blazing barrels in built-up areas at night is not hard to understand. The steps taken to proscribe or control bonfire culture were, however, but a subset of the general increasing disapprobation of unlicensed activity in public space manifest throughout the nineteenth century. As we have seen, there had always been those opposed to plough bullocks, to rough music, mumming, lent crocking and any forms of popular justice, but the pace of persecution notably increased during the course of the century. The habits of disobedience that festive practice taught were no longer to be tolerated, especially since the tumults and political controversies of the time so clearly demonstrated the potential of festive practices to operate as the seedbeds of disorder. All gatherings of the common populace outside the context of national ceremonial or patriotic endeavour began, to some, to be deeply suspect.

Many communities were either stripped of their traditional festivities and pastimes or were forced to remodel them in ways that did not threaten the new Victorian order. In some places those practices were already so decayed that they could be displaced by simple proscription. In others the proscription had to be accompanied by considerable force. Malcomson's study of the bull running at Stamford serves as a comprehensive study of the eventual success enjoyed by central authority, assisted by professional policing, in suppressing an activity that clearly enjoyed the support of a considerable portion of the town's population.[61]

The list of what was lost in terms of popular recreations and customary practices in the nineteenth century is long indeed. For example, 1847 saw the suppression of the Shrove tide football at Derby, 1852 the last Cotswold Games, 1857 the last scouring of the white horse at Uffington, 1858 the last election of the May Queen at Kirtlington, 1863 the last garland procession on Oxmoor – unfortunately one could go on and on. Innumerable fairs disappeared during this period. Somerset, for example, had some 180 fairs in 1729 and this number actually increased to around 300 by the end of the century but almost all were lost during the nineteenth century, leaving only 34 by the 1930s.[62]

In some places, practices could not be terminated by a single act of outright proscription but fell victim to the case-by-case application of law. Whether it was that magistrates were increasingly willing to hear complaints, or that complaints

---

61 R. W. Malcolmson, *Popular Recreations in English Society, 1700–1850* (Cambridge: CUP, 1973).
62 D. K. Cameron, *The English Fair* (Stroud: Sutton, 1998), p. 214.

were increasingly made, as the nineteenth century advanced one reads of more and more defendants being brought to court for offences perpetrated during the course of traditional practice. So for example, during the second half of the nineteenth century there were a number of successful prosecutions of lent crockers in Somerset and Dorset who had (allegedly) caused criminal damage by the throwing of their shards.[63] As with many similar practices the tradition was a long time dying but by the end of the nineteenth century, in Somerset at least, it seems to have been extinct.

In yet other instances, substitution was employed, groups being cajoled or bribed to adopt new, less-threatening practices that would indeed, in time, come to be regarded as authentic and antique. Harvest homes are a case in point:

> The harvest home is no more. We have instead harvest festivals, tea and cake at sixpence a head in the schoolroom, and a choral service and a sermon in the church . . . There are no more shearing feasts; what remain are shorn of all their festive character. Instead, we have cottage garden produce shows. The old village 'revels' linger on in the most emaciated and expiring semblance of the old feast. The old ballad-seller no longer appears in the fair.[64]

By the final three decades of the nineteenth century, harvest homes had been almost entirely replaced by the altogether more sedate harvest festival, which seems to have been invented in the West Country in the 1840s.[65] With their disappearance went booting and some of the authority of the harvest lord. Bushaway points out that the attack on popular customs arose not simply from a desire to suppress them per se but from a desire to remake social relations from 'a positive attempt to construct or recreate an image of rural society in which relations between the classes took the comforting form of deference and paternalism rather than the "new" forms of antagonism and conflict'.[66]

It would be too simplistic to say that whilst those on the bottom clung tenaciously to their traditions, all those on the top were determined to extinguish them. In Wales, for example, the impulses towards suppression came substantially from the chapel and from reformed 'working class' opinion itself. Conversely, socially powerful actors sometimes intervened to protect popular activities. Cameron gives the delightful example of the Camberwell Fair under threat from middling elements and

---

63 See, for example, the prosecution at Crewkerne in 1858 reported in W. G. Willis Watson (ed.) *Calendar of Customs, Superstitions, Weather-Lore, Popular Sayings, and Important Events Connected with the County of Somerset* (Somerset: n.p., 1920), pp. 64–5. The practice is reported by Watson as having been in abeyance since about the end of the previous century, p. 56. See also J. S. Udal, *Dorsetshire Folklore* (Hertford: Stephen Austin and Sons, 1922), pp. 24–5.
64 S. Baring-Gould, *Old County Life* (London, Methuen and Co., 1890), p. 280.
65 Bushaway, *By Rite, Custom, Ceremony and Community in England, 1700–1880*, p. 175.
66 Bushaway, *By Rite, Custom, Ceremony and Community in England, 1700–1880*, p. 159.

magistrates in 1806. The threat was effectively scotched by a philanthropic but clever counter-threat from the sympathetic lord of the manor. If the fair was abolished he would instead turn the area into cottages for the labouring poor. The interest of middling groups in ridding the neighbourhood of the three days of the fair seems to have dissipated at that point![67] Nevertheless, in 1856 the fair disappeared after the area was bought by subscription by a committee established to abolish it. The Camberwell case illustrates the point that traditional fairs and other activities continually had to resist attempts upon them, whereas the abolitionists had only to prevail once to achieve their purpose for all time. A new order of society was coming into being, one in which it was said that: 'Happiness does not consist in booths and garlands, drums and horns, or in capering about a Maypole. Happiness is a fireside thing, it is a thing of grave and earnest tone, and the deeper and truer it is, the more it is removed from the riot of mere merriment.'[68]

The practice of rough music naturally became one of the particular targets of reformers. So, for example, the vestry of Upton St Leonards in Gloucestershire passed a resolution in 1858 that: 'The practice of assembling with a rough band to the annoyance of individuals and disturbance of the public is an evil which ought no longer to be suffered. This meeting therefore pledges to use its utmost power to discourage and put an end to this practice.'[69] According to Robert Storch: 'The custom of stang riding was particularly distasteful to Victorian respectables. It was first of all an open public affair always accompanied by disorder: marching, chanting and shouting.'[70]

Against such activity a number of legal remedies were theoretically available. Obviously, if the victim had actually been seized, a battery had occurred and if injury had resulted a relevant offence under the Offences against the Person Act 1861 or its precursors might be charged. There were sundry other criminal offences that might occur during the course of an incident of rough music, such as criminal damage. A counterclaim from Canterbury that continued customary practice and made skimmingtons a lawful method of disgracing a cuckolded husband was dismissed in 1876,[71] and some old cases suggested that a civil action might be brought against the perpetrators by the victim. In *Mason v Jennings* in 1680,[72] a hackney cab-driver, who had allegedly allowed himself to be beaten by his wife, had brought an action against the man who had orchestrated a skimmington against him. The man was seeking damages in compensation for the fact that, the allegation against him now being

---

67 Cameron, *The English Fair*, pp. 215–16.
68 Howitt, *The Rural Life of England*, p. 420.
69 Burne, 'Parish Gleanings from Upton St Leonard's, Glos.', pp. 236–9.
70 R. D. Storch, 'The Policeman as Domestic Missionary: Urban Discipline and Popular Culture in Northern England, 1850–1880', *Journal of Social History* 9:4 (1976), pp. 481–509 at p. 489.
71 *R v Roberts* (1876) 2 Keb 578.
72 Mich. 32 Car. 2. 1680 B.R.

common currency, none of his former customers would use his services. The plaintiff succeeded but was not, however, awarded the damages he sought.

Although statute did not deal specifically with rough music per se, as the nineteenth century advanced there was a whole raft of legislation that could be employed against performers, clustered around the contention that the activity either constituted an illegal obstruction or else occasioned a breach of the peace. Several useful offences were found within the Highways Act 1835. There was an offence of 'wilfully obstructing the free passage of the footway, by causing a crowd to assemble',[73] one could also be summonsed for playing games on the highway 'to the annoyance of inhabitants',[74] and those driving floats, carriages or rush carts could be charged with hindering the free passage of other vehicles.[75] It was an offence to use abusive or merely insulting words or behaviour that were either intended to provoke a breach of the peace, or that simply had occasioned one.[76] There was also a more general offence of using obscene language in a public place.[77] Some of the offences were rather vague, such being 'a loose, idle and disorderly person found disturbing the public peace',[78] others were more specific such as discharging fireworks in the street.[79] If these were rather minor offences there was no shortage of them and Alfred Williams complained in 1918 that:

> The villagers blame the police regulations for the extinction of the old festivities, by prohibiting all concourse in the streets and open spaces, and driving the feasters and revellers into far-off fields and obscure corners, they brought about the death of the old fairs and amusements. In many cases the village clergy took a leading part in smashing up the old games, without increasing their congregations, however; it is common knowledge that the churches in country places are barer and emptier than before.[80]

As above, the key to the proscription of music lay in the operation of the new police. Robert Storch asserts that the new police were very active in this respect and believes that for them it was a reputational issue. They were inclined to ignore activities that, although unlawful, were nonetheless quiet and invisible but:

---

73 Highway Act, 1835 s.72, (5 and 6 Wm. IV, Ch. 50.)
74 Ibid.
75 Ibid., s. 78.
76 Met. Police Act, 1839 s.54 (13).
77 For example, Met. Police Act, 1839 s. 54 (12) (2 & 3 Vic., Ch. 47) and Towns Police Cl. Act, 1847 s. 28 (10 & 11 Vic., Ch. 47).
78 Borough Police Municipal Corp. Act 1882, s. 193 (45 & 46 Vic., Ch. 50).
79 Towns Police Cl. Act 1847 s. 28 (10 and 11 Vic., Ch. 89), Explosives Act, 1875, s. 80. (38 and 39 Vic., Ch. 17).
80 Alfred Williams, *Villages of the White Horse* (London: Duckworth, 1918), p. 214, cited in Bushaway, *By Rite, Custom, Ceremony and Community in England, 1700–1880*, p. 160.

> It was quite otherwise in the case of football through the town, stang-riding, Guy Fawkes celebrations, or other highly visible lower class fetes. Either the police acted to suppress them or they faced severe loss of face and were open to the charge that they were failing in one of their primary missions, the preservation of municipal order and decorum ... The police proved to be a weapon well attuned to the task of terminating the popular fete with all its connotations of disorder, drunkenness, sexual license and property damage.[81]

He notes the particular use of the charge of 'breach of the peace' to suppress such activity in the West Riding of Yorkshire,[82] and the anxiety that the ceffyl pren excited amongst the Cardiganshire magistrates: 'Because stang-riding and similar customs represented survivals of old forms of popular justice or self-policing or else were used as vehicles for social protest, because they symbolically short-circuited all modern agencies and bureaucracies of established authority, the police and magistrates were ruthless in their attempts to put them down.'[83]

This may perhaps be true of areas of the West Riding, but as a statement of the general state of affairs in England and Wales it is rather problematic – not least because the preceding chapters have been full of examples, many of them from the later nineteenth century, in which skimmingtons and stangings seem to have been performed without any form of interference from authority! The picture seems to have been a great deal more mixed and the resolve of police and magistrates a great deal less firm than is suggested by Storch. True, there were many occasions in which the police and the magistrates did indeed interfere. It was claimed in 1860 that charivaris against wife-beaters had been common in Surrey and Sussex, but that an occasion upon which a gentleman was severely injured by a fall from his frightened horse induced the magistrates to intervene and the police 'silenced for ever the rough music'.[84] Two skimmingtons were alleged to have happened in Yorkshire in July 1863, the first being unmolested, the second leading to the prosecution of a number of the participants for obstructing the highway.[85] In 1882 the prosecution of the members of a 'stag hunt' at Hatherleigh in Somerset was predicated upon the earlier decision in *Papping v Maynard*[86] that the hunt was a game within the meaning of the Highways Act.[87] The skimmington staged against a wife-beater in Welburn in 1883 was similarly declared an illegal obstruction of the highway.[88]

---

81 Storch, 'The Policeman as Domestic Missionary', p. 489.
82 See *Leeds Mercury*, 28 May 1857 for one such occasion at Oxspring, Barnsley.
83 Storch, 'The Policeman as Domestic Missionary', p. 490.
84 *Notes and Queries*, 2nd series, vol. 10 (15 December 1860), p. 476, letter from Mr A. A.
85 *Notes and Queries*, 3rd series, vol. 4 (11 July 1863), p. 37.
86 *Papping v. Maynard*, 27 J.P. 745.
87 *Somerset County Gazette*, 8 July 1882.
88 Reported by Isaac Taylor, *Folklore* 1 (1883), pp. 298–9.

On the other hand, magistrates sometimes displayed a degree of tolerance that hardly justifies a picture of ruthless suppression. Indeed the suggestion is rather that they were sometimes in sympathy with the participants. At Welburn, for example, when the leaders of the skimmington were summonsed a petition was drawn up and signed by most of the most influential villagers denying that any obstruction had been caused and arguing that the old and worthy custom deterred men from beating their wives. The magistrates, whilst declaring that the activity was illegal, let the men off all fines and costs.[89] There were gentlemen who were still prepared to argue that rough music had a social utility. One such was a Mr P. S. C. who lamented in 1860 that although he had more than once witnessed 'riding skimmicking' [sic] he had not seen it for a number of years and 'the practice will ere long give way before the civilisation we are so proud of; one characteristic of which is, that, while it gives ample scope to skulking vice, it suppresses every demonstration that can jar upon the nerves of the fastidious.'[90] J. S. Leicester remarked that the custom of stanging remained in fashion at Northallerton and that: 'The magistrates declined to interfere with the old custom so long as no property was damaged; and before the introduction of the rural police they scarce had any alternative but to wink at it.'[91] When Owen Owens was actually dragged from his house in Anglesey in 1887 and paraded tied to a ladder through the village of Rhostrehwfa, the police did indeed intervene to release him, but whilst the magistrates knew the culprits they apparently allowed them to escape unpunished.[92]

Storch notes the particular alarm created by the employment of the ceffyl pren in Cardiganshire in 1837 and some vigorous attempts at its suppression. Whilst this was certainly the case, I have also shown that there was at least one occasion on which the police were quite prepared to stand by and tolerate the proceedings so long as no property was damaged.[93] Whether this was because they saw no harm in the proceedings, or more practically because they believed that the risk of getting manhandled or sparking a riot outweighed the wrongdoing observed, is a moot point. After the 'tin-kettling' at Ventnor in 1844 (see Chapter 5) the parish constable freely confessed that he had not gone up to the disturbances because he thought that his presence 'would do no good' and a rural police officer similarly 'considered his interference would be no use'.[94] The *Illustrated Police News* reported in 1876 that when effigies of two gentlemen who had participated in a prosecution at Maidstone were paraded through the streets of Woolwich and Plumstead, 'police were on standby but did not

---

89   Ibid.
90   *Notes and Queries*, 2nd series, vol. 10 (20 October 1860), p. 319.
91   Leicester, 'Riding the Stang', pp.122–26 at p. 113.
92   Ibid., p. 126.
93   See HO 52/35/153 fol. 450, December 1837, Statement of the Mayor and Justices of Carmarthen as to the complaint of Mr David Davies.
94   *Hampshire Advertiser & Salisbury Guardian*, 22 June 1844.

interfere'.[95] During the mock burial of an adulterer at Bugle in Cornwall in 1905, 'The police were present but their services were not required.'[96] It was still the case that in 1930 the inhabitants of Woodley in Berkshire were able to parade in front of the house of a wife-beater for three days without the police doing anything other than observe.[97] Edwin Grey witnessed three instances of rough music in Hertfordshire at the end of the nineteenth century and remarked:

> I understood the unwritten law concerning these affairs to be that the music makers could, if they so wished, perform on three successive nights, that they must keep on the move, that one could make as much noise as they wished, but that the names of the offenders or the nature of the offence must not be shouted out. With these conditions observed, it was affirmed that no police officer could interfere; if this was so I cannot say, but certainly no police or any other officer interfered or made an appearance, so far as I can remember at any of the rough music parades that I witnessed.[98]

This account is particularly interesting since it seems to suggest that communities adapted their practice to meet the challenge of the authorities. It was presumably difficult to argue that an obstruction of the highway was occasioned if the crowd did not stop but continued to move along the road, or equally if they gathered on private land. Similarly, if the offender was not named then a breach of the peace was more difficult to establish. At Honely near Huddersfield in 1857 the inhabitants actually asked for permission from the county police to ride a stang for an adulterer.[99] Probably the most important adaptation made by the crowd in response to the changing temper of the times, however, was their abandonment of the earlier practice of actually forcing the malefactor to participate in the parade. With some notable exceptions this became rare during the second half of the nineteenth century.[100] William Henderson remarked upon this when, in 1879, he observed that: 'Originally the offender was himself compelled to ride, but, as the law became stronger and the liberty of the subject was more respected, some young fellow of powerful lungs and obtuse sensibilities was selected as his deputy.'[101]

It seems, then, that there were some concessions made to the new police but it is easy to overexaggerate the police's capacity to intervene in such events during the run-up to the First World War. County forces were small to start with and had large

---

95 *Illustrated Police News*, 18/11/1876.
96 Peacock, 'Burial in Effigy', pp. 405–6.
97 Seal, 'A "Hussitting" in Berkshire, 1930', pp. 91–4.
98 Grey, *Cottage Life in a Hertfordshire Village*, p. 161.
99 *Leeds Mercury*, 1857.
100 Tentatively I would say that the vigorous tradition of physically laying hands upon sexual malefactors seems to have persisted longer in Wales than in England.
101 Henderson, *Notes on the Folk-Lore of the Northern Counties of England and the Borders*, pp. 29–30.

areas to cover in a time before mass transportation. For example, the county constabulary for Surrey had only seventy officers at its foundation in 1851 – ten years later its mobile force was chiefly dependent upon its employment of twenty-nine bicycles. Even when the police did try to prevent incidents of rough music they did not always have the manpower to prevail. Around 1868 an 'oosit' was held at Ramsbury in Wiltshire against an unfaithful husband, the affair consisting of a rough music parade outside the home of the malefactor. Leading the parade was a man holding a horse's skull whose jaws could be made to open and close at the tug of a string. The affair lasted three or four days with the crowd increasing every night. The police then tried to suppress the gathering but they were simply unable to do so.[102]

Bushaway observes of the customary calendar that by the end of the nineteenth century it had been 'annexed by the Victorian middle class, purged of its disagreeable features and restored as a respectable medium for the expression of social order within the village community in which concepts of "Merry England" actually represented a new form of deference'.[103] This is naturally a very generalised summation of a very complex situation but seems to be substantially correct. Accomplishing this 'pacification', however, stretched the Victorian police to the limit. Very many attempts to suppress popular recreations or sports ended with reports such as those written at the conclusion of an attempt to suppress street football at Nuneaton on 1 March 1881, to the effect that the crowd had been large and the police had been 'roughly handled',[104] or indeed, as at Lewes earlier in 1847, 'seriously hurt'.[105] Under such circumstances one can readily imagine that preventing the gathering of a crowd to burn a badly made effigy or bang on some saucepans might not have appeared to be a law enforcement priority. Perhaps this was all the more so because the victims of such activity were very likely to be characterised by authority as being in any case morally deviant and perhaps undeserving of protection. Furthermore, it seems that it was not always easy for those outside the affective reach of such demonstrations to understand their real impact, hence the supposition that they were harmless so long as no one was actually assaulted and no property was damaged.

Ultimately, the police prevailed against many of the tumultuous but set-piece popular festivals and recreations precisely because they were predictable. Very large numbers of people were involved but, in time, the police were able to deploy large numbers of officers, special constables and even troops to counter them. They knew, for example, that they had to be in Guildford every year on 5 November, not 5 October or 10 June and so on. Skimmingtons and stangings were much more difficult

---

102 Cunningham, 'Moonrake Medley', pp. 278–80.
103 Bushaway, *By Rite, Custom, Ceremony and Community in England, 1700–1880*, p. 180.
104 E. H. Coleman, 'Football at Nuneaton, Warwickshire', *Notes and Queries*, 6th series, vol. 3. (12 March 1881), p. 207.
105 A. Beckett, *The Spirit of the Downs* (London: Methuen & Co. 1949 repr.), pp. 178–80.

to suppress due to the fact that, certainly since as far back as this survey goes, they bubbled up from popular culture at irregular intervals and at unpredictable locations. As such, commentators sometimes concluded that since no instance had come within their own knowledge in recent times then the activity must now be extinct or at the very least dying away. John Brand accompanied this in 1793 by a rather naive (or ironic?) estimation of the power of the authorities:

> There used formerly (and I believe it is still now and then retained) to be a kind of ignominious procession in the North of England, called, 'Riding the Stang'... This custom bids fair not to be of much longer continuance in the North, for I find, by the *Newcastle-upon-Tyne Courant* for 3 August 1793, that at the Assizes at Durham the preceding week, 'Thomas Jameson, Matthew Marrington, George Ball, Joshua Rownstree, Simon Emmerson, Robert Parkin and Francis Wardell, for *violently assaulting* Nicholas Lowes, of Bishop Wearmouth, *and carrying him on a Stang*, were sentenced to be imprisoned two years in Durham Goal...' The law taking such cognizance of the practice, it must of course terminate very shortly.[106]

A hundred years later the stang was still happening in the north of England. Similarly, although the skimmington allegedly disappeared in 1860 from Surrey and Sussex, Frederick Mant witnessed one at Egham, Surrey in 1873.[107] Olivia Woolley reported a case from Copthorne, Sussex around 1951![108] One gets the sense that rough music was capable of surviving as a very powerful motif in popular culture even though individual communities rarely experienced it. It remained a latent possibility so long as there were old heads in the district who could still remember a performance. When a ceffyl pren was staged at Llechryd in 1837 it was the first for a generation.[109] It might be an accident of record but skimmingtons and stangings are ever prone to pop-up in communities where there is no record of there having been one before.

Much had changed, though, by the end of the nineteenth century. It was by then scarcely possible for a private individual to take control of a town centre, as at Tewkesbury in 1805,[110] even less so for a criminal gang to drag alleged malefactors out of a public place and beat, abuse and parade them publicly and unchallenged

---

106 J. Brand, *Observations on Popular Antiquities Chiefly Illustrating the Origin of our Vulgar Customs, Ceremonies and Superstitions*, 2 vols (London: Bentley, 1813), vol. 1, p. 107.
107 F. W. Mant, 'Skimmington: Wooset: Ousel Hunting', *Notes and Queries*, 4th series, vol. 11 (22 February 1873), p. 156.
108 Olivia S. Woolley, 'Rough Music in Sussex', *Folklore* 69:1 (1958), p. 39.
109 *Carmarthen Journal*, 28 July 1837, cited in Jones, 'Popular Culture, Policing, and the "Disappearance" of the Ceffyl Pren in Cardigan, 1837–1850', p. 26.
110 Matthews, 'A Tax Riot in Tewkesbury in 1805'.

through a town, as had happened at Deal in 1822.[111] Visiting upon a malefactor the sorts of physical harm observable in the first half of the nineteenth century and before was now so likely to result in swift official retribution that it was generally eschewed. Old systems of judgement such as the coolstrin court had passed too, and along with them many festive practices within which they were encased. However, as we saw in the previous chapter, there remained types of community that were long able to resist the general trend towards pacification, that continued in effect to police themselves. In rural society generally, the fact that rough music was performed so unpredictably, allied with the inadequacy of the mechanisms for its suppression, ensured that it survived into the twentieth century. By this time it had become for some merely an object of antiquarian curiosity, but for its performers it remained a very real and powerful response to social deviance. Moreover, performative and shaming culture had survived long enough in the open industrial villages and amongst close-knit occupational groups to guide the formation of a working-class culture in which shame continued to be a very powerful driver of social cohesion. Reputation remained almost everything in working-class communities of the early twentieth century and to be 'white-shirted', taunted with women's apparel or chased through the community with the cane was still to be subjected to a powerful psychological assault. It was a humiliation scarcely less painful than being forced to do penance in church or being displayed on a stang.

---

111 *Morning Chronicle*, 23 March 1822.

Aftermath

In 1979 Theo Brown reported in *Folklore* a rather curious incident that had happened some six years previously to two of her acquaintances, a vicar and his wife, who had at that time been living in a village in Devonshire. Brown described the cleric as an Oxford graduate who 'had worked most of his ministry in a suburban parish and knew nothing of country life'.[1] His wife was 'artistic, very well-meaning and nervous'. Eager to fulfil her role in the community the aforesaid wife had been active in the community but had unknowingly offended a portion of the village by stumbling into village politics. What followed had been rather odd. Some objects had been moved around in their garage but nothing had been taken, a dead cat had appeared in their garden and some silent phone calls had been received. When bonfire night came, however, they had determined to follow tradition and host the event at the vicarage:

> The village turned up but behaved in a curiously quiet and menacing way, watching the vicar's wife closely. Suddenly it dawned on her that the Guy on top of the bonfire was dressed to resemble her. One or two other odd things happened, and as the fire was dying down and the people were starting to go home, one of the men brushed past her muttering: 'Reckon as you won't sleep much tonight, missus.' It seemed a pointless remark, but it proved right, for all night long there were strange cat-calls and yappings in the garden from people hidden among the bushes.[2]

It comes as some surprise that a rural community should still be pursuing a local figure in this fashion in the second half of the twentieth century. In fact, though, there is rather good evidence that the old shaming rituals were still being remembered and occasionally being performed in village communities even after the dislocations caused by the First and Second World Wars.

Shame still did its work in Copthorne, Sussex around 1951 when Olivia Woolley

---

1 Brown, 'A Further Note on the "Stag Hunt" in Devon', pp. 18–21, at p. 20.
2 Ibid.

recalls that rough music was arranged for the benefit of a family in the village. The father had smacked a neighbour's son for hitting one of his daughters. The boy had subsequently developed pneumonia for which the chastiser had, somewhat inexplicably, been blamed. The rest of the villagers had gathered on a Saturday night to serenade the offender and had continued to do so for several days: 'The victims tried to stick it out, but it was too much for them in the end, and eventually they sold their cottage and moved from the district.'[3] An earlier incident was reported from West Hoathley in Sussex in 1947, where a young man in the village had become subject to a mild form of rough music and had been unwise enough to complain to the police. The identity of the performers had been known and the police had asked them courteously not to continue, whereupon vague noises became 'Pots and Kettles of all Keys' and continued for three successive nights. The constabulary seems to have been at a loss as to how to respond after the villagers had told them, unapologetically, 'It is our right.'[4] Joan Eltenton reported personal experience of yet another incident at Oxford in 1940. A woman from the Foreign Office, a Miss C., had been billeted upon her but had had an unfortunate tendency to get dressed and undressed without closing her curtains. One morning, 'I was suddenly aware of banging on saucepans, saucepan lids, kettles and anything else that could make a loud clattering noise, and realised it was directed at my house, and that a group of women had gathered in one garden and were shouting and screaming.' Far from being sensible that their demonstration might bring some sanction upon themselves, the crowd had also summoned a policewoman who interviewed both lodger and host: 'it was with difficulty that I eventually convinced her [the policewoman] that I had no reason whatsoever to query Miss C's general moral behaviour.'[5]

The above examples serve to demonstrate that, to a degree, the attempts to stamp out rough music culture in the nineteenth century had failed. Snell has observed that, 'community spirit remained a pervasive feature of English and Welsh local societies well into the early twentieth century, even though by then it often co-existed with, and was filtered through or augmented by, abrasive senses of class'.[6] In pockets of England and Wales, at least, that spirit endured even longer and with it still came an assertion that the community was authorised to judge those amongst it. It is that assertion that this study has been most interested in tracing – through the medium of rough music and associated behaviours. It was an assertion not merely predicated upon moral claims but reinforced by forms of fake legalism and false historical memory that nonetheless sufficed to give it authenticity. It is an astonishing

---

3 Woolley, 'Rough Music in Sussex', p. 39.
4 Alford, 'Rough Music or Charivari', pp. 505–18 at p. 511.
5 Joan M. Eltenton, 'An Experience of Rough Music', *Folklore* 99:1 (1988), p. 124.
6 Snell, *Parish and Belonging*, p. 499.

testimony to the vitality of that claim and, I would argue, the power of the fictive legal community, that well into the modern era the people of West Hoathley could still feel that it was their right to kettle a wrongdoer, or the good citizens of Oxford to shame an allegedly loose woman.

Yet in broader terms there is no doubt that rough music in rural communities was in decline during the final decades of the nineteenth century. The culprits were not so much the police officers as the railway, the bicycle and, eventually, the motor car. By the end of the nineteenth century those fierce local loyalties necessary to sustain the stangings and skimmingtons were fading away. The days when the liminal bounds of the parish accorded with the conceptual bounds of its ordinary inhabitants were passing. Some communities remained very insular but: 'Preoccupation after 1880 with national and imperial issues, in this most expansive phase of British history, came to make very local ties to place seem antiquated at all cultural levels. "Parochial", like "provincial", was one of the new disparaging words of the later nineteenth century.'[7] One signifier and driver of social change was the fact that intra-parochial marriages were now in steep decline. A survey has shown, for example, that some 80 per cent of the marriages in West Dorset in the ten years up to 1886 had been intra-parochial. However, between 1886 and 1896 this declined to just 50 per cent and by 1936 the figure was down to 30 per cent.[8] The key offender here was the bicycle, which made possible long-distance courting, and also the declining pugnacity of the times, which meant that the travelling wooer was less likely to be beaten up once he got to his destination. Snell argues that the declining attachment to parish can also be observed through the medium of gravestones: until 1890 the number of stones declaring the parish of the deceased was actually increasing but thereafter there was a rapid decline, people no longer seemed to think it important.[9]

Physical and social mobility, better communications, education and then the intermingling brought about by war and conscription changed rural society in ways impossible to pursue here. All this transformed the parish but also the history of shame. Shame depended upon the shamer and the shamed being enmeshed within the same system of social understandings, such that the participants knew what they were doing and the recipients had a full sense of what was being done to them. Shame was at its most powerful when the party shamed was trapped within a social nexus tuned to respond to it. Shame has an affective power, it changes what we feel about ourselves but it also changes what others feel about us and thus engenders consequences that can be economic, social, sexual, political and so on.

However, where the individual has the power to escape the nexus of the shaming

---

7 Ibid., p. 486.
8 Snell, *Parish and Belonging*, fig. 4.8, p. 200.
9 Snell, *Parish and Belonging*, fig. 8.2, p. 474.

community, or does not feel part of that nexus in the first place, then its power can rapidly evaporate. So it was with rough music. It had often appeared perplexing, even comical to those looking in from the outside, and as communities grew more diverse and life opportunities expanded so its affective reach was reduced. The case of our Devonshire vicar and his wife illustrates the bankruptcy of the practice in the eyes of a couple who were not dependent upon the community economically, socially or emotionally. The key act in the campaign of harassment did not speak to them in the way that the villagers intended – they failed to comprehend what it 'meant' on a deeper emotional and psychological level. Burned in effigy the wife did not flee, take to drink, pills or poison but, like her husband, remained simply perplexed and, entirely distanced from its affective content, called in a folklorist.

If shaming ritual survived with real vigour it was (and is?) most evident within organised labour, within those large and industrially powerful groups who were strong enough to hold themselves together and replicate a collective ethos. Such groups have often found themselves in opposition to the government, the status quo and with that the formal legal process – they have accordingly tried to hold on to their own methods of disciplining those within their ranks who break 'the rules'. The traditions of the colliers, quarrymen and their like have, however, inevitably suffered alongside the general decline of the heavy industrial base.

Their decline is in contrast, of course, to the ever-expanding industry that is British romanticism. This has now been fabricating and marketing images and texts of our past (and our rural history in particular) for so long as to create a yearning for a past that never in fact existed. Xenophobia, religious and social bigotry, general intolerance and an inadequate sympathy for the general failings of all mankind are all charges that can be laid against popular justice during the period under consideration. Much that was ugly seethed under the apparent tranquillity of the English or Welsh village. But there was also much that was good. There was a sense of place and belonging, of continuity and tradition that fostered support networks as reliable as anything dreamed up by the state, then or now. If tradition constrained the individual it also attempted to offer some protection to him or her against the aggrandisement of others and to give a sense of real value to those whose circumstances placed them, in terms of political or economic power, at the bottom of the social dunghill.

With the demise of 'mock courts' and rough music, the constitution of local communities as juridical mechanisms was lost. However, in respect of judging and applying the law, localism to a degree survives (for the moment) within our contemporary legal system in the form of the jury trial and the magistrates' court. The legitimacy of the law itself is, however, primarily defended upon the basis of what I call the democratic justice proposition. By this I mean that it is suggested that the system of democratic politics ensures that the laws that bind us are the creation of our representatives and must therefore be a reflection of that which we truly desire. Any tendency for abuse is allegedly constrained by the existence of an independent professional judiciary selected, again allegedly, on merit. I would not wish for a moment to deny the many advantages of this proposition. However, for someone like myself, who believes that, at its heart, law is but power mixed up with some logic and an awful lot of enchantment, then there may be some difficulties suggested by this otherwise advantageous idea. Law often fails to engage us because of its affective remoteness, the way that it is debated, created and implemented being far too distant from the lives of ordinary people to inspire in us any sense of ownership. The legal system seems upon occasion to have become the site of rules only tangentially connected to traditional moral values. Indeed I might provocatively suggest that it is an important cultural trope of our time that many of our institutions have become rather ineffectual at the same time as they have become wary of being 'too judgemental'. There is, though, a danger that if the law becomes too dispassionate, too abstract and too aloof, if it loses too many of its performative facets and it ceases to make moral, supernatural claims, that it may become entirely disenchanted in the eyes of those who must be persuaded to obey it.

Certainly, we now have a society that we are trying to govern much more by the application of formal rules than by an appeal to culturally generated emotional states such as shame. Whilst shame is not entirely displaced (and still governs some communities much more powerfully than others) we live in a world where convicted perjurers emerge from prison to appear quite unabashed on our television and radio chat shows. Incompetent or dishonest managers of our public companies boldly declare that they deserve the rewards that their power enabled them to extract. Hardly anyone seems to resign anymore upon being 'found out', and any conduct that is seen to be immoral by the lights of most of us, is readily defended upon the grounds that it is not actually, technically, provably, undeniably, 'against the law'.

Given the independent liberty I enjoy, the freedom of thought and, with that, the knowledge of many foul things that were done in the name of popular morality in the past, I am quite sure that I would not wish to see a return to rough music. One wonders, however, if a society can go too far in attempting to displace shame as both a public external and a private internal phenomenon. Can we maintain a society in which interpersonal relationships and normative behaviours are, it seems, to be increasingly regulated on the basis of systems of formal rules that define what we must do but which are affectively neutral?[10] Shame and public significations of shame, such as rough music, have been used by groups to discipline individual conduct for far longer than the latest fashions for process and the letter of the law. I finish, then, with no great conclusion, but merely an observation that whether we can sustain and govern a society based merely upon logic, rationality and the rule of law, whether we can indeed do without shame is, as yet, too early to say.

---

10 As I write this China has just begun to experiment with a new law apparently forcing children to visit their elderly parents.

Select Bibliography

Alford, V., 'Rough Music or Charivari', *Folklore* 70:4 (1959), pp. 505–18.

Anon. *Holderness and the Holdernessians: A Few Notes on the History, Topography, Dialect, Manners and Customs of the District by a Fellow of the Royal Historical Society* (London: Trubner and Co., 1878).

Axon, W. E. A., *Cheshire Gleanings* (London: Simpkin, Marshall and Co., 1884).

Baker, A. E., *Glossary of Northamptonshire Words and Phrases,* 2 vols (London: J. R. Smith, 1854).

Bamford, S., *Passages in the Life of a Radical* (London: A. M. Kelly, 1967 [1844]).

Banks, S., *A Polite Exchange of Bullets: The Duel and the English Gentleman, 1750–1850* (Woodbridge: Boydell, 2010).

Baring-Gould, S., *The Red Spider* (London: Chatto & Windus, 1887).

——*Old County Life* (London: Methuen and Co., 1890).

Beckett, A., *The Spirit of the Downs* (London: Methuen & Co., 1949 repr.).

Behagg, C., 'Custom, Class and Change: The Trade Societies of Birmingham', *Social History* 4:3 (1979), pp. 455–80.

Blakeborough, R., *Wit, Character, Folk-Lore and Customs of the North Riding of Yorkshire* (London: Henry Frowd, 1898).

Bloom, U., *Whitchurch, The Changed Village* (London: Chapman and Hall, 1945).

Blundell, N., *Nicholas Blundell's Diary and Letter Book, 1702–1728*, ed. Margaret Blundell (Liverpool: Liverpool University Press, 1952).

Booth, A., 'Popular Loyalism and Public Violence in the North-West of England, 1790–1800', *Social History* 8:3 (1983), pp. 295–313.

Brand, J., *Observations on Popular Antiquities Chiefly Illustrating the Origin of our Vulgar Customs, Ceremonies and Superstitions*, 2 vols (London: Bentley, 1813).

Brewer, J., 'The Misfortunes of Lord Bute: A Case-Study in Eighteenth-Century Political Argument and Public Opinion', *The Historical Journal,* 16:1 (1973), pp. 3–43.

Briggs, K. M., *The Folklore of the Cotswolds* (London: B. T. Batsford, 1974).

Brown, T., 'The "Stag Hunt" in Devon', *Folklore,* 63:2 (1952), pp. 104–9.

——'A Further Note on the "Stag Hunt" in Devon', *Folklore,* 90:1 (1979) pp. 18–21.

Burne, C. S., 'Guy Fawkes Day', *Folklore,* 22:4 (1912).

Burne, M., 'Parish Gleanings from Upton St Leonard's, Glos', *Folklore,* 22:2 (1911), pp. 236–9.

Burne, S., *Shropshire Folk-Lore: A Sheaf of Gleanings* (London: Trubner and Co., 1883).

Burnett, J., 'The Baking Industry in the Nineteenth Century', *Business History* 5 (1963), pp. 98–9.

Burnett, T. A. J., *The Rise and Fall of a Regency Dandy: The Life and Times of Scrope Beardmore Davies* (London: John Murray, 1981).

Bushaway, B., *By Rite, Custom, Ceremony and Community in England, 1700–1880*, 2nd ed., (London: Breviary Stuff Publications, 2011).
Cameron, D. K., *The English Fair* (Stroud: Sutton, 1998).
Capp, B., 'English Youth Groups and the Pindar of Wakefield', *Past and Present* 76 (1977), pp. 127–33.
Cawte, E. C., 'It's An Ancient Custom But How Ancient?', *Aspects of British Calendar Customs*, ed. Theresa Buckland and Juliette Woods (London: Folklore Society, 1983).
Chambers, R., ed., *The Book of Days: A Miscellany of Popular Antiquities; in Connection with the Calendar, including Anecdote, Biography, & History, Curiosities of Literature and Oddities of Human Life and Character*, 2 vols (London: Chambers, 1888).
Chandler, K., 'The Abingdon Morris and the Election of the Mayor of Ock Street', *Aspects of British Calendar Customs*, ed. Theresa Buckland and Juliette Wood (London: Folklore Society, 1983), pp. 119–36.
Chesterton, G. L., *Revelations of Prison Life* (London: Hurst and Blackett, 1856).
Clark, A., *Women's Silence Men's Violence: Sexual Assault in England, 1770–1845* (London: Pandora, 1987).
Cobbett, W., ed., *Parliamentary History of England from the Norman Conquest to the Year 1803*, 36 vols (London: R. Bagshaw, 1806–20).
Cockburn, J. S., 'Patterns of Violence in English Society: Homicide in Kent 1560–1985', *Past and Present* 130 (1991), pp. 70–106.
Coleman, E. H., 'Football at Nuneaton, Warwickshire', *Notes and Queries*, 6th series, vol. 3 (12 March 1881).
Courtney, M. A., *Cornish Feasts and Folk-Lore* (Penzance: Beare and Son, 1890).
Crawford, R., 'English Georgic and British Nationhood', *English Literary History* 65:1 (1998), pp. 123–58.
Cromartie, A., 'The Idea of the Common Law as Custom', *The Nature of Customary Law*, ed. A. Perreau-Saussine and J. B. Murphy (Cambridge: CUP, 2007), pp. 203–27.
Cunningham, B. H., 'Moonrake Medley', *Wiltshire Archaeological Magazine* 50 (1943), pp. 278–80.
Curtis, G., ed, *A Chronicle of Small Beer: The Early Victorian Diaries of a Hertfordshire Brewer* (London: Phillimore, 1970).
D'Archenholz, M., *A Picture of England: Containing a Description of the Laws, Customs and Manners of England. Interspersed with Curious and Interesting Anecdotes* (Dublin: P. Byrne, 1790).
Davis, J., 'A Poor Man's System of Justice: The London Police Courts in the Second Half of the Nineteenth Century', *Historical Journal* 27:2 (1984), pp. 309–35.
Davis, N. Z., 'The Reasons of Misrule: Youth Groups and Charivaris in Sixteenth-Century France', *Past and Present* 50 (1971), pp. 41–75.
Douglas, D., 'The Durham Pitman', *Miners, Quarrymen and Saltworkers*, ed. R. Samuel (London: Routledge & Kegan Paul, 1977), p. 207.
Eltenton, J., 'An Experience of Rough Music', *Folklore* 99:1 (1988), p. 124.
Etherington, J. E., 'The Sociology of a Recurrent Ceremonial Drama: Lewes Guy Fawkes Night 1800–1913', unpublished PhD thesis, The Open University, 1988.
Evans, G. E., *Ask the Fellows Who Cut the Hay* (London: Faber, 1956).

Farrer, O. W., 'The Marblers of Purbeck', *Papers Read Before the Purbeck Society, 1855* (Wareham: C. Groves, 1856).
Faulk, B., 'The Public Execution; Urban Rhetoric and Victorian Crowds', *Executions and the British Experience from the 17th to the 20th Century*, ed. William B. Thesig (Jefferson, N. Carolina: McFarland, 1990), pp. 77–91.
Fisher, C., *Custom, Work and Market Capitalism: The Forest of Dean Colliers, 1788–1888* (London: Croom Helm, 1981).
Fisher, G., 'The Birth of the Prison Retold', *Yale Law Journal* 104:6 (1995), pp. 1232–324.
Fletcher, A., and J. Stevenson, eds, *Order and Disorder in Early Modern England* (Cambridge: CUP, 1985).
Gier-Viskovatoff J. J., and A. Porter, 'Women of the British Coalfields on Strike in 1926 and 1984: Documenting Lives Using Oral History and Photography', *Frontiers: A Journal of Women Studies* 19:2 (1998), pp. 199–230.
Gilbert, A. N., 'Law and Honour Amongst Eighteenth Century British Army Officers', *Historical Journal* 19 (1976), pp. 75–87.
Girard, R., *Violence and the Sacred* (Baltimore: Johns Hopkins University Press, 1977).
Gomme, A. B., 'Skimmington Riding', *Folklore Journal* 1 (1883).
Goodwyn, E. A., *Selections from Norwich Newspapers, 1760–1790* (Ipswich: privately printed, n.d.).
Gorsky, M., 'James Tuckfield's "Ride": Combination and Social Drama in Early Nineteenth-Century Bristol', *Social History* 19:3 (1994), pp. 319–38.
Greenslade, M. W., ed., *A History of the County of Stafford, Vol. 14: Lichfield* (Oxford: OUP, 1990).
Greer, A., 'From Folklore to Revolution: Charivaris and the Lower Canadian Rebellion of 1837', *Social History* 15:1 (1990), pp. 25–43.
Grey, E., *Cottage Life in a Hertfordshire Village: How the Agricultural Labourer Lived and Fared in the Late 60s and 70s* (St Albans: Fisher Knight, 1935).
Gutch, Mrs, *Country Folklore vol. iv. Examples of Printed Folk-lore Concerning the East Riding of Yorkshire, Collected and Edited by Mrs Gutch* (London: Folklore Society, 1912).
Hale, Sir Matthew, *The History of the Common Law of England*, ed. C. M. Gray (Chicago: University of Chicago Press, 1971).
Hall, J. G., *A History of South Cave and of Other Parishes in the East Riding of the County of York* (Hull: Edwin Ombler, 1892).
Hammerton, J., *Cruelty and Companionship: Conflict in Nineteenth-Century Married Life*, (London: Routledge, 1992).
Hammond, J. L. and Barbara Hammond, *The Village Labourer* (London: Longman, 1978).
Hare, C., 'The Skeleton Army and the Bonfire Boys, Worthing, 1884', *Folklore* 99:2 (1988), pp. 221–31.
Harland J. and T. Wilkinson, *Lancashire Folk-Lore, : Illustrative of the Superstitious Beliefs and Practices, Local Customs and Usages of the People of the County Palatine* (London: Frederick Warne, 1867).
Hay, D., P. Linebaugh, J. G. Rule, et al., *Albions Fatal Tree: Crime and Society in 18C England* (London: Allen Lane, 1975).

Henderson, W., *Notes on the Folklore of the Northern Counties of England and the Borders* (London: Folklore Society, 1879).
Hendrix, R., 'Popular Humor in the "Black Dwarf"', *Journal of British Studies* 16 (1976), pp. 108–28.
Henriques, U. R. Q., 'The Rise and Decline of the Separate System of Prison Discipline', *Past and Present* 54 (1972), pp. 61–93.
Higson, J., 'Riding the Stang', *Notes and Queries*, 5th series, vol. 5 (25 March 1876).
Hindle, S., 'Custom, Festival and Protest in Early Modern England: The Little Budworth Wakes, St Peter's Day, 1596', *Rural History* 6 (1995), pp. 170–71.
Hislop, R. O., *Northumberland Words. A Glossary of the Words used in the County of Northumberland and on the Tyneside* (London: English Dialect Society, 1892).
Hobsbawm, E. J., and G. R. Rude, *Captain Swing* (London: Lawrence and Wishart, 1970).
Hockaday, F. S., 'The Consistory Court of the Diocese of Gloucester', *Transactions of the Bristol and Gloucestershire Archaeological Society* 46 (1924), pp.195–287.
Holdsworth, W., *History of English Law* (London: Methuen, 1964).
Hole, C., 'Winter Bonfires', *Folklore* 71:4 (1960), pp. 217–27.
——*British Folk Customs* (London: Hutchinson, 1976).
Home Coleman, E., 'Football at Nuneaton, Warwickshire', *Notes and Queries*, 6th series, vol. 3 (12 March 1881), p. 207.
Hone, W., *The Year Book of Daily Recreation and Information* (London: Thomas Tegg, 1864).
Howitt, W., *The Rural Life of England* (London: Longmans, 1840).
Humphries, S., *Hooligans or Rebels? An Oral History of Working Class Childhood and Youth 1889–1939* (Oxford: Blackwell, 1981).
Ibbotsen, D., 'Custom in Medieval Law', *The Nature of Customary Law*, ed. A Perreau-Saussine and J. B. Murphy (Cambridge: CUP, 2007), pp. 151–75.
Ingram, M., 'Juridical Folklore in England Illustrated by Rough Music', *Communities and Courts in Britain, 1150–1900*, ed. C. W. Brooks and M. Lobban (London: Hambledon Press, 1997), pp. 61–82.
Ireland, R., *'A Want of Order and Good Discipline': Rules, Discretion and the Victorian Prison* (Cardiff: University of Wales Press, 2007).
Jewitt, F. W. L., 'On Ancient Customs and Sports of the County of Derby', *Journal of the British Archaeological Society*, vol. 8 (1851), pp. 201–2.
Jewitt, L., 'The Pillory and Who They Put In It', *Reliquary* 1 (1861), pp. 209–24.
Jones, D. J. V., 'Distress and Discontent in Cardiganshire, 1814–1819', *Ceredigion* 5:3 (1966), pp. 280–9.
——'The Scotch Cattle and their Black Domain', *Welsh History Review* 5:3 (1971), pp. 220–49.
——*Before Rebecca: Popular Protest in Wales, 1793–1835* (London: Allen Lane, 1973).
Jones, R. N., 'Popular Culture, Policing, and the "Disappearance" of the Ceffyl Pren in Cardigan, 1837–1850', *Ceredigion: Journal of the Cardiganshire Antiquarian Society* 11:1 (1988–9), pp. 19–39.
——'Women, the Community and Collective Action: The Ceffyl Pren Tradition', *Our Mother's Land: Chapters in Welsh Women's History, 1830–1939*, ed. Angela V. John (Cardiff: University of Wales Press, 1991), pp. 17–42.

Kenny, C., 'The Lawless Court of Essex', *Columbia Law Review* 5:7 (1905) pp. 529–36.
Kent, J. R., '"Folk Justice" and Royal Justice in Early Seventeenth-Century England: A "Charivari" in the Midlands', *Midlands History* 8 (1983), pp. 70–85.
King, P., 'The Summary Courts and Social Relations in Eighteenth Century England', *Past and Present* 183 (2004), pp. 125–72.
Knight, L., *Oil Paint and Grease Paint: The Autobiography of Laura Knight*, vol. 1 (Harmondsworth: Penguin, 1936).
Langford, P., *A Polite and Commercial People: England, 1727–1783* (Oxford: OUP, 1989).
Laqueur, T., 'The Queen Caroline Affair: Politics as Art in the Reign of George IV', *The Journal of Modern History* 54:3 (1982), pp. 417–66.
Leicester, J. S., 'Riding the Stang', *Monthly Chronicle of North-Country Lore and Legend*, 1:3 (1887), pp. 122–26.
Little, C. B., and C. P. Sheffield, 'Frontiers and Criminal Justice: English Private Prosecution Societies and American Vigilantism in the Eighteenth and Nineteen Centuries', *American Sociological Review* 48:6 (1983), pp. 796–808.
Lobban, M., 'Custom, Common Law Reasoning and the Law of Nations in the Nineteenth Century', *The Nature of Customary Law*, ed. A Perreau-Saussine and J. B. Murphy (Cambridge: CUP, 2007).
MacMaster, N., 'The Battle for Mousehold Heath, 1857–1884: "Popular Politics" and the Victorian Public Park', *Past and Present* 127:1 (1990), pp. 117–54.
Madan, M., *Thoughts on Executive Justice, with Respect to our Criminal Laws, Particularly on the Circuits* (London: J. Dodsley, 1785), pp. 148–50.
Malcolmson, R. W., *Popular Recreations in English Society, 1700–1850* (Cambridge: CUP, 1973).
Mant, F. W., 'Skimmington: Wooset: Ousel Hunting', *Notes and Queries*, 4th series, vol. 11 (22 February 1873), p. 156.
Marshall, W., 'The Review and Abstract of the County Reports to the Board of Agriculture: Vol. IV, Midlands Department' (York, 1818).
Matthews, S., 'A Tax Riot in Tewkesbury in 1805', *British Tax Review* 337 (2002), pp. 437–44.
Mayhew, G., *Tudor Rye* (Falmer: University of Sussex, 1987).
McCalman, I., *Radical Underworld: Prophets, Revolutionaries and Pornographers in London, 1795–1840* (Cambridge: CUP, 1988).
Merfyn Jones, R., *The North Wales Quarrymen, 1874–1922* (Cardiff: University of Wales Press, 1982).
Miller, W. I., *Humiliation and Other Essays on Honor, Social Discomfort, and Violence* (Ithaca: Cornell University Press, 1993).
Millingen, J. G., *The History of Duelling: Including Narratives of the Most Remarkable Personal Encounters that Have Taken Place from the Earliest Periods to the Present Time*, 2 vols (London: Richard Bentley, 1841).
Minchinton, W. E., 'The Beginnings of Trade Unionism in the Gloucestershire Woollen Industry', *Trans. Bristol and Glos. Archaeological Soc.* 70 (1951), pp. 134–5.
More, H., *Village Politics: Addressed to all Mechanics, Journeymen and Day Labourers in Great Britain by Will Chip, a Country Carpenter*, 5th edn (York: G. Walker, 1793).

Morgan, D. H., 'The Place of Harvesters in Nineteenth Century Village Life', *Village Life and Labour*, ed. R. Samuel (London: Kegan Paul, 1975) pp. 29–72.

Murphy, J., 'Habit and Convention at the Foundation of Custom', *The Nature of Customary Law*, ed. A. Perreau-Saussine and J. B. Murphy, pp. 53–78.

Neeson, J. M. *Commoners: Common Rights, Enclosure and Social Change in England, 1700–1820* (Cambridge: CUP, 1993).

Newman, L. F., 'Some Notes on Life in East Anglian Villages in the Early Part of the Nineteenth Century', *Folklore* 56:2 (1945), pp. 285–354.

Nicholson, J., *The Folk Speech of East Yorkshire* (London, Simpkin, Marshall and Co., 1889).

Odell F. J., 'Wife Sales', *Notes and Queries*, vol. 151 (6 November 1926), p. 340.

Outhwaite, R. B., *The Rise and Fall of the English Ecclesiastical Courts, 1500–1860* (Cambridge: CUP, 2006).

Owen, E., *Old Stone Crosses of the Vale of Clwyd and Neighboring Parishes* (London: B. Quaritch, 1886).

Paley, R., 'An Imperfect, Inadequate and Wretched System? Policing London before Peel', *Criminal Justice History* 10 (1989), pp. 95–130.

Paley, W., *The Principles of Moral and Political Philosophy* (New York: B. and W. Collins, 1835).

Palmer, R., *The Folklore of Shropshire* (London: Logaston Press, 2004).

——*Folklore of Warwickshire* (Gloucester, Tempus Stroud, 2004).

Parry Okeden, W. H., 'The Agricultural Riots in Dorset in 1830', *Dorset Natural History and Archaeological Society* 52 (1930), pp. 90–1.

Paz, D. G., 'Popular Anti-Catholicism in England, 1850–1851', *Albion* 11:4 (1979), pp. 331–59.

Peacock, A. J., 'Village Radicalism in East Anglia, 1800–1850', *Rural Discontent in Nineteenth Century Britain*, ed. J. P. D. Dunbabin (London: Faber, 1974), pp. 27–61.

Peacock, M., 'Burial in Effigy' *Folklore*, 16:1 (1905), pp. 405–6.

——'Burial in Effigy', *Folklore* 16:4 (1905), pp. 463–4.

Peate, I. C., 'A People's Court', *Folklore*, 56:2 (1945), pp. 273–4.

Poole, R., 'The March to Peterloo: Politics and Festivity in Late Georgian England', *Past and Present* 192:1 (2006), pp. 109–54.

Porter, E., *Cambridgeshire Customs and Folklore* (London: Routledge, 1969).

Price, R. N., 'The Other Face of Respectability: Violence in the Manchester Brickmaking Trade, 1859–1870', *Past and Present* 66:1 (1975), pp. 110–32.

Proffatt, J., 'The Fire at Tranter Sweatley's: A Wessex Ballad by Thomas Hardy', *Appleton's Journal* 14 (1875) p. 594.

Rappaport, E. D., '"The Halls of Temptation": Gender, Politics, and the Construction of the Department Store in Late Victorian London', *Journal of British Studies* 35:1(1996), pp. 58–83.

Reaney, B., *The Class Struggle in Nineteenth Century Oxfordshire: The Social and Communal Background to the Otmoor Disturbances of 1830–1835* (Oxford: History Workshop Pamphlet no. 3, 1970).

Redwood, C., *The Vale of Glamorgan: Scenes and Tales amongst the Welsh* (London: Saunders and Otley, 1839).

Reed, M., 'The Peasantry of Nineteenth Century England: A Neglected Class?', *History Workshop* 18 (1984), pp. 53–76.
Richardson R. and B. Hurwitz, 'Joseph Rogers and the Reform of Workhouse Medicine', *History Workshop Journal* 43 (1997), pp. 218–25.
Rider, L., ed., *I Walked by Night: The Life of the King of Poachers* (London: Nicholson and Watson, 1935).
Roberts, G., *The History and Antiquities of the Borough of Lyme Regis and Charmouth* (London: Samuel Bagster, 1834).
Rollison, D., 'Property, Ideology and Popular Culture in a Gloucestershire Village 1660–1740', *Past and Present* 93 (1981), pp. 70–97.
Rowling, M., *The Folklore of the Lake District* (London: B. T. Batsford, 1976).
Rubinstein, D., *Before the Suffragettes: Women's Emancipation in the 1890s* (Brighton: Harvester Press, 1986).
Salmond, Sir John, *Jurisprudence: Or the Theory of the Law* (London: Stevens and Haynes, 1902).
Samuel, R., '"Quarry Roughs": Life and Labour in Headington Quarry, 1860–1920. An Essay in Oral History', *Village Life and Labour*, ed. R. Samuel (London: Kegan Paul, 1975) pp. 139–263.
Schubert, A., 'Private Initiative in Law Enforcement: Associations for the Prosecution of Felons, 1744–1856', *Policing and Punishment in Nineteenth Century Britain*, ed. Victor Bailey (New Brunswick, NJ: Rutgers University Press, 1981), pp. 25–41.
Scott, O. P., 'Memories of a Villager', *Nottinghamshire Countryside* 21:4 (1960–1), pp. 20–3.
Seal, G., 'A "Hussitting" in Berkshire, 1930', *Folklore* 98:1 (1987), pp. 91–4.
'Tradition and Agrarian Protest in Nineteenth-Century England and Wales', *Folklore*, 99:2 (1988), pp. 146–69.
Shoemaker, R., 'Male Honour and the Decline of Public Violence in Eighteenth Century London', *Social History* 26:2 (2001), pp. 190–208.
Shorter, E., *The Making of the Modern Family* (London: Collins, 1976).
Sketchley, R. F., 'Coronation and Proclamation of the Queen of the Gleaners', *Notes and Queries,* 2nd series, vol. 10 (13 October 1860).
Snell, F. J., *The Customs of Old England* (London, 1919) pp. 207–8.
Snell, K. D. M., *Parish and Belonging: Community, Identity and Welfare in England and Wales* (Cambridge: CUP, 2006).
Spalding K., *Tales and Traditions of Tenby* (Tenby: R. Mason, 1858).
Stevenson, J., *Popular Disturbances in England, 1700–1870* (London: Longman, 1979).
Stone, L., 'Interpersonal Violence in English Society 1300–1980', *Past and Present* (1983) pp. 22–33.
Storch, R. D., 'The Policeman as Domestic Missionary: Urban Discipline and Popular Culture in Northern England, 1850–1880', *Journal of Social History* 9:4 (1976), pp. 481–509.
——'Please to Remember the Fifth of November: Conflict, Solidarity and Public Order in Southern England, 1815–1900', *Popular Culture and Custom in Nineteenth Century England*, ed. R. D. Storch (London: Croom Helm, 1982), pp. 71–96.
——'Popular Festivity and Consumer Protest: Food Price Disturbance in the Southwest and Oxfordshire in 1867', *Albion* 14:3 (1982), pp. 209–34.

Suckling, A., *The History and Antiquities of the County of Suffolk, with Genealogical Notices of Several Towns and Villages* (London: John Weale, 1846).
Suggett, R., 'Festivals and Social Structure in Early Modern Wales', *Past and Present* 152:1 (1996), pp. 79–112.
Tate, W. E., *The English Village Community and the Enclosure Movements* (London: Gollancz: 1967).
Teulon-Porter, N., 'Rough Music', *The Countryman* 52:2 (1955).
Thomas, K., *Religion and the Decline of Magic: Studies in Popular Beliefs in Sixteenth and Seventeenth Century England* (London: Weidenfeld and Nicholson, 1971).
Thompson, D., *The Chartists: Popular Politics in the Industrial Revolution* (London: Pantheon, 1984).
Thompson, E. P., '"Rough Music": Le Charivari Anglais', *Annales: Economies, Sociétés, Civilisations* 27 (1972), pp. 285–312.
——*The Making of the English Working Class* (Harmondsworth: Penguin, 1986).
——*Customs in Common* (Harmondsworth: Penguin, 1991).
——'Rough Music Reconsidered', *Folklore* 103:1 (1992), pp. 3–26.
Thornber, W., *The History Of Blackpool and its Neighbourhood* (Poulton: Blackpool and Fylde Historical Society, 1837).
Udal, J. S., *Dorsetshire Folklore* (Hertford: Stephen Austin and Sons, 1922).
Underdown, D., 'The Taming of the Scold: The Enforcement of Patriarchal Authority in Early Modern England', *Order and Disorder in Early Modern England*, ed. A. Fletcher and J. Stevenson, (Cambridge: CUP, 1985), pp. 116–36.
——*Riot, Revelry and Rebellion: Popular Politics and Culture in England, 1603–1660* (Oxford: OUP, 1985).
Walker, A., *Yorkshire Miscellany* (Huddersfield: The King's England Press, 2000).
Walsh, W. S., *Curiosities of Popular Customs and of Rites, Ceremonies, Observances, and Miscellaneous Antiquities* (London: J. B. Lippincott Company, 1914).
Walshingham, T., *Historia Anglicana*, ed. Henry Thomas Riley, Rolls Series, 2 vols (London, 1863–4), ii, p. 65.
Wareham, A. F. and A. P. M. Wright, *A History of the County of Cambridge and the Isle of Ely: Volume 10: Cheveley, Flendish, Staine and Staploe Hundreds (North Cambridgeshire)* (London: Victorian County History Society, 2002).
Warner J. and F. Ivis, '"Damn You, You Informing Bitch": Vox Populi and the Unmaking of the Gin Act of 1736', *Journal of Social History* 33:2 (1999), pp. 299–330.
Warren, C. H., *Happy Countryman* (London: Geoffrey Bles, 1939).
Watson, W. G., ed., *Calendar of Customs, Superstitions, Weather-Lore, Popular Sayings, and Important Events Connected with the County of Somerset* (Somerset: n.p., 1920).
Webb, S. and B., *The History of Trade Unionism* (London: Chiswick, 1920).
Wells, R., 'The Revolt of the South-West, 1800–1801: A Study in English Popular Protest', *Social History* 2:6 (1977) pp. 713–44.
Wiener, M. J., 'Judges v Jurors: Courtroom Tensions in Murder Trials and the Law of Criminal Responsibility in Nineteenth Century England', *Law and History Review* 17:3 (1999), pp. 467–506.
Williams, A., *Villages of the White Horse* (London: Duckworth, 1918).

Williams, D., *The Rebecca Riots: A Study in Agrarian Discontent* (Cardiff: University of Wales Press, 1955).
Williams, E. A., *Hanes Mon Yn y Bedwaredd Ganrif ar Bymtheg* (Llangefni: Cymdeithas Eisteddfod Gadeiriol Mon., 1927).
Williams, G. A., 'The Insurrection at Merthyr Tydfil in 1831', *Trans. Hon. Soc. of Cymmrodorion* 2 (session 1965), pp. 227–8.
Williams, G. W., 'The Disenchantment of the World: Innovation, Crisis and Change in Cardiganshire c.1880–1910', *Ceredigion* 9:4 (1983), pp. 303–21.
Williams, R., *History and Antiquities of the Town of Aberconwy* (Denbigh: T. Gee, 1835).
Wood, H. C., 'The Diaries of Sir Roger Newdigate, 1751–1806', *Trans. Birm. Arch. Soc.* (1962).
Woolley, Olivia S., 'Rough Music in Sussex', *Folklore* 69:1 (1958).

Manuscript Sources

Ambleside Public Library
Ambleside Oral History Group, Transcript GQ. Interview with Malcolm Tyson 8th Jan. 1998.

Bodleian Library
MS. Oxford Diocesan Papers, c. 657, fos. 21–22.

British Library
BL Add. MS. 21800, fos. 281, 284[v].
BL Add. MS. 41313, fos. 3–4.
BL Add. MS. 41313, fo. 80.
BL Add. MS. 27802, fo. 53.
BL Add. MS. 27813, Letter of June 1795.
BL Add. MS. 27826, fo. 172.

Centre for North-West Regional Studies (Lancaster)
Elizabeth Roberts Oral History Archive: *Neighbours* i/v with Mrs D. I. P.

Derby Central Library
Derbyshire Deeds vol. x ms 3555.

Kent History and Library Centre
Q/SI West Kent Mich. 1708 ff. 9, 12.

Lincolnshire Archives
2 SIB/4/37 & 38   Correspondence regarding Sir William Manners 28 April 1797

Litchfield City Council Records
D. 35   Bailiffs accts. 1704–84, p. 445
D.126   Acct. bk. 1666 – 1895 acct. 1666-7

214   SELECT BIBLIOGRAPHY

London Metropolitan Archives (Corporation of London Records Office)
COL/CC/01/01/013/ ff. 141 v, 143 27th May 1578 – 9 March 1529.

London Women's Library (LSE)
396/4b   Bristol Women's Party. Letter to Mrs Chibnall 12 November 1918.

National Archives: Public Records Office
HO 42/23   Letters and Papers 1792–3
HO 42/35   Letters and Papers 1st June–31st August 1795
HO 42/145   Letters and Papers 1st July–31st August 1815
HO 52/9   Counties Correspondence Public Disorder Monmouth – Somerset 1830
HO 52/10   Counties Correspondence Public Disorder Stafford – Sussex 1830
HO 52/19   Counties Correspondence Public Disorder Middlesex – Stafford 1832
HO 52/35   Counties Correspondence Public Disorder Stafford - York and Wales
KB 21/48   Kings Bench Rule Book 1802–1807
SP 36/50   State Papers Domestic 1739–1748
SP 36/136   State Papers Domestic 1st October 1756–31st December 1756
WO 40/17   War Office Papers 1802
WO 71/50   Judge Advocate Court Martial Records March 1st 1765–31st July 1767
WO 81/111   Judge Advocate Letter Books 1864–1865

National Archives of Scotland
JC 26/1031   Punishments: Use of Brank 1858.

National Library of Wales
GSD 4/753/3   Case of James David 1802.
MS. 2172B   Adpar Police Book 1870–74.

Norfolk Record Office
T. C., 50., 5   Bulwer of Heydon Family Papers.
T. C., 50., 7   Bulwer of Heydon Family Papers.
T. C., 50., 9   Bulwer of Heydon Family Papers.

Somerset Archive and Record Service
DD\HP/23.   Misc. Papers notes of a skimmington held at Bradford 1790.
DD\WHb/A/86   Letter of Sir Robert Peel to Thomas Assheton Smith.
DD\X\Port/1   Will of Jasper Porter of Enmore, 1779 d. 1781.
A\CMQ/2/22   Somerset Voices Archive interview with Bob Hiscox.

Suffolk Record Office (Bury St Edmunds)
EE 500/27/1   Programme for Bury Festival 17 Jun 1814.

Wiltshire Record Office
Petworth Archive   Letter of W. Tylor to Lord Egremont 27th July 1831.

Newspapers and Journals

All the Year Round
Appleton's Journal
Bayswater Chronicle
Berrow's Worcester Journal
Birmingham Mercury
Bristol Journal
Bristol Mercury
Bury and Norwich Post
Byegones
Caledonian Mercury
Cambrian Quarterly Magazine
Cambridge Chronicle and Journal
Carmarthen Journal
Ceredigion
Chambers Edinburgh Journal
Cornwall Royal Gazette
Countryman
Craven Herald
Daily Telegraph
Devon and Exeter Gazette
Dorset Natural History and Antiquarian Field Club
Durham Chronicle
Eastern Weekly Press
Examiner
Folklore
Forester
Freeman's Journal and Daily Commercial Advertiser
Gazeteer and new Daily Advertiser
Gentleman's Magazine
Grub Street Journal
Hampshire Advertiser and Salisbury Guardian
Hampshire Courier
Hampshire Telegraph and Sussex Chronicle
Hull Packet and Humber Mercury
Illustrated London News
Illustrated Police News
Ipswich Journal
Journal of the British Archaeological Society
Kentish Gazette

Lancashire Gazette and General Advertiser
Leicester Chronicle
Leicester Journal
Leeds Mercury
Lincolnshire, Rutland and Stamford Mercury
Liverpool and Lancashire General Advertiser
Liverpool Mercury
London Chronicle
London Daily Post and General Advertiser
London Evening Post
Manchester Times
Middlesex Journal and Evening Advertiser
Monthly Chronicle of North-Country Lore and Legend
Morning Post
Newcastle Advertiser
Newcastle Chronicle
Northampton Mercury
Notes and Queries
Nottingham Evening News
Nottingham Guardian
Once a Week Periodical
Oxford Chronicle
Oxford Journal
Oxford Times
Oxford University and City Herald
Political Register
Read's Weekly Journal or British Gazeteer
Salisbury Journal
Somerset County Gazette
Stamford News
Standard
Star
Sussex Advertiser
Sussex Notes and Queries
Torquay Directory and South Devon Journal
Times
Transactions of the Bristol and Glos. Arch. Soc.
Transactions of the Devonshire Association
True Briton
Welshman
Western County Magazine
Wiltshire Archaeological Magazine
Worcester Herald
Worthing Gazette

Worthing Intelligencer
Y Genedl Gymreig
Y Werin
Yr Eco Cymraeg
Yr Herald Cymraeg
York Herald and General Advertiser

Cases

Ex Parte Leversedge Standard 1st February 1867.
Mason v Jennings (1680) T Raym 401, 83 ER 209.
Papping v Maynard 27 J. P. 745.
R v Crutcher Morning Post 12th August 1822.
R v Mead and Belt (1823) *York Herald and General Advertiser* 26th July 1823.
R v Roberts (1876) 2 Keb 578.
Willock v Windsor 3 Barnewall & Adolphus 43, 1852.

Index

adjudication 21, 47
Alford, Violet 86, 90
arbitration 21, 45–6
Assessed Tax Act 1819 123
Assheton, Thomas 81
authorities
  collaboration with xi–xii, 196
  professional policing x, 9
    suppression of informal justice traditions 193–8
  proscription of rough music traditions 190–9
  punishments 32
  toleration of rough music 74, 97
    patriotic burning of effigies 180–1, 183, 187, 189
  use of informers 109–11, 118

Behagg, Clive 166
Black Act 1723 149
Blackstone, William 14, 16
Bloom, Ursula 97–8
Bonfire Boys 40, 185, 187–90
bonfire culture xi
  political resistance 182–90
bonfires 7, 10, 181
booting 52–4, 191
branks vii, 27, 30, 90
'breach of the peace' 132, 134, 193–4, 196
Briggs, Katherine M. 92
Brown, Theodora 91, 96–7, 200
Burne, Charlotte 30, 71
Burne, Margaret 90
Bushaway, B. 48, 53–4, 64, 146, 149, 191, 197

Canada
  marriage 87
    restitution 86
Catholic Relief Act 1780 177
Cawte, E. C. 48
ceffyl prens 9, 58, 60–1
  reasons for use 130
  suppression 131
  variations 129–30
Capp, B. 39
Chandler, Keith 48
Chapel
  suppression of festivities 190–1
charivaris
  France 38
charters 34–5
child protection 103
Church courts 31
  decline 137
Clark, Anna 103
Cobbett, W. 36
collective solidarity 17, 43, 164, 171–3
  bargaining power 49–50
  economic interests 111–14, 124–5
  occupational solidarity 68, 139
  school strikes 171–2
common law 8–9, 12
  courts 7, 43, 45
    duties 6
  customary rights and 8, 13–16, 61
  duelling 55–6
  moral authority 14
  origins 14–15
common rights 143
  bonfire societies 185
  perambulations 151–2
compensation 146, 192
  alternative to prosecution 21, 86
conflicts of law 54–5
  duelling 55–6
  legal pluralism 43, 45
coolstrins 46, 57, 91, 199
  abandonment 136
court-leets 6, 23, 44, 140
  duties 6
courts
  activities 46
  ad hoc courts 54–5

Church courts 31, 137
common law courts 6, 7, 43, 45
conflicts of law 54–6
coolstrin courts 46, 57–8, 91, 199
   abandonment 136
court-leets 6, 23, 44, 140
deanery courts 31
duties 6
'lawless' court 57
London police courts 9, 45–6
manor courts 8, 15–16, 44–5, 149, 162–3
occupational courts 45
pie poudre courts 46–7
stannary courts 6, 44
summary courts 45
swainmotes 6, 44
verderers' courts 6, 44
criminal law 20, 29
   administration of justice 22–3
   prosecution societies 20–1, 46–7
   prosecutions 20–1
Cromartie, Alan 13–14
customary rights 6–7, 139
   common law and 8, 13–19
   jurisdictions 9
   legitimising 47–8

D'Archenholz, M. 29, 54–5
Davis, Jennifer 9, 21, 45
Davis, Natalie Zemon 38
declining traditions
   Church courts 137
   festivities and public punishment 30–1
      judicial ridings 28–9
      mock courts 203
      plough-bullocking 184–5
      skimmingtons 197–8, 202
      stang ridings 192, 194–5, 197–9, 202
   impact of industrialisation xii, 37, 202
   social mobility and 202
Defoe, Daniel 29
Dickens, Charles 90
duckings vii, ix, 8, 18, 30, 38, 72, 90, 115

economic interests 107–9, 124–5
   informers 109–22
   laissez-faire 2, 125, 140
   sponsorship of rough music 123–4

effigies xi, 76, 79, 124
   burning 94, 98, 138, 166
      political figures 18, 176–81, 189
   parading 91, 95
   types 59–60
enclosure
   resistance 85, 127–8, 139, 141, 149–51
Enclosure Act 1812 127
Enclosure Act 1815 127
Evans, George Ewart 37
extortion 6, 64, 162
   Ad Montem celebrations 65
extra-marital relations 94–6

fact v belief dichotomy viii, 3–5, 11–13
Faulk, Barry 7–8
festivities 7, 92
   authority control 190
   bonfire culture xi, 7, 10, 181, 182–90
   campaigns against 175–6
   chastisement and 92–3
   harvest festivals 153, 191
   harvest suppers 7, 56, 153
   judicial nature 23, 47, 68
      Plough Monday 66
   public punishment and
      decline 30–1
   rough music and xi, x, 7
      symbolic performances 17–19
   suppression 190–9
food price protests x, 85, 127, 141–5, 155, 164, 181
see also political resistance
forces of order
   lay-officers 10
   military 10, 107, 110, 136–7, 142, 187–8
   police xi, 9, 13, 21, 29, 41, 66, 80, 119–20, 133, 137–8
      resistive communities 158–9, 170
      suppression of rough music 193–9
   posse comitatus 10
   professional policing x, 9
      suppression of informal justice traditions 193–8
Fortescue, John 14
France 110
   Abbayes de la Jeunesse 38
   charivaris 38, 62

France (*cont.*)
  husband-beating 90
  remarriage of widows
    restitution 86
  wife-beating 99
free market 2, 17, 25, 125, 140–3
  food price protests x, 85, 127, 141–5, 155, 164, 181
  see also price fixing
friendly societies 34–5, 156
Fulbecke, William 14

gender behaviour vii, xi, 83
  ceffyl pren 130
  changing attitudes ix, 91, 93, 103
  reputation and gender mockery 167–8
  transgender behaviour 84
  see also women
Gier-Viskovatoff, Jaclyn J. 170
Gin Act 1736 116–17
Girard, René 84
gleaning 50–1, 139
  legitimacy 51
  rights 158, 164
  unlawful
    sanctions 52
Gomme, Alice B. 91–2
Gorsky, M. 165–6
Greer, Allan 86
Grey, Edwin 76, 196
guilds 34–5, 165

Hale, Matthew 14
Hammerton, James 93
Hardy, Thomas 76, 87, 101, 105
Hare, C. 185–6
Harris, John 105
harvest festivals 153, 191
harvest suppers 7, 56, 153
Hay, D. 14
Henderson, William 75, 76–7, 196
Hendrix, Richard 154–5
Highways Act 1835 193–4
Hislop, R. O. 63
Hobsbawm, E. J. 138, 154–5
Hogarth, William 175
Holdsworth, William 43–4
Humphries, S. 172

Ibbotson 16
informal justice vii–viii
informers
  background 109–11
  press gangs 110
  punishment 120–21
  smuggling 111–12
Ingram, Martin vii, 24–9, 138
Ireland, Richard 53
Ivis, Frank 116

Jackson, Georgina 30
Jones, David 127–8, 129, 130
Jones, Merfyn 167–70
Jones, Rosemary 58, 130–2, 134, 136–7
judicial ridings vii, 62, 178
  City of London 24–9
  decline 28–9
  false pardoning 25
  hurdles 29, 29n31
  offences
    dishonest practice 24–6
    sexual impropriety 26–7
    social deviance 27–32
  penance 31
  pilloryings and 29
  price-fixing 25
  weights and measures 24–5
judiciary
  independence 203–4
juridical community
  judge of the Court of the Admiralty 44
  judges 43
  justices of the peace 8–9, 21, 43
  Lord Chancellor 43
  Master of the Rolls 44
  see also courts
juridical systems
  inequality 22
  official v unofficial ix
justices of the peace 8–11, 28, 179
  arbitration 21
  role 9–10

katzenmusik 62
Kelly, Richard 96–7
Kendrick, William 59

Kent, Joan 28
Kilday, A. 30
King, Peter 45

laissez-faire 2, 125, 140
   food price protests x, 85, 127, 141–5, 155, 164, 181
   free market 2, 17, 25, 125, 140–3
law
   community expectations and 5
   legal fictions 2–8
   local interpretation 5–6
   normative values 4–5
   obedience 4–5
Lee, Laurie xi, 104, 159
legal beliefs viii, 2
   fact v belief dichotomy viii, 3–5, 11–13
   legal fictions 2–8, 12
legal pluralism 43, 45
legal professionals
   judges 12–16, 22, 43, 48, 53–4
   lawyers viii, 2, 3–4, 6–7, 13, 15
Leicester, J. S. 69
Lobban 16
local patriotism 33–8
   see also parochial loyalty
loyalty 179, 181
   obedience and 17
   see also parochial loyalty; solidarity

McCalman, Ian 154
MacMaster, Neil 160, 162–3
Madan, Martin 22–3
magistrates
   see justices of the peace
maintaining social hierarchy 99–101
Malcolmson, R. W. 190
marital relations
   changing attitudes 92–4
   cuckolds 91
   extra-marital relations 94
   scolds ix
   wife-beaters ix, 92
   see also gender behaviour; marriage
marriage
   compensatory expectations 85–6
      Canada 86, 87
      England 86

      France 86
      Wales 86
   disparity
      age 86, 87
      social standing 86
   France
      remarriage of widows 86
   pre-marital sex 88–9
   refusal to marry 89
   wrongful conduct
      skimmingtons 89–90
      wives 92
   wife-beating 92
   wifely insubordination 92
Marshall, William 44
Mill, John Stuart 150
mobility xii
   decline of rural communities 202
   social mobility xii, 202
mock courts 6, 23, 43, 58–9
   decline 203
   origins 43
Molland, Lawrence 97
moral policing 83–5, 89, 103–6
   abduction of offenders 72–4
   moral authority of the crowd viii, 8, 12–13, 62–3, 70, 72, 76
   legal authority distinguished 13
More, Hannah 16–18, 153, 174
Municipal Corporations Act 1835 161
Murphy, James 15

Nash, D. 30

O'Gorman 177, 178–9
obedience
   loyalty and 17
open villages x, 156–60
otherness 34, 37–8
   outsiders x–xi, 36–40, 43, 105–6, 159, 162
Outhwaite, R. B. 31
outsiders x–xi, 36–40, 43, 105–6, 159, 162

Paine, Thomas 16–18, 60, 111
   effigy burning 177–9, 181
Paley, Ruth 20–1
Paley, William 20

parochial loyalty 33
　occupational loyalties and 34–5
　otherness 37–8
　parish boundaries 34–5
patriotism 175–6
　violence 178
　symbolic violence 177–8
Peek, Welldon 96–7
Peel, Robert 81
penance
　social correction 31–2
perambulations 11
　boundary setting 35, 149
　common rights 150–2
　Swing Riots 146
pie poudre courts
　initiation of outsiders 56–7
pillorying
　offences leading to 30–1
　political pillorying 29
Plough Monday 7, 11, 69, 84
　'entrepreneurial activities' 66–8
plough-bullocking 11, 67–8
　decline 184–5
Police Act 1856 159
policing
　informers 120
　professional policing x
　　impact 9
　suppression of informal justice
　　traditions 193–8
　see also moral policing
political resistance
　effigy burning 180–1
　England 138–53
　　economic crisis 139
　　festive elements 152–3
　South Wales 127–38
　ceffyl pren 127–38
Poor Relief Act 1662
　impact on parochial loyalty 33
popular justice
　see informal justice
Porter, Abigail 170
price fixing 140–1, 142
　food price riots x, 85, 127, 141–5, 155, 164, 181
　free market 2, 17, 25, 125, 140–3

laissez-faire 2, 125, 140
　see also political resistance
processions
　celebrations 63–4, 70
　informal justice vii
　judicial ridings vii, 24–9
　perambulations 11
　　boundary setting 35, 149
　　common rights 150–2
　　Swing Riots 146
　punishment 64, 70–1
professional policing x, 9
　suppression of informal justice
　　traditions 193–8
promiscuity ix, 104
　ceffyl pren 136–7
prosecution societies 20–1, 46–8
protest
　skilled collective labour 155
　see also political resistance; processions

Queen Caroline affair 182–3

Rappaport, Erika 125
Rebecca Riots x, 92–3, 129, 132, 134–6
Redwood, C. 58
reform of popular culture 190–9
　authority control 190
　legal remedies 192–3
　suppression of festivities 190–1
reputation xi - xii, 33 173, 187
　professional police force 193
　shaming and 76
　working-class respectability 167, 173–4, 199
　see also shame and shaming rituals
resistive communities x, 154–74
　common rights 156–8
　fair pricing 155
　food riots 155–6
　mining communities 155–6
　ritualism 165–6
　trade societies 165–70
　　discipline 166–7
　urban v rural communities 156
Roberts, George 69, 89–90, 98
Rollison, David 41
rough music
　decline 202

definition vii, 62
evolution xi
festivities and xi, x, 7
forms 62–4
gender reversal 83–5
legal remedies 192–3
legitimacy 11
magistrate approval 10–11
methods 72–6
nature of performances 71–2
origins 62, 63
proscription 192–9
regional practices xi, 63
reporting of 71
sponsorship 122–6
symbolic performances 17–19
trivialising 71
use of effigies 76, 78–80
violence 65–6, 77–9
see also duckings; skimmingtons; stang ridings
Rude, G. R. 138, 154–5

Samuel, Raphael 77, 156, 158–60
scold's bridle vii, 27, 30, 90
Scotch Cattle gangs 128
   origins 129
   South Wales 85
Scott, Oswald P. 67–8
Seal, Graham 135, 148
self-governing communities 161–4
sexual offences 85–105
shame and shaming rituals vii, ix–xi, 18–19, 27–32, 63–71, 78
   informers 109–10
   labour organisations 203
   proscription xi
   ridings 24–7
   rules vii, 6–7
   social discipline 7–8
   women's role 145–6
   see also reputation
shivaree 62
Shorter, Edward 99, 104
Skeleton Army xi, 40, 185–7
skimmingtons ix–x, 9, 28, 41, 48, 63, 70–2, 75–6, 92, 96, 98–101, 129, 194–5
   cuckolds 192

decline 197–8, 202
principle reasons 89–90
Snell xii, 34, 38, 201
social elite
   parochial loyalty 41–3
   sponsorship of rough music traditions 122–6
social hierarchy 99–101
social mobility xii, 202
solidarity 7, 17, 68, 139
   bargaining power 49
   economic interests 112
   geography and 164
   outsiders 43
   political resistance 81
South Wales
   ceffyl pren 127–38
   discontent 127–8
      industrial disputes 128–9
   political resistance 127–38
   resistance to Enclosure Acts 127 – 8
sponsorship of rough music 122–6
stang ridings 9, 11, 28, 41, 48, 62–4, 70, 72, 75–7, 96, 179
   decline 192, 194–5, 197–9, 202
   marital relations 92
   reporting 71
   rituals 146
stannary courts 6, 44
Statute of Artificers 1563 34–5
Stevenson, J. 36
Storch, Robert 142–5, 156, 192–5
Stuart, John (3rd Earl of Bute) 176–7
Suggett, R. 33
swainmotes 6, 44
Swift, Jonathan 90
Swing Riots x, 135–6, 146–7, 149, 155
   aftermath 148
   festive justice 147
symbolic performances 17–19
   revenge 115

Thompson, E. P. vii–viii, 11–13, 80, 93, 101, 150, 155
   Church and King burnings 180
   crowds 139–40
      moral authority viii, 12–13
   mob violence 179
   parochial loyalty 34

Thompson, E. P. (*cont.*)
  patriotism 179–80
  public unrest 139–42, 179
trade
  regulation 115–20
  free market 2, 17, 25, 125, 140–3
    food price protests x, 85, 127, 141–5, 155, 164, 181
  laissez-faire 2, 125, 140
    food price protests x, 85, 127, 141–5, 155, 164, 181
    free market 2, 17, 25, 125, 140–3
  see also price fixing
trade unions 34–5

unofficial justice
  see informal justice

verderers' courts 6, 44
violence 65–6, 77–9
  patriotism 178
    symbolic violence 177–8
  symbolic violence 177–8
  towards women
    growing intolerance 93–4

Wales
  ceffyl prens 9, 58, 60–1, 129–31
  Chapel
    suppression of festivities 190–1
  coolstrins 46, 57, 91, 136, 199
Warner, Jessica 116

Wells 155–6
Wiener, Martin 22
wife-beating 100, 103–5, 194
  changing attitudes to 92
  France 99
  Rebecca's daughters 135
wife-sale 101–3
wifely insubordination 92, 98–9
Williams, David 58, 134–6
Williams, E. A. 138
Williams, Gareth 37
witchcraft 73–4
Witchcraft Act 1736 73
women
  France
    husband-beating 90
    remarriage of widows 86
  popular protest 170–1
  price disturbances 144–6
  promiscuity ix, 104, 136–7
  protesters 144–6, 170–1
  wife-beating 92, 99
  wife-sale 101–3
  wifely insubordination xii, 90, 92, 98–9
Woolley, Olivia 198, 200–1

youths
  application of sanctions 38–40
  Abbayes de la Jeunesse 38
  entrepreneurial activities 67–8
  France 38
  inter-parish conflicts 36–7